"Most employees have no direct experience with the ultimate customer. They have little opportunity to see firsthand the results of their work. Roughly 75 percent of today's human capital operates behind the scenes. The problem is that this promising, overlooked resource is seldom tapped. Unleashing this hidden potential represents an enormous economic opportunity for America."
—**From the introduction to**
Managing the Hidden Organization

In a new era of labor-management relations and global competition, no company will be more successful than its workers. Getting the most out of the people who work behind the scenes is the key to your success, and these are the strategies to do it.

You don't learn about it in business school. You haven't read about it before in books. But the advice in this book may make the ultimate difference between your company's failure and success.

■ ■ ■

MANAGING THE HIDDEN ORGANIZATION
Strategies for Empowering Your Behind-the-Scenes Employees

TERRENCE E. DEAL, PH.D., is Professor of Education and Organizational Development at Vanderbilt University. He is co-director of the National Center for Educational Leadership. He consults with hundreds of organizations worldwide. He is co-author of *Corporate Cultures*, which now has been translated into eleven languages.

WILLIAM A. JENKINS, PH.D., is Vice-chancellor for Administration at Vanderbilt University and a faculty member at Vanderbilt's Owen Graduate School of Management. He delivers his culture and service excellence program throughout the country.

MANAGING
THE
HIDDEN
ORGANIZATION

MANAGING *the* HIDDEN ORGANIZATION

TERRENCE E. DEAL AND WILLIAM A. JENKINS

WARNER BOOKS

A Time Warner Company

Warner Books, Inc., 1271 Avenue of the Americas, New York, NY 10020

W A Time Warner Company

Printed in the United States of America
First Printing: March, 1994
10 9 8 7 6 5 4 3 2

Library of Congress Cataloging-in-Publication Data
Deal, Terrence E.
    Managing the hidden organization : strategies for empowering your behind-the-scenes employee / Terrence E. Deal and William A. Jenkins.
        p.   cm.
    Includes bibliographical references.
    ISBN 0-446-39456-4
    1. Organizational behavior.   2. Employee motivation.
3. Psychology, Industrial.   I. Jenkins, William A.   II. Title.
HD58.7.D42   1994
658.3'14—dc20   93-30520
                                                                         CIP

Cover illustration: Mark Fisher
Cover design: Julia Kushnirsky
Book design: H. Roberts

Contents

Acknowledgments and Preface

Most books begin with some opening words from the authors followed by an acknowledgment of the supporting cast. Because this book focuses on behind-the-scenes players, we chose to reverse the order. Although our names are on the front cover, a host of others have their fingerprints and footprints throughout the contents. Their assistance came in many forms: some chased down references and helped us with details; others interviewed people and observed them at work in our select group of organizations. Some generated rough drafts of examples. A few cheered us on when our energies or spirits were low. Others brought us down to earth when our egos soared too high, or offered constructive criticism when our prose was garbled and missed the mark. Each and every contribution is as much a part of this book as ours.

As the two now in the footlights, we acknowledge our hidden cast: collaborators Carole A. Runyeon, Barbara Holton, and Danielle Mezera for actively writing, editing, and never losing sight of the book's vision and soul; Homa Amin-madani for minimizing the logistical problems her erratic charge (Deal) often creates; researchers Tricia Cook, Sabrena Foreman, Laura Rickey, and Lawrence Singer, who truly were the eyes and ears for many facts and stories; Mac Pirkle, our theater expert, who gave us valuable insight; our opinion crew, Jon Gullette, Bob Lane, Richard Oliver, and Courtney Reynolds, who offered us professional advice and guidance; readers Joann DeMott, Sue Holmgren, Betty Price, and El-wyn Taylor for taking time to look over our work and make comments; assistants Eleanor Fuqua, Elizabeth Johnson, Sue Lewis, Marli Maloney, Carolyn McGee, Felisa Simmons, Priscilla Stewart, and Kelly Turney, who helped us with the nuts and bolts and searched libraries for secondary sources. Last but certainly not least, our close personal supporters Sandy Deal and Mary Ann Jenkins . . . we could not have done it without you. To all of you, we are ever grateful and want you to accept a well-deserved standing ovation.

As for us, we are a combination of oil and water. In most universities, executives make decisions and allocate resources while faculty think, teach, and write. Relations between the two groups are often strained or strident. However, beginning eight years ago, we became an uncommon pair because of our mutual belief that every employee has the potential to make a substantial contribution to an organization. Jenkins is the chief financial officer of a $1.2 billion enterprise with over 11,000 employees. A thinking manager, he leads the hidden cast at Vanderbilt University. Deal, a Vanderbilt professor, is a management thinker. He develops ideas about how organizations might work better. His concepts of corporate culture and reframing are widely known in management circles.

Both of us have consulted with a variety of organizations, including corporations, hospitals, universities, schools, and the military. While the scope of our consulting varies, each of us focuses on how organizations get the most from people and vice-versa. Combining our experiences, we began to see some patterns. Quite often, it's the visible people who get the attention, training, and recognition. In terms of size alone, this group is the tip-top of the organizational iceberg. People below the organizations' water line are often unseen, taken for granted, and in the rear when appreciation is given. We call this important group *the hidden organization*, the unseen cast without whom very little would ever get done. Being invisible has very little to do with being unimportant.

As we unveiled our concept of an organization as theater to CEOs, vice presidents, managers, and line workers, we witnessed an immediate recognition and understanding. Our differentiation between the onstage stars and backstage crew seemed to reveal something that they knew but couldn't articulate. Our words helped them capture their thoughts. Many were eager to explore possible applications. This strong positive affirmation confirmed that we were on target. Not only had we discovered another way of viewing organizations, we also seemed to have an idea that was practical, logical, and just made good sense. We are indebted to all of the executives, managers, and employees who have given their generous cooperation throughout our research. Their thoughtful discussions and useful feedback helped us forge principles for how the untapped resource of the hidden organization could be released.

This is a book about how organizations can unleash the energy and potential of workers operating behind the scenes. We hope our fusion of theory and practice has produced a set of grounded principles that will prove beneficial in advancing the performance and reputation of America's organizations.

Introduction— Tapping Hidden Resources

"Yes, I'm at the end of the line, but I have a smile in my voice."[1]

Telephone operator Faye Bartlett is representative of millions of employees in American organizations. Though vitally important, Faye is never seen by the public. But at least she has voice contact. Most employees have no direct experience with the ultimate customer. They have little opportunity to see firsthand the results of their work. Roughly 75 percent of today's human capital operates behind the scenes.[2] Unleashing this hidden potential represents an enormous economic opportunity for America.

The problem is that this promising, overlooked resource is seldom tapped. Working backstage often means being last in line as far as recognition and rewards are concerned. This is one reason why America's businesses, hospitals, and schools are in big trouble. Managers are preoccupied with quick-fix solutions, short-term results, and a belief that rational analysis and restructuring can solve any problem. This mind-set leads many managers to sterilize the human side of organizations. They believe that strategy, decisions, and structure are really all that matter. In a recent divestiture of a small company in IBM's portfolio, upper management assured employees that nothing would change with a shift in ownership. A backstage worker articulated why most employees felt differently:

> "Imagine being a small boy taken for a walk by your father. He takes you to a stranger's house and says, 'This is where you will live from now on. Don't worry. It's an equivalent house, and he's an equally good father. Good-bye.' "[3]

To these employees, feelings and attachments count too. This sentiment was echoed by Tim Epps, vice president of Human Resource Services, Saturn Corporation: "I don't know how America got to this state of top-heavy bureaucratic management, but it doesn't work."[4] It doesn't work because it ignores people—especially the faceless crowd the public never sees.

How do we begin to harness the potential and creativity of people in hinterland positions? A first step is to abandon our rational, mechanistic views that see organizations as erector sets. As a philosopher observed centuries ago, the world is what our thoughts make it. If that's true, our current ways of thinking about organizations aren't making them work very well. Now is a good time to consider new images that may help us achieve the improvements we want.

In helping leaders find ways to uncork the potential of their backstage employees, we present a different image—organizations as theater. From this perspective, every organization has its onstage drama—the product or service it features. As in every theater, it is very easy for the visible stars to receive all the glory—the limelight, the applause, and the official recognition. But in any theater, what appears in the stage light is only a small slice of the total action. Someone has to sell tickets, get the audience seated, and cater to their need for refreshment or relief. In theatrical terms this is called the front-of-house. Behind the scenes another group makes other important contributions to the audience's ultimate experience. Without lighting technicians, wardrobe dressers, makeup personnel, and stage managers, the theater would falter or flop. Away from the theater itself, accountants, marketing representatives, set designers, and artists swell the ranks of the hidden support personnel. People the audience see are just a small part of the total ensemble that make a successful theater work. Thinking about an organization as theater helps leadership become aware of a large group of employees who often feel neglected. Frequently, they don't receive kudos for their efforts. As a result, they have little understanding about the purpose or impact of what they do.

To pursue this metaphor in more detail, we studied organizations recognized for extending leadership attention to backstage employees. From their experiences and practices, supplemented by others reported in the wider management literature, we distilled several principles for tapping the potential of rearward employees. The principles sound simple. And they are. They are based on good, solid, common horsesense that has become far too uncommon in America's leadership ranks.

The real challenge is incorporating and applying the principles with consistency. This is not a cookbook where following a well-tested recipe will ensure good results. The principles are guidelines designed to spark the creativity of leaders and provide a blueprint to outline generic considerations. The leader's job is to adapt the blueprint to fit the local situation. This requires a long-term view and a commitment to stick with it. Most people in backstage roles have had their fill of fads that come and go. They know that often managers seize on solutions and then try to find a corresponding problem to solve. Today's solution quickly becomes tomorrow's castaway in favor of what's currently in vogue. Most have learned to wait and lay low until today's hot management initiative fades away. Their caution also has its costs. If they lay low, it is very obvious that they won't work hard. And if they don't work hard, it is unlikely that the organization will produce very much. Even if the volume of production is high, it is very unlikely that anything of high quality will result.

There will be a significant payoff to any organization's bottom line if the potential of this hidden cast can be liberated. Guaranteed profits are not necessarily the objective of the book. However, lower costs, better services, and heftier profits are an inevitable by-product of paying more attention to the legions of people who operate in an organization's wings.

The book is written for leaders of any organization—from a Fortune 100 corporation to an entrepreneurial, family-owned start-up company. The ideas provide a framework for growth, as well as for change. By leaders, we do not mean only those in formal leadership positions. Any manager, supervisor, or employee can profit from reading the book. It is intended for leaders at all levels—not just those at the top of the chain of command. Nor are the ideas limited to any particular sector. We have included examples from many different environments: business, health care, education, and the military. We believe that the principles apply across the board.

No organization can realize its potential unless all its people are in tune with and committed to the main drama—whatever the onstage performance intends. To succeed, organizations, like theaters, need to spotlight more than the stars. When backstage contributions are respected and recognized, unseen employees will respond in terms of hard work, loyalty, dedication, and a commitment to an excellent performance. The hidden cast is a powerful resource. We believe that giving unseen people more attention will help restore America's ability to compete in a global marketplace.

■ PART I

Looking Behind the Scenes

CHAPTER 1
Somebody Nobody Knows

The Back Roads of America

America is made up of millions of people. Their individual lives weave together our society; their work comprises our country's economic foundation. Some of their lives and careers are visible and well-known. Politicians, movie stars, athletes, and corporate executives are in full view of the American public. Favorably or not, these stars are recognized for what they do. Yet, for every individual in the spotlight, there are thousands of others whose exploits go unheralded:

> "I'm a machine," says the spot-welder. "I'm caged," says the bank teller, and echoes the hotel clerk. "I'm a mule," says the steelworker. "A monkey can do what I do," says the receptionist. "I'm less than a farm implement," says the migrant worker. "I'm an object," says a high-fashion model. Blue-collar and white call upon the identical phrase: "I'm a robot." "There is nothing to talk about," a young accountant declares.[1]

These people are frustrated. Their work will never receive either widespread acclaim or criticism. They compose a large, faceless crowd. Yet this anonymous, unrecognized mass is the backbone, if not the very soul, of the country. Without these people, neither the stars nor, for that matter, our society could exist.

Charles Kuralt, in his book *On the Road with Charles Kuralt*, chronicled the exploits and the escapades of these faceless people on America's back roads. To him "the back roads connect up a country that still seems rather fine and strong and enduring. . . . You don't read about this America in your morning paper. But it's there."[2] Not only is it there, this hidden world is filled with exciting characters whose lives, works, and avocations are often more interesting and authentic than those we read about in the newspaper or watch on the nightly news. Kuralt's writing gives these people faces and names: the Bird-Lady of St. Petersburg, Florida; the Singing Mailman from Magoffin County; Oakland's Gumball King; the Kite Flier from Farmland, Indiana; the Toy Fixing Man from Cedarville, California;[3] all common people doing exceptional things. Theirs is a collection of heartwarming *small miracles* that any American can identify with and derive inspiration from. Kuralt said, "Americans are up to all sorts of surprising things. You never know what—until you go out and take a look."[4]

The Backstage of Organizations

The back roads and byways of the nation are not the only obscure places where faceless people do fascinating things. All organizations have their own out-of-the-way places where hidden efforts are seldom recognized or publicly displayed. Every hospital, business, school, university, religious order, or military has an unseen cast of characters. Without these people, nothing of much significance would ever be accomplished. A handful of company executives or frontline people who serve the public, clients, or customers directly are in the limelight. Many others, like Kuralt's secret gallery, are hard at work and out of view.

Studs Terkel, author of *Working*, first brought this invisible cast to our attention. Much like Kuralt's fond portrayal of America's back roads, Terkel found dignity and majesty in people's everyday, ordinary work life.

> [Work] is about a search, too, for daily meaning as well as daily bread, for recognition as well as cash, for astonishment rather than torpor; in short, for a sort of life rather than a Monday through Friday sort of dying. Perhaps immortality, too, is part of the quest. To be remembered was the wish, spoken and unspoken, of the heroes and heroines of this book.[5]

Terkel found these heroes and heroines in a variety of occupational roles. A stone mason remarked:

> "I can't imagine a job where you go home and maybe go by a year later and you don't know what you've done. My work, I can see what I did the first day I started. All my work is set right out there in the open and I can look at it as I go by. It's something I can see the rest of my life."[6]

Even in less-skilled jobs, Terkel found people whose work was satisfying and meaningful. A janitor noted:

> "I carry on my jacket, it says: Hoellen, Building Engineer. But I'm a janitor. An engineer is just a word

that people more or less respect. I don't care. You can
call me a janitor. There's nothing wrong with a janitor."[7]

Our own research supports Terkel's portrayal of these
hidden people who find meaning in what they do. They derive
satisfaction in being a part of a high-quality organization. For
example, an operating technician at Saturn, America's new
and highly successful auto manufacturer, passionately indicated that there is much more to her job than riding on the
"skillet" to assemble a car: "The people, all the workers, came
here to Saturn because of the cause, the vision that they can
make a better car."[8]

As another example, consider the attitude of a stone arti-
san who works on the uppermost levels of St. John's Cathedral
in New York City—a project under way for one hundred
years: "I know my carving is up there and that's all that matters. And I know it's going to be up there for a long, long
time. That's enough for me."[9]

To many others like these two, a job provides more than
a paycheck. It's a way of life, an opportunity to make a contribution, to make a difference. They are motivated by a sense
of pride and a meaningful connection with *their* organization.
They work hard because they want to, not because they have
to. In a very real sense, they find the same sense of immortal-
ity in what they do on the job as they experience with children,
family, or country. A fireman in Terkel's book summed it up:

"The firemen, you actually see them produce. You see
them put out a fire. You see them come out with babies
in their hands. You see them give mouth-to-mouth when
a guy's dying. You can't get around that shit. That's real.
To me that's what I want to be. . . . I worked in a bank.
You know, it's just paper. It's not real. Nine-to-five and
it's shit. You're lookin' at numbers. But I can look back

and say, 'I helped put out a fire. I helped save
somebody.' It shows something I did on this earth."[10]

But what happens when one's work is not so visible? How
do people feel when their efforts go unrecognized over long
periods of time? What do people do when the monotony of
their work engulfs its potential meaning? For every person
Terkel met who was excited, committed, and satisfied with
his or her work, he found countless others who were bored,
disenchanted, demoralized, and discontented. Terkel is not
alone in uncovering such disturbing patterns. Our meander-
ings through several contemporary organizations confirmed
his observations. Along with Terkel and others, we also
learned that disaffected people often respond to their circumstances in less than productive ways. Their negative response
limits what an organization is able to produce.

Costs of Backstage Neglect

Of the over 100 million people employed in America, 75 percent are unseen, unheard, and frequently unappreciated or
unrecognized.[11] A quote from a *Wall Street Journal* article
reveals a philosophy typical of many organizations: *"We'll treat
them like a piece of equipment. When they stop being productive, we'll just bring in somebody new."*[12] Such an attitude has
its costs. No human being likes to be treated like a piece
of equipment or disregarded like a disposable object. These
legions of hidden people fight back when they are neglected
and often in highly counterproductive ways.

1. **They retire on the job.**
    Think about what 75 million people working at
50 percent of their potential can subtract from

America's gross national product (GNP). A box assembler at a Ping-Pong plant, for example, amused himself by "doing the job with his eyes closed,"[13] taking pride that his foreman could not tell the difference. A process clerk from Terkel's study described how he and his coworkers socialized a strict new boss to informal patterns of arriving late, leaving early, and taking a long lunch:

> "You know how the game is played. Tomorrow you might need a favor. So nobody would say anything. If he'd want to find out what time someone came in, who's gonna tell him? He'd want to find out where someone was, we'd always say, 'They're at the Xerox.' Just anywhere. He couldn't get through. Now, lo and behold! We can't find him anywhere. He's got into this nice, relaxed atmosphere . . . (laughs). He leaves early, he takes long lunch hours. We've converted him."[14]

2. **They conform to policies and rules even when counterproductive.**

A young clerk in an insurance company noticed an error in a customer's policy. Rather than insuring the store for $165,000 for fire damage and $5,000 for vandalism, the policy had the figures mistakenly reversed. Worrying about the customer's future if a fire should occur, she took the problem to her supervisor. Her supervisor responded angrily:

> "Listen, for all I know he took out the insurance just to burn down the store himself. . . .
> Goddamn it! They don't explain this stuff to me. I'm not supposed to understand it. I'm supposed

to check one column against the other. . . . If
they're going to give me a robot's job to do, I'm
going to do it like a robot."[15]

If the store burns down, the store's owner, the
company, and the field agent who sold the policy
will suffer the consequences. Operating behind the
scenes, the clerk was just trying to do her job. Next
time, she'll follow the rules to the letter and let
someone else take the blame.

In an American car plant, the job of one
assembly line worker was to install windows. At the
same job for several years, she had learned to install
windows in nearly half the time the company's
engineers said it should take. By skipping
unnecessary steps, she was able to perform her
assigned task more quickly and efficiently. By doing
so, she had more time for herself. When
supervising engineers walked by, she would quickly
revert to standard procedures. Just another
deceptive, unmotivated American worker? Look at
her side of the story:

"Why would I tell them that I can cut the
installation time in half. They wouldn't listen to
me. In their eyes, I am just a dumb assembly
line worker. They have the college degrees—
what would I know? When they are around, I
just do it the way they say it's supposed to be
done. Once they are gone, however, I go back to
my own method. Besides, with all the extra
time, I can read the newspaper or spend time
talking to the other workers. They don't care that
their methods are outdated. They are the

engineers. They never ask us how our jobs are or solicit worker ideas or opinions."[16]

The assembly line worker did what she was told. No one will ever know how much the company lost in revenues because its workers conformed to the company's counterproductive rules. The American automobile industry is beginning to figure it out.

3. They are absent frequently.

Absenteeism costs American businesses millions of dollars each year. Employees are absent on average almost two days a month. Retail stores have an average absentee rate of 6.7 percent; government agencies average 5.2 percent.[17] While some absences are due to sickness or other legitimate reasons, many people miss work simply because they would rather be someplace else. As one disgruntled employee proudly told us:

> "Look, I take every 'mental health day' that I can get away with. Most of my 'illnesses' occur on either Friday or Monday. That way, my family can get in a three-day weekend of sailing. It's our boat, not my job, that I live for."[18]

4. They intentionally sabotage or steal.

The fiendish escapades of disgruntled automotive workers are particularly well documented. At General Motors' Lordstown, Michigan, plant, workers admitted to dropping ignition keys down gas tanks and setting work gloves on fire in locked trunks. They wanted to see how far the cars would get on the assembly line before being discovered. For extra entertainment they scratched a new car's paint with sharp instruments. They took great delight in their ability to undermine the system: "It's only a car. It's more important to just stand there and rap. With us, it becomes a human thing. It's the most enjoyable part of my job, that moment. I love it!"[19]

In another example outside the automobile industry, an angry employee of a well-known oil company erased a data base worth millions of dollars.[20] He got mad and got even. No one will ever know why it happened. If the company doesn't care, why should he?

Such perverse responses also occur undetected in the service business. At a fine restaurant, a worker secretly put dishwasher soap in the sugar bowl, then feigned innocence when the customer burned his mouth. An angry middle-aged switchboard operator of a competing hotel chain cheerfully greeted callers with "Holiday Inn" instead of identifying her own company.[21] She did it *for a lark*. At a retail store, a discharged employee, believing she was treated unfairly, taped razor blades between her fingers and slashed twenty thousand dollars' worth of overcoats before she was caught.[22]

These are dramatic, well-documented examples. What about those of smaller significance that are never discovered? At surprising and increasing rates, employees can play out their fear and anger through theft, sabotage, and embezzlement. It is a pervasive problem specialists say adds up to billions of dollars annually. Richard

Holinger, an associate professor of sociology at the University of Florida, states: "A loss that a big firm could absorb could put a small firm out of business."[23]

The end results of all these examples are the same: unhappy, angry, and unproductive employees intentionally ruin products and services. Ultimately they can ruin an organization.

5. People backstage also strike.

When Yale's clerical and technical staff walked out in 1984, the university's prestige and internal cohesion were damaged significantly.[24] Eastern Airlines mechanics played a major role in bringing the airline to a standstill in 1989 and ultimately contributed to Eastern's demise. In the cold winter of 1990, the New York *Daily News* heated up when its delivery drivers walked off their jobs.[25] The walkout halted delivery for the 1.18-million-circulation newspaper, causing severe damage for both management and unions, as the corporation replaced union workers with newly hired nonunion workers. Sadly, the New York *Daily News* now hovers close to bankruptcy as it has been unable to recoup the financial losses it incurred during the strike.

6. They leave.

The cost of employee turnover in America is more than $11 billion annually. The average cost per replacement is ten to twenty times the weekly wage rate for hourly employees. When a salaried worker earning forty thousand dollars per year

leaves employment within the first six months, it
costs a company eighty thousand dollars—double
the person's salary.[26] "Take this job and shove it" is
one way many workers express their disaffection. A
very common strategy for those whose jobs are not
connected directly to clients or customers is to leave
at precisely the time when their organization's front
line would feel it most. They leave letting people
know just how important their unseen efforts really
are.

In countless ways, people in the hidden cast make their
presence known—often in highly destructive ways. But
should the blame rest solely on them? As one executive remarked recently, "You can't treat [employees] like a commod-
ity and expect them to treat the customer like a king."[27] Nor
can you expect them to come to work, work hard, or remain
as loyal and committed employees, without some sense that
they are valued and appreciated. It would be one thing if
employees were not inherently motivated to do a good job.
But as Barbara Garson, author of *All the Livelong Day*, observed, "The most dramatic thing I found [in two years of
intensive study] was quite the opposite of non-cooperation.
People passionately want to work."[28] It is often not the employees, but the organizations in which they work that contribute to the pathologies—especially for those not in the
limelight or mainstream of the business.

Our objective here has been to get people's attention.
This is a first step, but certainly not the last. There are too
many books in print that dish out the criticism without identifying other possibilities. Our main task is to identify what can
be done to improve the situation.

New Leadership Opportunities

Oxford Chemicals has a sales force of over a thousand people. These salespeople canvass businesses selling chemicals and cleaning supplies. As a former employee stated:

> "The problem was that the sales force got most of the attention because it was a sales-driven company. Therefore, the factory people who mixed, packaged, and shipped the chemicals, did not get much regard. When I was there, I tried to make sure they got some notice, but in hindsight, I see that I did not work on it as much as I should have. I think if the factory workers had gotten more attention, we would have had less problems with product quality and delivery."[29]

The problem with this insight is that it came in hindsight. To recognize problems before they arise and fix things before they occur is one way leaders can unleash the potential of their behind-the-scenes work force. The one–ten–one hundred rule demonstrates such opportunity.[30] If workers prevent a defect or service failure, it will cost the company one dollar. If the product is discovered defective during the inspection, it will cost ten dollars. However, if the product or service reaches the customer, the failure will cost a hundred dollars. This hundred-dollar loss does not include the expensive loss of the customer's potential business or loyalty.

People in backstage positions are the foundation of any organization. Problems occur when they feel ignored, devalued, or unwanted. Recognizing and promoting hidden cast members provides for a vital infrastructure of productive people. Stronger, focused efforts yield high-quality products or services, ultimately resulting in higher profits. More executives need to explore their organization's back roads and byways through the eyes of a Charles Kuralt or a Studs Terkel. To improve quality and cut costs, they need to identify the unseen people whose efforts are essential but unsung. But as Kuralt stressed, you have to "go out and take a look."[31] Taking a look and then taking action may be a very profitable thing to do.

The Backstage Bottom Line

As we have hinted, engaging people outside the mainstream loop can have a substantial impact on financial performance. The sheer number of employees who operate in rearward positions make small contributions of large magnitude. Assume that an average American company can increase net productivity 10 percent through conscious effort to manage the hidden organization more effectively. At an annual salary of roughly $25,000 [average American salary in 1992], a department of a hundred people could generate $250,000 in savings. A middle-size company of a thousand people would realize a $2.5 million improvement. These amounts flow directly to the bottom line. Given that three-quarters of the American work force is behind the scenes, the United States has within its grasp almost $200 billion in economic value, all by paying more attention to a neglected part of its work force.[32]

■ CHAPTER 2

Identifying the Hidden Organization

Limitations of the Universal Pyramid

As noted, many contemporary managers see organizations as highly rational, two-dimensional erector sets that can be controlled mechanistically. It's very straightforward. First, you allocate responsibilities horizontally and create well-defined roles. Then, you coordinate efforts through vertical channels of authority and control. When circumstances change, you reshuffle roles and responsibilities or redo the layers. Many managers view organizations this way, and this is why they are, at best, effective managers. They spend much of their time defining goals, specifying objectives, clarifying roles, assigning or reassigning authority, and determining rewards based on formal evaluations.

This imagery centers attention mainly on bureaucratic issues. What responsibilities do you have? To whom do you report? How many people report to you? Are you middle or upper management? Or are you merely one of the many in the "lowerarchy"? One's value is measured by where one fits into the prevailing pyramid. A vice president gets a bigger office than a manager. A manager is more valuable than a line supervisor. Below this level, most people become part of a nameless, faceless, powerless mass. To advance a career, one must move up the ladder, expand his or her span of control, or find a promotion by moving to another organization. Those in the lowerarchy often work behind the scenes. Being concealed in conventional organizational terms, usually means being downwind, the last in a long chain of rewards and recognition.

America is now waking up to the fact that human organizations are more complicated than this. They are *human* organizations, highly dependent on people. They are delightfully surprising and deceptive. Compliance does not necessarily follow command. Change does not always make things much different. Taking another obvious jump, a person's contribution is not always determined by their placement in the formal pecking order. Everyone, at least those who have been with an organization for very long, knows how vital are the efforts of technical and support people. Their important contributions become obvious only when they are not done—or are done halfheartedly or improperly. Invisible roles such as these are often left off the organizational chart. They are lumped together in two-dimensional illustrations that distort or obscure their importance. As a consequence, their efforts fall outside the typical manager's scope of attention.

This managerial myopia severely constricts the necessary field of vision. Not only are these invisible support roles growing in importance, but the obscure group is growing in size, becoming too large to be overlooked. These unseen support functions grew significantly between the years 1950 and 1960. Since then, due mainly to the growing complexity of running a business, these technical and support roles have ballooned. Take, for example, the federal government. What we see in the newspapers or on TV is only a fraction of the people who conduct the official business of our country. The bulk of our government consists of support people and "staffers." This large group is rapidly increasing in size and influence. When it comes to seeing who really runs America, the public sees only a small tip of a gigantic policy-making iceberg. This creates a troubling crisis.

How can managers identify these unseen people and understand better where they might fit? The prevailing structural imagery needs to be supplemented by other ways of looking at human organizations. We need new metaphors to help identify and deal with people who are invisible but vital to an organization's performance. We need leadership to make sure that unseen people, along with their more visible contemporaries, are motivated, satisfied, and productive.

Organizations as Theater

Metaphors or images shape how we define situations, what course of action we choose, how we evaluate the results and decide what to do next. These images or maps determine how we diagnose and respond to problems and opportunities. Because of this they are of great practical consequence. What we see determines what we do. In seeking imagery to help managers think about the hidden side of organizations—people seldom noticed and rarely seen—the concept of theater emerges as a promising alternative. While others have considered organizations *as* theater, we treat organizations *as if* they are theaters to distinguish between the stars and those behind the performing areas. The alternative mental map illuminates some promising new territory that often falls outside management's field of vision.

Nearly everyone has been to a live theater performance.

The center of attention is the drama onstage. The audience comes to see and experience something special and extraordinary. The spotlight shines on the cast onstage. Dennis Brisselt and Charles Edgley, in their book *Life as Theater*, assert:

> "Normally in the theater, as elsewhere, the performer is foreground; in particular, it is the lead actor who attracts the most attention. All the other aspects of the production are transparent in the sense that they support the star. It is possible, of course, for the star to be upstaged by another performer (accidentally or otherwise) or by an element of the set or effects."[1]

When the star(s) and other important members of the supporting cast are not the focal point, it creates a problem both for the cast and the audience. Bit-part actors, the set, or dramatic stage effects should provide background, not attract overt attention. In the theater lead actors, not the supporting cast, are the centerpiece. They receive applause from the audience and are praised or panned by the critics. But if one looks behind the curtain or thinks about what has to happen before the curtain opens, the outcome of the performance is highly dependent on a host of other people who work outside the spotlight and without audience attention or acclaim. Take for example this observation on the set designer, offered by Mac Pirkle, artistic director of the Tennessee Repertory Theatre:

> "A designer who comes to a show comes in total anonymity. Nobody in the audience knows who they are. They don't care who this person is. Yet when the curtain goes up and the applause happens, the designer feels great. They know part of the reason it is happening is because what they have done."[2]

Anatomy of a Theater

To any theatergoer, the primary motivation is to experience ordinary things in an extraordinary way. During a performance the audience's attention is focused on the play, the stage, and the actors. The director uses these three elements to attain the desired effect. Those falling outside the conscious attention of the audience are the other two parts of the theater: front-of-house and backstage.

Front-of-House

Anyone entering a theater first encounters people who are responsible for getting the audience in position for the performance. These people take money and coats, sell us programs and drinks, and help us find our seats in the auditorium. Among others, these people include box-office staff, ushers, refreshment vendors, and the house manager. None of these front-of-house workers are readily welcomed onstage. In clarifying further the impersonal front-of-house activities, Pirkle commented:

> "You get out of the car, you walk to the theater, you haven't bought your tickets yet so you have to stand in line and buy them. You have some relationship there. You get your programs. Do you want a drink? If you wore a coat, what do you do with that? Then someone helps you find your seat. The lights dim and the overture starts. . . ."[3]

While visible to the audience, these front-of-house workers are often treated as nonpersons. Like servants, waiters, chauffeurs, and bus drivers, they help people get what they need or guide them to where they need to go. They are there without formal acknowledgment. Too much of a departure from this peripheral status can have a negative effect. Think about an overly zealous usher's impact on your enjoyment of a dramatic play. The job of a front-of-house worker is secondary to the performance; yet without a solid front-of-house, you have no theater.

Backstage

Even further removed from the audience are those whose work is unknown to the public. Backstage workers include stage managers, assistant stage managers, stagehands, lighting technicians, electricians, wardrobe and makeup personnel, prop persons, and stagehands. While none of these individuals are ever seen by the audience, they are an integral part of a successful performance. People in the wings create the support, setting, and intangible qualities that make the action onstage dramatic and meaningful.

Something out of place on the set—such as a sound or lighting problem or a visible glitch—can distract the audience from the magical moment of the fantasy the actors are seeking to create. As Jim Cavanaugh, an actor turned author, recalls:

"My first play at a large community theater was the behemoth *Gypsy*, with 19 sets, 60 performers and a running crew of 25. Musicals ran 22 nights at this theater; running crews were flexible within that time. Prop girls, grips, flymen, makeup crews, electricians and the like worked on as many or as few performances as they wished. The mistaken assumption was that the actors' onstage glory gave them more stake in showing up night after night than did the unsung backstage workers' glorious toil. . . .

"On closing night I was passing through the backstage area during the busy second act when the chief prop girl, who hadn't worked the show for several nights, ran up to me with an armload of spears for the first burlesque-house scene. 'Oh, thank God!' she gasped. 'Where do these damn things go?' Closing night: twenty-two performances for the chief prop girl."[4]

While most behind-the-scenes activity goes unnoticed, errors have a noticeable impact on the performance onstage. Take the important role of the dresser:

"If I'm onstage in one costume—my pajamas—and have to come back in formal wear because I'm going to a ball—it's not that easy. I've got 45 seconds. You can't do it by yourself. The minute you walk off stage, somebody rips your clothes off—probably with velcro. They take your shoes off. You stand there doing what you can to let them dress you. And then you walk out calm and cool like you're going to a ball. You've just been in absolute pandemonium. You've given your life to someone else for that 45 seconds knowing they'll do their job right and get you back to where you're supposed to be."[5]

In the world of theater—*where you are only as good as your last performance*—the drama onstage depends on private contributions as well as on the ease with which the front-of-house positions the audience. If Jim Cavanaugh's statement is true—"Backstage is where the heart of the play is found"[6]—then consider the following table of organization (figure 1[7]) from a production organization where more than two-thirds of the roles are performed out of the public's view.

Some of these roles are connected to the drama itself. Think about set design. The construction often takes place

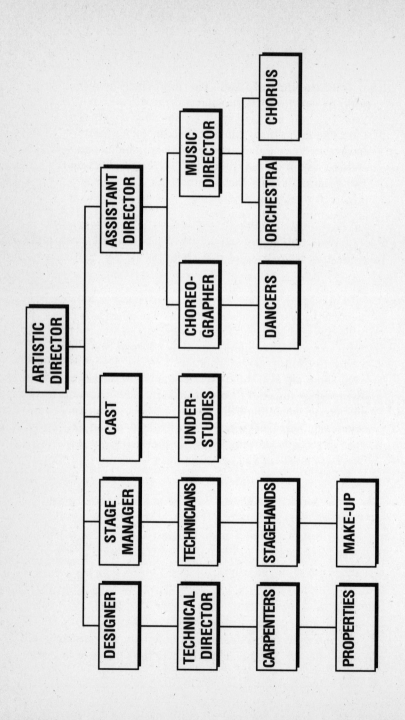

away from the theater itself. Then, as Mac Pirkle notes, it is "loaded in" in three to four days.

> "It's like taking an architect and compressing the construction time into four days. And for the designer to see it loaded into the theater and be able to clean up the little things that are wrong and get the facade exactly right. [It's a crucial time.] Some of the reinforcement comes from the director him or herself saying: 'That's got it, you've gotten that one great. The house right there is great.' The ultimate satisfaction comes from seeing that the whole project went off right."[8]

Important behind-the-scenes roles do not end with the large unseen cast in the theater's immediate wings. Other remote employees are headquartered away from the actual theater. These people provide the marketing, printing, accounting, billing, casting, set shop, administrative, and other services that create the stage and keep the theater clean, filled, and profitable. Others are not directly connected with the actual theater. Often they have only a sketchy understanding of what a theater does. Unlike those in the immediate theater who derive satisfaction from watching the drama, these employees may not feel emotionally attached to the theater. They tend to identify more strongly with their own specific occupation or profession, and this can be detrimental, says Pirkle:

> "There's a danger in our business to compartmentalize it so that the accountant or marketing person doesn't need to know anything about the play. I believe that if the accountant at Tennessee Repertory Theatre doesn't care, we're shot."[9]

If one compares the number of workers onstage with those in the front-of-house or backstage, it is easy to understand why theaters rely more heavily on unseen people than on those actually seen by the audience.

In the Chicago Bulls' organization, attention focuses on five show-time players. The spotlight captures the antics of Michael Jordan and the NBA Bulls' Coach, Phil Jackson. Efforts of assistant coaches, trainers, and other front-of-house workers are rarely noticed—nor are the concealed contributions of accountants, clerical staff, janitors, and video technicians. These are not even a remote afterthought on the part of the fans. Yet the hidden Bulls' organization is five times larger than the player roster.[10] Without these employees, the team would not exist. There would be no nightly performance.

The critical management choice is whether to focus attention mainly on the visible stars or to refocus attention and redirect resources to human capital that operates out of view. In the world of theater, that choice is clear: *either manage or flop*. Rewards that come to the actors onstage are constant, obvious, and uplifting. Others rarely receive applause or critical reviews. Their recognition and rewards must come from someplace else. If not recognized or rewarded, they often will withdraw their support and the theater will, figuratively or literally, flop.

Identifying the Hidden Organization

Thinking about organizations as if they are theaters helps identify obscure roles and clarify issues overlooked by traditional management imagery. This is important since most organizations have only a few people onstage.

Front-of-house people are visible to customers or clients but essentially seen as nonpersons. In hospitals, for example, front-of-house people make subtle appearances. Admitting clerks, receptionists, and volunteers greet patients and guide them to their room. Technicians draw blood, orderlies empty bedpans, custodians clean rooms, and kitchen workers serve meals—often without much interchange with patients. Becoming too prominent could upstage physicians or nurses, who are the primary actors in the patients' world.

Most work backstage is hidden from public view. Although these people are essential, they are often treated like ghosts. Management pays little attention to them and rarely worries about their needs—even though their invisible work leaves powerful tangible tracks on the organization's performance. Pilots depend on aircraft maintained by mechanics. Waiters receive kudos for the quality of food prepared by cooks. Marketing representatives take bows for slide presentations actually put together by the graphics department. No organization could exist without the unseen contributions of people who work behind the performing area.

Anatomy of a Flight

Many leaders or managers spend most of their time with the 25 percent of the people who are part of the main drama. Successful organizations, such as American Airlines, have learned that this modal mind-set is obsolete. They pay attention to managing their hidden human resources. For every visible American flight attendant, there are over two hundred American employees whom a passenger may never see or whose existence may be unknown to customers.[11] But their hidden performance is just as vital as the visible efforts of those on the line.

Consider a typical flight on American. The gate agent announces that it is time to board Flight 85 from New York City to Dallas. Before boarding, porters, ticket agents, and gate agents deal with baggage, seat assignments, and upgrades. How well they do can influence the attitudes that passengers bring aboard. As passengers board the plane, cabin attendants do everything possible to make everyone feel comfortable and safe. During the flight, the cockpit crew provides periodic updates of progress toward the final destination. Although the pilot and first officer may be somewhat visible during the boarding process, they are now out of sight in the cockpit charting the way. The captain usually offers a personal good-bye as passengers disembark. But during the flight, the quality of service and the passenger's peace of mind are almost totally in the hands of the flight attendants. In flight, members of the cabin crew are the only official representatives of the airline visible to passengers. Exclusive of turbulence or technical problems, they determine how customers will experience the flight. Flight attendants receive plaudits when passengers are satisfied and incur their wrath when things go wrong. Irrespective of the nature of the problem, flight attendants are the frontline in-flight representatives of American Airlines. They are the significant people who are at center stage when the curtain rises and falls. In large measure their performance influences whether or not passengers will choose to fly American Airlines again.

Prior to, during, and after the in-flight drama, there are hundreds of others whose behind-the-scenes efforts are critical to a successful flight. They took your reservation, programmed your destination, cleaned and fueled the aircraft, disposed of sewage, made minor repairs, edited the *American Way* magazine, planned and prepared meals, loaded baggage, determined departure schedules, guided the plane from the terminal to the taxiway, and gave the final release to federal air traffic controllers. They are the unseen players with whom the average passenger may never have direct contact: ramp clerks, dispatchers, crew schedulers, crew chiefs, cutters, mechanics, ticket lifters, ramp managers, baggage handlers, line crews, computer programmers, zone planners, secretaries, editors, lawyers, and accountants. While these people are not onstage, their efforts contribute, directly or indirectly, to the success of a flight. Although unseen, their importance is quickly noticed when their job is not done or not done well. The flight crew will receive official credit or blame. Their performance either made or flawed the flight as far as the passengers are concerned. But the hidden contributions are just as essential.

The Untold Story of Desert Storm

Airline companies are not the only organizations where unseen people make or break a successful performance. By most accounts, the performances of the U.S. military in the Desert Storm campaign were exemplary. In fact, Operation Desert Storm was one of the most successful military campaigns in history. It accomplished its immediate objective and did so with fewer casualties than any other major campaign: total U.S. troops killed, 184 (in World War II 407,318 were lost); total U.S. troops wounded, 213 (during World War II 670,000 were wounded).[12]

Media coverage of the operation focused mainly on the frontline heroes: pilots reporting the results of successful bombing raids; smart bombs dropped through airshafts with pinpoint accuracy detonating strategic targets inside; troops equipped with the latest in modern weaponry, engaging and defeating entire Iraqi units equally well equipped; and naval vessels bombarding targets on land with radar-guided missiles. One easily can remember a war won entirely by combat troops, airmen, sailors, and modern weaponry—the stars in the theater of war. They received nearly all the well-deserved attention and the glory. But were frontline heroes and sophisticated technology the whole story?

What about the military planners at Central Command? Few Americans realize that since 1983, seven hundred military personnel had been developing strategies for the Middle East. In 1988, Gen. Norman Schwazkopf and his staff designed a coordinated strategy to counter a possible Iraqi invasion of Kuwait. Without that plan some believe the operation could have been a fiasco. As Lt. Gen. John Waller of Central Command remarked, "We have found that military options are too complicated to wing it."[13] Without plans the outcome of the war would not have been so favorable to our interests. Without the planners there would have been no plans. Behind-the-scenes people were crucial to the operation's success, yet virtually ignored in its media coverage and celebratory aftermath.

The planners were not the only ones whose contributions to Operation Desert Storm were overlooked. Consider the success of the Twenty-fourth Infantry Division (Mechanized).[14] In four days, 16,530 men, 290 Abrams tanks, 270 Bradley fighting vehicles, 72 155mm howitzers, 9 multiple-launch rocket systems, 18 Apache attack helicopters, and 6,000 transport vehicles plunged deeply into Iraqi territory in what one American officer labeled, "the greatest cavalry charge in history."[15] The Twenty-fourth destroyed airfields, tanks, and Republican Guard divisions while sustaining only minimal casualties. The commander of the Twenty-fourth's First Brigade appropriately commended the troops: "These young soldiers are simply splendid. They have performed miracles."[16]

The miraculous events did not all begin at the time the attack was launched. Even before the Twenty-fourth Infantry crossed into Iraqi territory, Maj. Gen. Barry McCaffrey, commander of the infantry, watched miracles unfold.[17] Prior to the attack, a briefer from the Aviation Brigade reported the operational levels of equipment and aircraft. Major General

McCaffrey listened as equipment was classified as 100 percent, 98 percent, and 99 percent operational. These levels were nothing short of miraculous, particularly in view of the harsh desert conditions. Afterward, in a humble but proud voice, the general commented: "What you are seeing is the result of superhuman labor by the mechanics, seven days a week, 18 and 20 hours a day. What a magnificent job; what magnificent soldiers."[18]

Equally magnificent was the logistical support the frontline troops received. During one of the last military moves before the invasion, the Twenty-fourth Infantry's logisticians moved 460,000 gallons of fuel, 108,000 gallons of water, 59 tons of food, 3,420 tons of ammunition, 16.5 tons of medical supplies, and 50 tons of miscellaneous supplies in just eight days.[19] An officer of the Twenty-fourth Infantry Division's Support Command said, "Just the computer printouts for the plans, supplies, and spare parts would fill up this headquarters tent."[20]

The performance of the logistical units was on par with the frontline troops but earned very little public applause or recognition. The logisticians were the ones who dug the latrines, cooked and served meals, and hauled ammunition and water. The work was not glorious but was crucial to the success of those who received the glory. As Col. Jim King noted, "You have to be flexible and innovate; some doctrine works, some doesn't. We are plowing new ground as logisticians."[21]

Just as we looked at the anatomy of a flight to highlight the hidden efforts of people, let's take a look at some of the unseen and unsung heroines and heroes who made Desert Storm a success.[22]

- Maj. Tim Timmons, main supply officer for several engineering battalions, scrounged and traded to keep his men well equipped. He traded plywood for oil; air filters for long underwear; and tents for the use of forklifts and trucks. Why did he work so hard and trade so wisely? He noted, "It comes down to one thing—supplying your soldiers."

- Sp. Kathleen Gonsman cooked for the 937th Engineering Group. Her upside-down cake and muffins were a welcome relief from MRE (meals, ready to eat), and the good food helped keep the morale of the troops at a high level.
- Sgt. Todd Burnett led a squad to clear mine fields. His work kept other troops from being blown to bits. His goal was to bring his squad back alive. As a leader and role model to his men, Todd did everything possible to make sure the squad got their mail, hot showers, and decent rations.
- Maj. Nelson Wiegman, an orthopedic surgeon in a forward MASH unit, helped set up a frontline field hospital within two hours after the war began.
- Capt. Katherine Cook led her 541st Service and Supply Company (156 people) in providing fuel and other supplies to thousands of tanks, trucks, and personnel at the front lines. One soldier said, "She takes care of everybody."
- Sergeant Ski, the point man of the Thirty-seventh Engineering Battalion, plotted his unit's course through the desert. Using his Global Positioning System "whiz-box" and following goat trails, he found four hundred water wells and charted the main supply route into Iraq. He was known not only for his outrageous behavior but also for his ability always to deliver the goods to his battalion.
- Maj. Ben Romer, a rabbi, ministered to the spiritual well-being of the troops and encouraged them to fight bravely and safely.

Despite adverse weather and geographical terrain, these efforts behind the lines contributed greatly to the Allies' victory over Iraq. These soldiers kept the frontline fighting men and their machinery at peak levels. The examples of unsung heroes of war could go on endlessly. Their jobs were not glorious acts of gallantry that immortalize warriors in the annals of warfare; but without plans, food, equipment, and water, the warriors would never have been able to fight effectively.

Extending the American Airlines and Desert Storm Examples

American Airlines and the U.S. military are not the only organizations that depend heavily on a host of invisible workers. Such efforts are critical to the success of any organization. In retail businesses, it is the warehouse workers, buyers, catalog designers, and advertising personnel who support the salespeople on the floor. Custodians, secretaries, food service employees, and purchasing agents help shape how well teachers perform and children learn in our schools. Maintenance workers, personnel staff, systems analysts, account clerks, crafts people, and technical specialists contribute as much to the overall image of our universities as do deans and professors. Pilots, retail salespeople, physicians, lawyers, and marketing representatives are visible performers. But for the stars to shine, it takes the dedicated help of many others, operating obscurely and inconspicuously, out of sight.

Variations in Backstage Motivation and Effort

The motivation and commitment of people backstage varies greatly among organizations. In a large insurance company a typist commented:

"This is just a job—a paycheck. I could not care less about what I do. I have been here for four years and no one has even told me 'Good morning' or asked about my life. My only hope is that the slipshod way that I do my work frustrates those heads-in-the-clouds jerks. They don't care about me; I couldn't care less about them."[23]

In contrast, at a well-known hospital, one of us was given a tour by the head of housekeeping. In the laundry room she described how carefully the workers fold the sheets, and noted, "We know that there is a connection between our care and patient care."[24] As the tour concluded, the elderly lady was asked what it would take to get her to leave her job. She responded with obvious emotion: "Son, they are going to have to carry me out of *my* hospital."[25]

Each individual was representative of the attitude of other employees. Differences in the collective performance were striking. It was obvious why the insurance company was in trouble over the quality of its product and losing money. On the other hand, the hospital was recognized as one of the best in the state and had just completed its fifth straight year in the black.

Consider also the differences in motivation and commitment of people in two retail businesses we visited. In the first, a warehouse employee remarked:

"Why do I work here? It beats the hell out of me. If you want someone to tell you why the place sucks why not ask one of those high-paid executives in the 'Taj Mahal.' To earn those salaries, they must know something. What they don't know is how I can screw things up without anyone ever noticing—or caring.[26]

The response of a warehouse employee in another organization was conspicuously different:

"This is a family. We all work together to get the job done. The people on the floor need me and I need them. I could never deal with customers; I like it right here where I am. Everyone is important here."[27]

Employees who are committed, motivated, and say that "everyone is important here" contribute significantly to the effectiveness of any business. Behind the scenes, they contribute energy and enthusiasm and go well beyond what is expected in supporting the ensemble onstage. When these workers are alienated, uninspired, and don't know why the hell they work here, they are in a position to botch things up by giving a minimally adequate performance or committing conscious acts of slowdown or sabotage.

Leading the Hidden Organization

Once identified, the hidden organization requires leadership. This is a key difference between high-performing and low-performing groups. The hidden organization is a large and often underutilized resource. Leaders who want to tap its potential must consider several questions:

- How many employees operate onstage? How many employees work in areas unknown to the public?
- Is leading unseen people different from directing and influencing the main performers and supporting cast onstage?
- Do the same basic leadership principles apply?
- How can the company make the linkage between concealed efforts and overall company performance more visible?
- How does a sense of belonging and appreciation develop?

- What is the value of having/making people behind the scenes feel that their jobs are more than just jobs?
- How can they become part of the enterprise and know that they are appreciated?
- How can they find out how they are doing and how they might do their jobs better?
- How can they be included in important events and be made to feel special from time to time?
- Can work behind the scenes be fulfilling and add value to a backstage worker's life?

Several successful companies have learned an important lesson: you cannot neglect people just because their contributions are less visible or indirectly related to the product or service. They must be recognized for their contributions just as often as the stars. The best companies identify and pay special attention to people in obscure but highly important roles.

■ CHAPTER 3
Gathering Information

Over the years, we have consulted with or studied well over five hundred organizations of all types. Each had an important group of players onstage. Each also had an impressive crew operating behind the scenes. In some organizations, we were the only ones who seemed to know and appreciate the hidden cast. In others, managers were aware of and in touch with their more obscure operations. In reviewing our experiences, we began to see some patterns in effective backstage leadership. We distilled these into some generic principles. We then set out to test these more systematically. Our research took three forms.

1. **Detailed case studies:** We selected several
   companies with reputations in providing leadership
   for their hidden cast. We conducted in-depth
   interviews with their personnel. To supplement
   intensive field visits, these companies supplied us
   with corporate literature, policies, philosophies, or
   stories. To make sure that we were not limiting

ourselves to organizations in a specific sector, we
chose an airline, a hotel/entertainment company, a
new automobile manufacturing firm, an ice cream
plant, a retail sales organization, and a nonprofit
entity for our intensive studies.

2. **Hands-on examples:** Other organizations also
   provided illustrations. This group included
   industrial corporations, diversified service
   companies, financial consulting companies, and
   nonprofit entities. In each, we had either direct
   experience as researchers, consultants, interviewers,
   colleagues, clients, or consumers. These
   organizations offered positive—and occasionally
   negative—examples of effective policies and
   practices. Only positive examples are cited by name
   in the book. Negative illustrations have been either
   altered to protect the organization's identity or
   drawn from secondary sources.

3. **Extensive secondary research:** In developing our
   ideas and principles, we relied extensively on
   examples from other studies, books, and articles.
   Brief biographies of these organizations, in addition
   to our detailed case studies and hands-on examples,
   are found in appendix A.

Evolution of the Principles

As our research evolved, some of our initial ideas were dis-
carded because they did not apply across diverse settings.
Others were added as we discovered promising practices our
earlier experience had overlooked. Still other principles were
modified as we were able to look more closely across organizations. The result is a short list of principles we feel apply

across the board. We believe that the principles provide a blueprint for any organization that wishes to pay attention to its behind-the-scenes employees as a means to maximize performance, reduce costs, and improve financial results. In this chapter, we preview the principles. In subsequent chapters, each principle will be explored in depth.

Principles of Backstage Leadership

- **Finding a backstage champion.** At least one member of top management needs to be an advocate for the hidden cast in order to acknowledge the needs, problems, and accomplishments of unseen people. This person can highlight, support, and give purpose to the important roles people play behind the scenes. Champions can provide much-needed lines of communication between upper management and other employees.
- **Linking backstage to the core mission.** People who understand the end result work harder and smarter than those unable to see how their efforts contribute to the *big picture*. Presenting and reinforcing an organization's core mission and values in easily understood language gives behind-the-scenes work more meaning. A common mission links backstage and onstage workers into a cohesive ensemble, each member concerned about the quality of the overall performance. Mission and values must become an integral part of an organization's daily operations.
- **Hiring the best.** Many companies go to great lengths to hire top-flight management staff and frontline employees. An equally rigorous process needs to be developed when selecting candidates for positions behind the lines. Having the top performers behind as well as in front of the curtain is a strategic advantage. Hiring the best requires an intensive process of sharing organizational

values and mission upfront, holding numerous interviews, checking references, stressing personal compatibility, and offering incentives to hire and retain top-flight people.

- **Commanding and commending customer service.** Frontline people are taught to please the customer at all costs. Hidden efforts are equally important and contribute indirectly to top-quality customer service. People in backstage roles also need to be taught to serve customers. Their *customers* are often the frontline personnel. How well they serve the onstage cast makes a crucial difference in how well satisfied paying customers are with the service they receive.

- **Broadening the base of ideas.** Every employee, visible or not, views business processes, procedures, and practices from a slightly different vantage point. Everyone has ideas that can contribute to the company's well-being. Placing a premium on suggestions, irrespective of their origin, is an important source of continuous improvement. Workers in the background can contribute ideas that result in savings or significant advances in quality. They always have ideas for performing their jobs better. They may also have suggestions on how the main performance can be improved. Regular solicitation of ideas lets these people know that they are an important part of the enterprise.

- **Trusting while helping.** It is important to trust employees to do what is right. But constant feedback, continual improvement, and rewards for a job well done are especially important for people whose work is not highly visible. It is important to maintain a balance between giving people autonomy and trust and providing evaluative feedback for them. In addition, job incentives often inspire people to perform better. Employing trust, feedback, and incentives enables hidden workers to feel they are worthy, valued, and needed members of the ensemble.

- **Avoiding the "that's not my job" syndrome.** Employees who can perform more than one function give an organization strategic flexibility. While it is important for people backstage to know their jobs, it is equally important for them to step over formal boundaries when needed to perform other essential duties. Through motivation, recognition, and rewards, people should be encouraged to broaden their specific job responsibilities, to assume more diverse roles, and become intimately involved in overall company quality. Enhancing customer service, for example, is everyone's job. It makes no difference whether efforts are directly related or visible to the customer. Doing one's own job well is not always enough.

- **Right things, not tight rules.** There is tension between individual needs and established rules. Effective behind-the-scenes people, particularly, have little tolerance for filling out forms and dealing with excess red tape. Having to accept rules rigidly can be especially frustrating when one's work is hidden from public view. Emphasis on doing things right rather than on doing the right thing can shift attention from an organization's more important vision and values.

- **Don't steal the show.** In some organizations it is possible for the backstage crew to upstage those in more visible roles. Providing visibility and applause to hidden people is important, as long as it does not take the spotlight away from others. By providing ample recognition to *all* employees, organizations can create and maintain an enjoyable, satisfying workplace for everyone.

- **Appropriate tools guarantee top efforts.** Providing state-of-the-art equipment—be it computers and telephones or floor cleaners and lawn-care products—is critical in maintaining people's morale and productivity. Providing the best equipment lets employees know they are important in the eyes of the organization despite the fact they are out of the public's eye. Additionally, top-flight equipment helps attract and retain these people by offering ease and sophistication in the working environment.

- **Dressing the hidden cast.** Invisibility does not reduce the importance of titles, office space, and an appropriate appearance. While those in the limelight receive titles, offices, and perks, others often go unnoticed. Little things mean a lot in any human organization. Symbols such as name tags, desks, and pagers can add significance to any effort. Uniforms can be as symbolic as the costumes key actors wear in front of the audience. Being identified, recognized, and respected creates an air of pride and a welcome sense of belonging.

- **Celebrating hidden achievements.** Those onstage receive continuous applause and feedback for a job well done. They also receive constant criticism that helps them improve. Behind the curtain, people often are not publicly recognized for superior performance, nor are their efforts visible to the discerning eye of important critics. Regularly and publicly celebrating invisible accomplishments conveys a sense of appreciation. It also lets others know about important contributions that enhance the main performance. Regular celebrations provide opportunities for stars and the rest of the cast to mingle. This reminds everyone that an effective human organization is only as strong as its weakest individual link. In many ways, celebrations are more important to people in the wings because they often provide the only occasions where their efforts are recognized.

How can these principles be applied to improve the quality of work life for people who operate outside public view?

The following chapters offer examples, diagnostic questions, and do's and don'ts from exemplary organizations. Many of these principles and examples also apply across the board. But our focus is on people who work in an organization's shadows. Most organizations need to develop a strategy and action plan for improving their backstage operations. The principles outline some important approaches to consider.

■ PART II

Getting Started Backstage

■ CHAPTER 4
Finding a Backstage Champion

The term *champion* has a clear meaning in most organizations. It is a label most often equated with leadership. To champion a cause is to lead the way. Champions are passionate leaders. Whatever they do is done with contagious gusto and zeal. They are the advocates of an organization's core services or products.

Ray Kroc of McDonald's, for example, was a champion of hamburgers. "You've got to be able to see the beauty in a hamburger bun"[1] was his way of communicating a vision of something special. Others saw two pieces of bread wrapped around a piece of chopped beef. Kroc looked beyond the obvious to grasp another dimension. He developed a passion for hamburgers. But he is not alone. There are others who see beauty in whatever is important in the hidden byways and backwaters of an organization.

Ben & Jerry's Ice Cream is a master ice cream and frozen dessert maker. The company's passion for ice cream is humorously inscribed on the T-shirts of employees: "One life to lick. What a long strange dip it has been."[2]

Champions get just as excited as Ray Kroc, Ben Cohen, and Jerry Greenfield about their own objects of passion. As Pat Shappert, head of housekeeping in the 1,891-room convention hotel at Opryland, also home of the Grand Ole Opry and a major theme park, remarked, "I make my living from dirt."[3] She is proud of her cleaning team. She obviously sees a more positive side to what most of us try to avoid. In fact, she has initiated an intense competition among housekeeping staffs of all Nashville hotels. The group that can clean a bathroom the quickest or make a bed the fastest has become a source of regional pride. It is an alternative source of reward for employees in an essential profession that is revered by so few. Not only does this paragon motivate her own people, she is renowned for reminding hotel executives to pick up paper in the lobby or insisting that her housekeeping staff receive their share of recognition. People like Shappert represent the interests of hidden employees with upper management. They are at the executive round table when important decisions are made and make sure that being invisible does not equate with being at the rear when resources are divvied up.

Without someone to support the cause, it is easy for obscurely placed employees to be ignored. They are treated as disinterested objects rather than as interesting people. The best organizations encourage protectors across management levels to voice concerns of employees who often go unheard. Bill Agee, CEO of Morrison Knudsen Corporation, commented that "when people are treated like costs, they become nothing more than costs; when people are treated like investments, they yield high returns."[4] Who are these people? They are right under the nose of anyone familiar with an organization's hinterland. One of the first steps toward a better program of managing hidden human resources is to find and encourage existing leadership behind the scenes.

Portrait of a Backstage Champion

Larry Kreider had an unimpressive-sounding title. He was Service Merchandise's vice president of Nonproductive Supplies until his title was changed to vice president of Purchasing.[5] Service Merchandise realized his former title was misleading; he is hardly nonproductive. Kreider describes himself as "the ultimate energetic person, always full of nervous energy, thriving on the excitement of work." Kreider believes in hard work and knows that his responsibility for a product doesn't end at the loading docks. Only when it arrives safely and on time at the Service Merchandise stores does he consider his job done.

Kreider is in charge of buying the little things that all stores need to do business. By any stretch of the imagination, his job—buying toilet paper, cash register tapes, carpet, equipment setups, and office furniture—is not glamorous. But his undertaking is not really that unusual. Every company, whether a corporation, hospital, school, or branch of government, has people who focus on the operational side of business rather than dealing directly with the product or service. Without these logistically oriented people, an organization cannot survive for long. Even direct-contact people who are motivated and responsive to the client or customer depend upon their support. Combat units quickly lose their motivation and battle readiness when basic needs are not met. Logistical support, as we witnessed in Desert Storm, is essential. The same is true in other less life-threatening situations.

Larry Kreider is not an obvious hero. A white male in his midforties, he comes from a broken, lower-middle-class family in the Northeast. His college career ended without his earning a degree. But somewhere along the line, he discovered the passion for hard work and learned the ability to make things happen. He credits a mentor from previous days, and Service Merchandise itself as the two major influences in his life:

> "He hired me and took me under his wing. We really got along well, I really looked up to him and he taught me a lot. And then, Service Merchandise presented the golden opportunity to rise above my educational limitations.
> Here I worked myself into a meaningful job and a way of life."[6]

Kreider firmly believes his job is to make people in the store—those who serve customers—more effective. His two top priorities are providing state-of-the-art equipment and being open to new ideas. These help him and his backstage team eliminate unproductive steps or methods in the stores.

Because he has been on the front line himself, Kreider understands and appreciates the invisible contributions of his Service Merchandise rearward procurement team. He looks for ways to help others succeed: "I try to second-guess my employees in order to help them avoid unexpected pitfalls. Two of my favorite sayings are 'Get with the program before it gets you,' and 'Don't assume—make it happen.' "[7]

Kreider is typical of many leaders of people who work astern. Although his efforts make a substantial difference, he works in a simple, understated office. While apparently well-organized, his work space is small and almost stark. He is quick to say, "I'm not looking for pretty—it's a place to perform my tasks."[8] Despite his spartan surroundings, Kreider becomes invigorated as he talks about his staff and how they assure that the employees in all Service Merchandise's 330 stores have what they need when they need it.

A recent Memorial Day visit to one of the company's outlets provided evidence of the not-so-obvious talents of Kreider and his staff. All the essential sales promotion supplies were in place: signs, racks, packaging, pencils and forms, computers for ordering, and cash registers for ringing the sale. But this was only the immediate and visible evidence of the accomplishments. Behind the public veneer there were toilet paper in bathrooms, light bulbs in fixtures, as well as oil on the rollers of the conveyor belt that carries merchandise from storeroom to customer checkout. Supplies whose importance is known only by their absence were available and working. Kreider and his staff provide virtually everything needed in all Service Merchandise stores. As one associate put it, "He provides the ceiling and lights above my head, the carpet beneath my feet, and everything in between."[9]

Kreider joined Service Merchandise ten years ago. It is his third Fortune 500 career. His job changes do not reflect an attempt to move upward to escape hard work. Like most of his employees, he is not afraid to roll up his sleeves and get the job done. His operation has a reputation for solving problems before they emerge. Kreider's success, in his view, comes from his long-term people—many of whom have been with the company longer than Kreider. He measures his effectiveness from the informal feedback he receives up, down, and across the organization. He learns how well he is doing at the coffee pot, in the hallway, and through informal thank-yous that come from onstage employees at Service Merchandise.

Two of Kreider's employees, a purchasing manager and a purchasing agent, described him as "supportive but a get-the-job-done kind of a guy."[10] The purchasing manager commented on Kreider's ability to "be a good leader and not a dictator. Larry's photographic mind helps him monitor every phase of the operation. He's open to ideas, hears you out, and gives you the freedom to disagree."[11] The purchasing agent agreed:

"Even in the highly paced environment, Larry is very consistent, very organized, and very confident. We are a total group here, there is so much comaraderie, we know each other well. Larry knows our jobs but so do we—we know what needs to be done and we do it. So many times managers or bosses take the credit for employees' work, but Larry always gives the credit where credit is due."[12]

The purchasing agent closed the conversation with the ultimate compliment: "Everyone in the organization wants to work in Larry's department."[13]

Kreider's leadership abilities are not confined to his immediate operation. He openly supports Service Merchandise's company-wide rites and celebrations. He attends the annual picnic for hourly associates as well as the annual black-tie dinner for salaried associates. His group is an integral part of Service Merchandise's long-term involvement with the Muscular Dystrophy National Charity and the Jerry Lewis Telethon. His buyers solicit vendors. Individual associates make contributions, and entire stores solicit customers for "Jerry's Kids." Service Merchandise's values of community pride and involvement are supported and cherished across the board. Kreider champions his crew that works in the background, but appreciates company-wide events that ensure everyone plays in harmony.

Through its indirect contributions, Kreider's rearward operation makes an important addition to Service Merchandise's bottom line. Recent calculations estimate that his operation saves the company almost $2 million yearly. The amount is equivalent to the profits of four retail outlets.

Kreider's unadorned philosophy is simply stated:

"I believe in hard work. With no education, I have compensated by working hard. I am not a cry-baby, not a whiner. When something does not work out, I simply take it back to the drawing board and get the job done."[14]

A Different Profile of Similar Character

In a different setting, in a style of her own, Donna Kane provides another example of what protectors of people who work in aft positions can do.[15] Kane is a vice president for Corporate Planning at Jewish Hospital HealthCare Services (JHHS) in Louisville, Kentucky. Her philosophy is summed up by the Golden Rule, ingrained in her formative years: "Do unto others as you would have them do unto you." She tries to follow that time-proven adage and carries it with her into the work environment.

Kane understands and values the role of backstage people and the vital shadowy support they provide to any quality health-care organization. In most hospitals, physicians and nurses—the obvious care-givers—are credited with providing patient care and generating revenues. But many others indirectly affect the quality of care as well as the health of the bottom line: housekeepers, lab technicians, dieticians, accountants, admitting clerks, analysts, engineers, buyers, pharmacists, and maintenance workers. All these unseen efforts support those who deal directly with patients. Kane has high regard for the hidden cast:

"Backstage workers are often more cooperative, while onstage players may be temperamental and demand more attention. Support personnel are expert at playing caring, supportive roles. Those individuals understand the importance of coordination, cooperation, and the sensitivity required in a successful team effort. Too often, squeaky professional wheels get the grease, while staff workhorses are taken for granted."[16]

By all accounts, Kane is a passionate supporter of obscure care-givers. She formally and informally goes out of her way to communicate respect and cooperation among all groups as vital ingredients in quality patient care. Manager Karla Thompson's account reinforces some of Kane's champion characteristics:

> "Donna is seen as a role model for many different individuals. She goes beyond the scope of her responsibilities by offering career advice to employees, even those who do not work for her. She is also interested in individuals' welfare and personal satisfaction outside of the workplace."[17]

She welcomes the opportunity to speak to Ambassador Groups—the hospital's formal designation for people who have been recognized for outstanding performance. She writes personal notes to individuals who go the extra mile for patients of the Jewish Hospital organization. A former employee, who credits Kane with her career advancement and development, supports the positive profile of Kane's management style:

> "Donna always cared about every individual. She has been both a role model and mentor to me and others. Whether you are a beginning secretary, a middle manager, or the CEO makes no difference to her. Donna inspired me to heighten my perceptions of what can be achieved by professional women. She was always quick to support the underdog and especially employees whose efforts usually go unnoticed."[18]

Jewish Hospital makes sure that its mission of service and quality is widely known. The Jewish Hospitality Program, started in 1980, was the hospital's initial effort to broadcast patient-care values widely. Kane led the team that developed this inaugural program and was responsible for its day-to-day management. The program includes employee education, guest relations, and an aggressive communication effort.

In its initial kickoff, posters featured all members of the health care team—both foreground and aft. Pictures of lab technicians and business office employees, as well as physicians and nurses, were placed throughout the hospital. The posters and pictures were changed every two months. By visibly recognizing people, especially the unsung heroes and heroines, this pictorial display reinforced the idea that all members of the team are important.

Today, the Ambassador Program, an extension of the Jewish Hospitality initiative, provides even more comprehensive hospitalwide recognition. Monthly, supervisors, patients, and peers acknowledge people who have done an exceptional job of providing superior service to patients, families, or co-workers. Each month, fifteen or twenty exemplary employees are recognized. They have breakfast with the hospital's president and receive a gift. At the end of each year, monthly honorees are recognized at an Ambassador Banquet, a black-tie affair with both dinner and entertainment.

The Ambassador Program and its forerunner, Jewish Hospitality, are combined service-recognition and employee-relations programs. As Kane explains:

"The feeling is that if people like being here, then they will go out of their way to help other people. Every day, in a hospital environment, there is someone walking down the hall lost who needs some special assistance. There are employee training programs designed to instill and instruct employees, whether a housekeeper, accountant, doctor, or nurse, to stop and ask that lost person, 'May I help you please?' And then to go a step further if they cannot help them—go find someone who can. This is a great service attitude that replaces entirely the old excuse 'It's not my job.' "[19]

The philosophy and value of "Jewish Hospitality" infuses Jewish Hospital HealthCare Services from boardroom to ward floors. Everyone takes pride in his or her work. At JHHS, widespread commitment ensures that patients, the ultimate clients, themselves feel the warm, cheerful hospitality.

Champions of the covert cast also realize the importance of fair compensation. JHHS has a compensation program designed to recognize all members of the health care team. Kane believes the human resource philosophy of JHHS is a contributing factor to the success of the organization. She believes one of the biggest mistakes an organization can make is to reduce backstage personnel or their salaries without carefully evaluating the impact.

Kane feels that the role of a leader is to understand employees and determine their special needs. Being a good listener and communicator plays an important role in building a strong work team. Kane sums it up:

"The employees I work with are first and foremost a team. We all sit down together, regardless of titles, discuss the projects we've got going—and then relate them to the bigger picture—as to what is going on with the total hospital system. The all-important tool of my management style is effective communication."[20]

The Key Stuff of Covert Champions

Although they work in different settings, Larry Kreider and Donna Kane have a lot in common. They are like countless others who protect and advance the interests of people working behind the scenes. Unless this undiscernible cast is represented in the inner circle, attention and rewards flow only to the visible stars. Imagine the outcome of the Desert Storm campaign without the absolutely magnificent logistical performance that we already have described. The widely acclaimed and publicly decorated heroes and heroines flew planes, manned ships, rode tanks, and fought skirmishes on the ground. But efforts of others behind the lines were deeply appreciated and acclaimed by those who passionately and fervently championed their logistical miracles. While these unapparent warriors did not always make front-page news, they at least knew someone had recognized them for being first-rate. Protectors of an organization's eclipsed work force:

- have a strong commitment to the concept of service and serving the company
- have an innate feeling and pride in the scores of people in the organization who are invisible
- are more than willing to talk about accomplishments of unseen employees
- are willing to roll up their sleeves and get involved at all levels of the organization
- look for ways to assure that the invisible accomplishments of backstage workers are celebrated so that these workers can enjoy some of the same limelight stars bask in regularly.
- are able to function in power parity with other top managers to aggressively assure that interests of backstage workers are not put on the back burner

- are passionate about "important grunt work," without which those at center stage would be unable to function

Designating and encouraging these champions are important for several reasons:

1. Hidden interests are publicly voiced.
2. People who work in the background are given examples to emulate as well as advocates to trust.
3. Upper management has a unified look, demonstrating that every function is essential for top company-wide performance.

Diagnostic Questions

1. Who are the backstage champions in our organization?
2. Are the areas where we have someone supporting the rearward operations more efficient and effective?
3. Are the traits described in this chapter characteristic of other champions? Are there opportunities to further develop these important advocates and role models?

■ CHAPTER 5

Linking Backstage to the Core Mission

Wings with Meaning

Textron Aerostructures, a division of Textron, Inc., builds wings for aircraft. Its core mission is to produce high-quality wings for all three major aircraft classifications (large commuter jetliner, small commuter jetliner, and small business jetliner). Assembling airplane wings is an exacting and complicated process. It requires the efforts of engineers, welders, riveters, surfacers, sealers, and countless others. While each is critical, none of these workers deal directly with customers. Their efforts are visible only to each other. In the past, many of these important people never experienced firsthand the flights Textron's wings keep aloft. Their efforts produced detached wings shipped somewhere else for final assembly. As a result, employees were only remotely connected with the final product. Seeing wings shipped is very different from observing them on an aircraft in flight.

Several years ago, the management of Textron was concerned about the morale of their workers. A bitter strike in

1989 left some deep and divisive scars. During the walkout, management and supervisory personnel rolled up their sleeves to keep the production of wings flowing. They were now worried about getting people back in touch with the company's core mission and values.

As part of a strategy to reinvest and reinvigorate its workers, management arranged an exhibition of several aircraft from the companies that bought and used Textron's wings. Employees and their families were able to see and touch the finished product. They watched the aircraft land and take off. Food, drink, and music made the occasion joyful and festive— a real celebration.

Textron's management used this event to call attention to the importance of high-quality wings and to instill a sense of pride in what the employees produced. C-130s and B-1 bombers are impressive aircraft. When individuals can actually see one, touch it, and imagine themselves or their relatives flying several thousand feet above the ground, it calls attention to just how important a rivet or seam can be. Someone's life can depend on how well a particular wing is put together. It is difficult to convey the importance of quality work in abstract terms. A tangible way to link work with results is particularly important if one's efforts are invisible to the ultimate client or customer.

Connecting Work with the Product or Service

It is easy for people in hinterland positions to lose touch. The connection between immediate work and the company's finished product is frequently indirect and rarely experienced firsthand. An airline mechanic who overlooks a mechanical problem does not have to face a planeload of frustrated passengers. A worker on an assembly line does not have to deal with an irate family whose vacation was spoiled by an automobile that quit on a deserted country road. It works the other way as well. A chef rarely sees the delight on the face of someone whose palette has been pleased by his or her culinary master-piece. A reservations agent may never know the emotional benefit experienced by a passenger able to arrive at a dying relative's bedside on time. When someone's immediate job becomes his or her primary focus, rather than the job's role in the overall scheme of things, performance rigidifies and deteriorates. The old adage "The operation was a success but the patient died" applies to more than just the medical profession. There are many people who go home pleased with a day's work, while disgruntled customers are irate about the service they received. "The in-flight service was perfect. It wasn't my fault that the plane was late or the bags were lost,"[1] said one flight attendant from an airline that recently went out of business.

In 1989, Booz Allen, a consulting firm, conducted a survey of 170 Fortune 500 companies. The survey revealed some chilling statistics about people's knowledge of wider corporate objectives.[2] Half the chief executives admitted that middle managers—never mind the rest of the employees—either did not understand corporate objectives or had only a partial grasp of what they were. Louis Harris, a marketing research firm, confirms what top management suspects: less than one-third of all employees think their management provides clear direction.[3] Many of America's organizations are failing because employees, especially those removed from frontline contact, do not see a connection between their work and why the company is in business. Raymond Smith, CEO of successful Bell Atlantic, stresses the importance of connecting work with purposes: "Almost any organization will succeed if the people feel empowered, are recognized for what they do, and understand the purpose of their jobs."[4]

How do organizations develop such a purpose? Some publish a mission statement. But many times the mission hangs on an obscure hallway wall. As a result, employees do not know what it says, let alone how its principles fit into their daily routine.

Our studies and others confirm the importance of a well-defined statement of purpose, one that is highly visible and intricately woven into the entire organization's social fabric. The core mission should be a part of every employee's informal job description. When taken to a deeper level, the core values are imprinted in the minds and hearts of employees. The mission becomes a living creed that connects work with something worthwhile.

People need to find meaning in their workplace just as they do in their personal lives. Let's examine how a mission statement can become the primary reason that employees want to work hard and do their job well, and how a psychic paycheck can supplement one's wages or salary.

Understandable Mission Statements

Mission statements need to be written in language that everyone understands. Statements of purpose and values are often written in the executive suite by people well removed from the primary audience of employees on the line. What appears as pure and passionate prose to executives is often perceived as inflated and boring bureaucratic gibberish by those for whom the statement of purpose is ultimately intended.

At Opryland, for example, a group of executives sat down to codify the principles that have made their enterprise so successful. After several days, they produced a rough draft of operating principles and were rightfully proud of their accomplishment. They adjourned for dinner and submitted the draft to a group of secretaries for typing. The next day the executives returned to inspect their masterpiece. To their surprise, a secretary remarked candidly that the principles sounded like "something a group of graduate students would write."[5] To the secretaries, the language left the meaning of the principles impenetrable.

In many companies, such insubordination from support staff would be cause for demotion or dismissal. But not at Opryland. An embarrassed, yet enlightened group of executives quickly gave the secretaries the responsibility of rewriting the document. As a result, Opryland now has a mission statement that is easy for everyone to understand and even easier for them to remember. Its participative authorship resulted in the following principles that are widely shared:[6]

Opryland, home of American music, is a unique, leisure-time entertainment organization. Live musical productions provide the foundation for a wide range of experiences appealing to a broad-based audience.

We are dedicated to maintaining long-term profitability and contributing to Opryland USA as the leading force in country music and to Nashville as a major vacation destination.

We intend to expand our market position through innovative marketing, creative product development and effective management, ensuring that our basic product, a visit to Opryland showpark, continues to improve in quality and perceived value.

Our commitment to entertain demands a positive attitude and pride in performance from all members of our team. Therefore, Opryland is dedicated to recognizing and rewarding the personal and collective achievements of all its employees.

Organizations take other innovative routes to assure that everyone's individual job is connected to a larger shared purpose. The simple phrase coined by Jan Carlzon, president and CEO of Scandinavian Airlines System Group—"We fly people, not airplanes"[7]—provides a purposeful focus for employees of the Scandinavian Airlines System. Even the employees who clean the brewing vats at Anheuser-Busch will tell you that the company stands for quality and pride. The logo of the Dodge Group, Inc., the developer of premier financial applications software, is an open hand. It signals to all employees that the company has an internal culture that is open, reaches out, and encourages supportive dialogue. The foundation of their open culture is communication. Frank Dodge, the CEO, meets with all employees on a periodic basis to share important information. Marketing plans, sales forecasts, competitive information, and financial information are discussed with the entire company. Dodge states:

"An open culture has a positive impact on the day-to-day operation of the company. When all employees understand the broad objectives of the company and how they fit into the overall process, the result is a higher-quality product/service."[8]

The important lesson is that one way or another, people—particularly those who do not occupy frontline positions—need to understand how their work makes a difference.

Repeating Mission and Values

Once formulated, organizational missions and values need to be communicated on a regular basis. TJ International (TJI), a lumber and home building supplier, takes great pride in its mission to serve others. TJI goes out of its way to reinforce its mission to the backstage employees. Walt Minnick, president and CEO, notes, "We have respect for the job that is done well. Every job is of equal importance and all associates [employees] are equal in importance."[9]

This notion of job and employee importance is highlighted in TJI's six Basic Business Values:

1. Unsurpassed customer service
2. Respect for associates
3. Defect-free quality
4. Technological leadership and innovation
5. Reasonable profit for growth and for the shareholders, and
6. Integrity in everything we do.[10]

These values are written and noticeable everywhere at TJI— on wall posters, on backs of business cards, and even on wallet pocket cards. TJI knows that company success starts with its employees. A final performance, be it a product or service, is either everyone's masterpiece or everyone's fiasco. Attaining shared meaning requires a concerted effort to make sure that a core mission is an ingrained part of every employee's job from the beginning.

Sometimes, linking backstage workers to their company's core mission is not so much a choice but a necessity. Take, for instance, Jack Stack, CEO of Springfield Remanufacturing Corporation (SRC), who, after taking the company private in 1983—and assuming an $8.9 million debt—recognized that in order for his company to survive, the SRC workers must "understand everything about the business and about the always-critical numbers."[11]

As a business, SRC remanufactures old diesel and gasoline engines and sells them to freight companies and others.

Posting over $1.3 million in earnings for 1991, SRC has redis-covered the benefits of a positive management–employee re-lationship.[12] Stack and his managers believed that in order for SRC to grow and become competitive in an already competi-tive environment, employees "had to understand [SRC's] fi-nancial information—to know how inextricably their futures were linked, not only to how they performed, but to how everybody performed."[13] It *has* paid off. As Stack notes, "Ev-erybody suddenly realized that we were in this together . . . that we all contributed to the big picture."[14]

Though SRC's story may be unusual in today's business world, it still highlights the importance of linking employees to their company's core mission. All employees, whatever their title or position, need to have a sense of belonging—a sense of loyalty—to their company. They need to understand what the company stands for. By investing employees in the core mission, an organization instills a sense of ownership. As Joe Smith, a worker at SRC observes, "It makes you want to come to work every day . . . because you can see that you are working for yourself."[15]

Extending the Understanding

A core mission needs to be spread and reinforced across all levels or areas. Backstage employees at Ford are encouraged to realize that "quality is job one" begins with them. Recently, Pepsi established the "Right Side Up Company,"[16] turning the standard hierarchical management pyramid upside down, thereby empowering employees. Each employee has been given a laminated copy of the "Right Side Up" vision state-ment. Pepsi wants all their employees, including rearward workers—mechanics, bulk drivers, or accounts payable peo-ple—to "exercise their freedom to act within their area of competence—take responsibility, accept accountability, exercise initiative and deliver results."[17]

The following companies also integrate the mission and core values into daily operations:

- Square D, a leading manufacturer of electrical equipment, established an in-house academy—Vision College.[18] All 19,200 employees of this company participated in a two-day program designed to clarify and reinforce the companys' three key beliefs: Service to the Customer, Quality Is a Way of Life, and Personal Accountability. Sessions not only included lectures on these beliefs but also exercises and problem solving. Each class was composed of employees from different geographic locations to further promote discussion and dialogue.

- Ben & Jerry's mission statement includes the product and their social and economic responsibility. The mission is part of their daily operations and is achieved through action. While their financial results indicate they are fulfilling their product and economic missions, it is their social mission—to be socially responsible inside and outside the organization—that sets them apart from most companies. Each year, 7.5 percent of Ben & Jerry's pretax profits go to worthy causes selected by both management and employees.[19] Several other actions, such as painting local fire hydrants, winterizing homes for the elderly, and creating special funds for local social causes, indicate employees do understand that social responsibility is a genuine part of their mission.

- At the well-known car rental conglomerate Avis, Inc., CEO Joseph V. Vittoria notes that "the key to success was getting all employees [12,400—one-third union members] involved."[20] Avis Human Resources personnel joined Vittoria in securing 100 percent employee participation through group meetings and videos that spread news of Avis's plan and its potential for sizable financial rewards throughout the company.

Strategies for Linkage

These organizations are successful because they capitalize on every available opportunity to reinforce their core missions and to underscore the contribution of all people. Reinforcing these values is important to employees who deal with a customer's or client's satisfaction or disgruntlement firsthand. But the generic aspects of these strategies need to be applied to people whose background work is equally important. To connect backstage efforts to frontline products or service, it is necessary to

- Put the mission and values in writing and distribute the philosophy to all people, not just management. Let everyone know what the company stands for in understandable terms.
- Send behind-the-scenes employees (even their families) newsletters that continually bring the organization's mission into focus, relating how each position fits into the overall purpose.
- Use a kickoff event to introduce or reinforce the values. Manugistics, a computer software and services company in Maryland, introduced their Elements of Excellence at a kickoff where each employee received a plaque on which the elements were etched:
  1. We treat others as we would like to be treated.
  2. Partnership with our clients results in superior products.
  3. Team success is more important than personal glory.

To further ensure the plaque became meaningful, the company created individual and team awards structured to reflect the elements.[21]

- Send quick informal notes or acknowledgments from the CEO or senior management team to backstage employees in appreciation for performances that contribute to core values. Usually, handwritten notes are best soon after the action occurs.

- Recognize backstage workers whose out-of-the-limelight jobs are essential to onstage performance. Letters of thanks and appreciation for behind-the-scenes work are almost always well received.

- When possible, bring people onstage for a thank-you on a job well done. This can be done by publicly acknowledging the contribution in front of an onstage group that is not aware of what goes on behind the scenes.

- Hold informal meetings with backstage workers. Breakfast meetings, pizza breaks, and rap sessions are important. Extra effort to meet with everyone, even odd-shift workers, goes a long way.

- Provide opportunities for backstage workers to see how the company's goods and services affect customers or clients. At General Motors' Saturn, facility workers are assigned randomly to a particular automobile that rolls off the assembly line. After a time they call the owners and ask how they like their new cars and if they have any problems that need to be fixed.

In our age of specialization, it is easy for people to become disconnected from an organization's ultimate product or service. Craftspersons, once responsible for an entire job, have been replaced by specialized technicians who handle only a small piece of the action—often performing the same operation over and over again. They often are removed from the *moment of truth* when a customer is either delighted or dissatisfied. In reality, each employee is a link in a tightly connected causal chain that determines whether the final product or service is of high or low quality. Any break in the chain will determine whether the consumer's experience is pleasant or disastrous. Sound leadership strategies make it possible for all employees to see and take pride in how their individual responsibilities affect the overall mission and purpose.

Diagnostic Questions

1. Do a large percentage of our employees understand our core mission and values? Do they believe in them? Have they taken them to heart? Does their understanding, acceptance, and commitment vary across different groups or types of employees?
2. Are planned programs and events reinforcing our core mission?
3. Do we have role models and stories that link people's work with our company's purpose? Do our formal leaders exemplify the core values?
4. Do employees refer to our mission and values when making decisions for the company? Are the mission and values reflected in everyday behavior?

■ CHAPTER 6

Hiring
the Best

Casting the Hidden Crew

Few organizations consciously search for and hire mediocre
employees. Most profess a policy of hiring the best talent
available. Hiring accomplished people is widely accepted as
one of the most important ingredients of sustained success.
Often, however, searching for the finest is confined to hiring
practices at the top. Rigorous selection procedures, prestigious search firms or individual headhunters, or costly visits to
universities with top M.B.A. programs are rarely used when a
position in the lowerarchy needs to be filled. "Fill the damn
thing and fire them if they can't cut it" is a philosophy that
many organizations employ when selecting people for positions astern.

   This strategy may work in the movie industry where bit
players are a dime a dozen. But in most organizations, it's
precisely where the problem begins. The amount of money
employees steal from the workplace, estimated at $50 billion,
pales in comparison to opportunities lost when employees are

randomly or carelessly selected to fill a position. As already noted, people are the foundation and lifeblood of any organization. Extra effort to make sure the right people are hired for all roles is common practice among top-performing organizations. Careful attention to hiring is applied across the board—not just when a management or an executive position needs to be filled. Visible people are hired with the understanding that advancement or changes in title or job duties will occur. People in the background should be interviewed and hired with these same goals in mind. Too frequently, behind-the-scenes people are hired for a specific position. If advanced or moved, they often "can't cut the mustard." This leads to demotions or terminations, never easy things to do. Finding the right people for an organization is crucial. It is important to select people who, after proper placement, can be moved upward or sideways instead of out.

Selecting top-notch people to fill unseen positions requires a process equal in intensity to that of casting starring roles. Who will be selected is determined as much by compatible values as by needed work skills. If a person does not subscribe to commonly held values, he or she will either shape up, ship out, or be pushed out. Auditions for backstage roles need to receive as much attention as those for selecting star performers or top managers.

Finding the Cream of the Crop

Top organizations take the hiring process very seriously. Donald D. DeCamp, vice president of Operations for Romac and Associates, Inc., a recruiting firm in Portland, Maine, notes, "Effective hiring procedures are 90 percent of the battle for reduced employee turnover, since they are aimed at placing the most suitable candidates in the environment where they will function most effectively."[1]

When DeCamp is talking about suitable candidates, he does not mean finding only those to fill top positions. He means selecting people who will fit in whatever job they are given. At American Airlines, for example, not just "top gun" pilots are carefully screened. Top performers are sought for every position. According to Al Becker, American's managing director of External Communications, "We try to hire the best person for every single position. Whether it's a baggage handler or a pilot, we must have the best. The quality of the people determine the quality of the airline."[2]

Appropriately screened people also tend to stay. American believes their low turnover rate of 4 percent can be attributed to the attention and commitment to a hiring process that assures the right people are placed in appropriate positions.[3]

At Cyprus Semiconductor Corporation, the company's proprietary advantage is seen as hiring better people than its competitors. Long-term success also requires they retain these talented, high-performing employees. Cypress's attention to hiring and retaining extends to all employees, not just those in top management. T. J. Rodgers, CEO, explains: "No one can bring in a new employee, no matter what their rank, without submitting a 'hiring book' that documents the entire process and gives comprehensive results of interviews and reference checks."[4]

At Cypress, no one is hired unless the system has been followed to perfection. Unless the file is complete and procedures followed to the letter, there is no hire. Rodgers emphasized his point recently when a vice president violated a cardinal rule by offering an employee a raise without following the hiring book's procedure. Rodgers "found a big pair of scissors, cut the book in half, and mailed it back to the executive."[5] The message was crystal clear: Follow the system and do it right.

Cypress has three beliefs that reflect their hiring philosophy. First, the only way to hire outstanding employees is for operational managers, before hiring, to do extensive searching and evaluating. The company's Human Resources Group plays a minor role in suggesting and evaluating candidates. No professional recruiters are used. Secondly, hiring is seen as an acquired skill. The more employees you interview and hire, the better your judgment becomes. Finally, Cypress goes out of its way to define a hiring process that is tough and fair. Only then will it be able to sort through the selection pool to uncover the unsurpassed talent.

Leaving No Stone Unturned

Other successful companies also place a premium on filling all positions with the most desirable person. Extended Systems, provider of products to enhance the life, capability, and functionality of computer resources, has a hiring philosophy that emphasizes finding people who fit the company's culture. Extended Systems requires 100 percent consensus on all new hires.[6] Any employee has complete and unquestioned veto power. Disney takes this "right fit" philosophy one step further. The company believes that their selection process is so thorough it will almost always produce a top performer. An employee who passes the rigorous selection process and performs below standards in the assigned position is not dismissed. Considerable time and effort is spent moving the employee until the right position is found.[7] For example, Don [a pseudonym] was hired to serve customers at the Disney Gift Shop in Orlando, a high-pressure and demanding retail assignment. After several months on the job, multiple customer complaints warranted two counseling sessions. Thereafter, a decision was made to transfer Don to the wardrobe and costume department. There he has no contact with paying customers but does issue work costumes to other employees. With the job reassignment, Don's performance and morale dramatically improved. He is well on the road to a successful Disney career.

Opryland's interview process also leaves few stones unturned. A backstage supervisor described his experience:

"When I interviewed here, I flew up from Florida and met six people on the first visit. I made five trips, had twenty-four interviews. I thought this was it. WRONG. I had to give a two-hour presentation to fifteen managers. At any time during those trips if anyone would have put the switch down, I wouldn't be here now."[8]

In an industry where recruiting and hiring commonly involve nepotism and the good-ole-boy network, Bill Agee of Morrison Knudsen is recognized for instituting an intense level of professionalism. The Human Resources Department culls dozens of candidates from hundreds of applicants. Then applicants go through a series of intensive interviews with various levels of managers and employees. Human Resources checks references and official documentation of employment and achievements. This process lets employees know they are special. As Agee says, "We hire the best. They know it and we know it."[9]

Rigorous selection processes also provide an opportunity to begin inculcating important values and beliefs. From the start, Disney goes to great lengths to convey its values to prospective employees. Prior to completing an application, an aspirant must preview a grooming tape. Women must not have tinted or highlighted hair, long fingernails, wear heavy makeup or earrings that dangle. For men, no long hair, no mutton-chopped sideburns, no makeup, and no earrings will be tolerated by the company. During Disney's recruiting and selection process, they convey their history, the importance of customer service, and their expectations.[10] This gives potential employees a chance to back out before they fail later. If there is any doubt that a potential employee will not work out, they are not hired. The Disney magic indoctrination begins immediately. When Euro Disney was opened recently, over one hundred thousand people were interviewed to fill fourteen thousand jobs.[11]

Reference Checks and Multiple Interviews

Exhaustive reference checks are a critical part of any rigorous selection procedure. Very often, those who appear to be the most promising candidates are actually those who show their best side in the interview. By checking references, a more complete picture can be drawn. Octel Communications, a manufacturer of voice-processing systems, requires their managers to spend at least an hour on the phone, with a minimum of three references each, per candidate. When checking references, in addition to discussing the candidate, they seek information concerning the work ethic and corporate culture of the candidate's reference company. When Director of Staffing Jim Robertson was asked whether Octel's extensive reference check process applies only to their top management recruiting, he replied:

> "Absolutely not. Everyone is checked—from the receptionist to the technician to the executive officer to the janitor. We are always extremely careful about hiring. This attention to hiring and using exhaustive

reference checks is our way to keep out people we feel
are ill suited rather than having to ask someone to leave
Octel after they have been hired."[12]

Octel reference-checking methods are paying dividends.
Their employee turnover is approximately 5 percent, about
one-half of other Silicon Valley high-tech companies.[13]

Frank Dodge, one of the two founders of McCormack
and Dodge (recently acquired by Dunn and Bradstreet) and
now the founder of Dodge Group, Inc., credits thorough background checks as a factor in his companies' success. He and
his associates not only talk with each prospective employee's
supervisors, they also check with their peers and subordinates. Each of these references provide a different perspective. It is imperative that the new hire fit into the existing
culture:

> "Any success I have had has been due to hiring good
> people for all of our positions, whether it be a staff
> assistant or key manager. While there probably is an
> element of luck in hiring, I credit most of my success to
> checking multiple references for every position I have
> ever hired—from programmers to managers. This
> philosophy has permeated both of the organizations I
> have led. Reference checks should not only be with the
> applicant's supervisor but with their peers and any direct
> reports. Many times I find applicants show different faces
> to their peers and/or employees than they show their
> boss. While I find a résumé and experience important, it
> is nowhere near as important as the kind of person they
> are. Comprehensive and thorough reference checks are
> the best measure of that."[14]

Organizations searching for superior people use other
innovative techniques in screening potential candidates. For

example, Disney borrowed a technique from the aircraft industry called peer review.[15] A current holder of a position, either backstage (i.e., accountant, seamstress, mechanic) or onstage (i.e., singer, salesperson, usher), knows what is required. He or she interviews three potential employees for an opening within their classification. The process provides the opportunity to see how people interact and how they respond to questions. Disney considers the peer review process so important that peer reviewers must undergo thorough training before participating. Michael Eisner, CEO of Disney, echoes the same opinions on other executives: "If there is any secret to our success, it is the fabulous people we've hired."[16]

Stevens Aviation, one of the largest and oldest aviation service companies, began a new hiring philosophy in 1992. They select only employees considered to be in the top 10 percent of their job category.[17] To ensure that they hire top talent, there are thorough reference checks and multiple interviews for all jobs, from shipping clerk to general manager. Finally, to emphasize this serious commitment, they require that one of the company's officers interview every prospective employee before an offer is made. Does this mean, for example, that the executive vice president would hop on a plane and travel to Dayton, Ohio, to interview an entry-level avionics technician? Executive Vice President Steve Townes replies:

> "Absolutely! It forces us out of headquarters and into the field where we need to spend more time anyway. It allows the top officers to deliver a consistent set of expectations and company values to new hires. It further allows us to define passionately 'the right stuff' that we expect of ourselves and our employees. It's a crucial element in our team building."[18]

Incentives to Remain

Once the most desirable people are identified and hired, they need incentives to stay. In addition to the draw of a unique culture, desirable working conditions, and a feeling of being able to make a difference, people want assurances that their basic economic needs will be satisfied.

A key to success for any organization is a low employee turnover rate. Employee turnovers "can cost from $3,000 to $185,000 per occurrence,"[19] according to John Hinrichs, president of Management Decisions Systems, Inc. On average, for all sectors, turnovers average "13%, [which costs] roughly $10,000 per employee."[20] In order to combat this costly situation, companies offer various incentives to employees, such as benefit packages or pay increases. Though these incentives are appreciated by employees, they sometimes fail in helping employees, particularly those in backstage roles, find reasons to stay on a long-term basis. Employees must feel a sense of belonging or ownership in their organization in order to remain.

Reflexite Corporation, a technology-based business, is already 59 percent employee owned and the percentage is on its way up.[21] Its CEO, Cecil Ursprung, contends:

> "Employees today are *better* educated. They want more than money—they want to be committed to something and they want some power over the decisions affecting their work lives. Give them that and they will repay the company a thousand times over."[22]

This is the basis for Reflexite's Employee Stock Ownership Plans. Because of this, employee participation is incorporated into the company's core mission, and as Ursprung says, "No

Reflexite employee is likely to forget the stake he or she holds in the company."[23]

Reflexite employees have more than monetary investment in the company. They have invested their hearts and loyalty, as indicated by the fact that their experienced employees hardly ever leave. For Reflexite, employee commitment has several benefits. First, Ursprung notes, "Employee ownership feeds profitability [because there is] a general willingness to run lean, since every new body dilutes the equity."[24] Second, the company attracts a wide range of outstanding people. Third, it retains them. The turnover of employees "who make it beyond the first year is virtually nil."[25] Finally, having an economic and psychological investment helps people work together under pressure. They know that dissension could cause their joint venture to lose money.

Ursprung sums it up by commenting on how he responds to other companies with an interest in buying Reflexite: "I listen politely, then generally respond in much the same way. 'It's interesting you should want to purchase Reflexite, because the company has already been sold.' 'Sold?' they ask. 'To whom?' 'To its employees.' "[26]

Like Reflexite, there are a growing number of companies that are adding stock option plans to motivate all employees. While such plans were once limited to top management, this is no longer the case. Pepsico, Inc., was the first major employer to implement a company-wide plan three years ago; however, it is now reported that approximately 5 percent of companies—such as Wendy's International, Merck and Company, Toys R Us and Du Pont—offer company-wide stock option plans to all levels of employees.[27]

Stride Rite is another example of an organization that recognizes the value of providing incentives for employees. Arnold Hiatt, recently retired CEO, instituted the company's first corporate children's day-care center in 1960. The center provides care for children of employees. It also serves needy children in the immediate area of the corporate headquarters. In addition, Stride Rite provides an adult day-care center for aging parents. Along with these programs, Stride Rite actively promotes employee fitness. Physical fitness centers are located in the corporate complex. All these incentives help retain many of the company's behind-the-scenes employees. Stride Rite knows that making investments in its people shows up on the company's economic bottom line. Incentives give the best people even better reasons for making a long-term commitment.

Themes for Hiring Backstage

In hiring top-notch people, successful companies follow several rules of thumb:

- Bring across-the-board attention to hiring top managers, employees who deal directly with the customer, as well as those with jobs the customers will never directly experience.
- Go to great lengths in the hiring process to tell your story; the values, the biases, and "the way we do things around here."
- Use peer review and multiple interviews.
- Match employee with employer and stress the importance of human qualities; the concept of right fit.
- Follow a thorough procedure for comprehensive reference checks.

Diagnostic Questions

1. Is the same care and attention given to hiring our behind-the-scenes positions as filling our key leadership slots?
2. Do our most productive departments seem to make better hiring decisions? If so, in what ways?
3. Do we pay as much attention to hiring (multiple interviews, peer review, right fit) as we do to firing?
4. What keeps our talented people here? Why do they leave?

■ PART III

The Critical Values of Backstage Management

■ CHAPTER 7
Commanding and Commending Customer Service

Customers—the Ultimate End

A recent *Wall Street Journal* survey asked consumers to identify what most annoyed them as recipients of goods and services.[1] The list of choices included common irritations, such as

- Waiting in line while other windows or registers are closed
- Being quoted one price, then learning the real price is higher
- Getting a sales call during dinner
- Learning that sale items are not in stock
- Staying home for delivery or salespeople who fail to show
- Poorly informed salespeople
- Salesclerks who are on the phone while waiting on you
- Salesclerks who say "It's not my department"
- Salespeople who talk down to you
- Salesclerks who can't describe how a product works

To most consumers this list should not be surprising. Many or all of its items frustrate everyone. But the survey responses also revealed another disturbing fact. A scant 1 percent of the respondents answered "none of the above." Evidently, beneath the surface of even seemingly satisfied customers, a few gripes are lurking. With all that has been written, discussed, and taught about the importance of customer service, it is difficult to imagine how this can be. Especially when there is substantial agreement among managers, entrepreneurs, and financial analysts that the quality of customer service has direct and significant financial impact.

A number of recent studies support the importance of customer service.[2] The aggregated facts speak for themselves:

- It is five times cheaper to keep an existing customer than to find a new one.
- Across America, one out of four customers are dissatisfied with the services or products they receive, yet only one of twenty-seven customers files a complaint.
- The average dissatisfied customer will tell ten to fifteen people about bad service. The average satisfied customer will tell two to three people about exceptional service.
- Companies rated highly for customer service charge on the average 9 percent more for their products and services than companies whose quality is rated poorly.

Given such overwhelming evidence, why is poor customer service still a prevalent problem? Our own experience is probably the best source of answers. All of us easily can recall our most frustrating story from the *Wall Street Journal*'s list of complaints. But usually we don't voice our objections to the company. We voice with our feet by leaving, never to return, or by broadcasting our beefs to our neighbors and friends. People in any buying decision have three options: loyalty, voice, or exit. We either sign up and stay, speak up, or sign off and ship out to another source. Unfortunately, loyal people are not nearly as forthcoming about their joys as exiting people are about their gripes. The end result is that companies that substitute marketing campaigns for quality customer service will not survive financially. Every dollar spent on marketing could be saved by focusing on customer satisfaction.

Serving the customer is everyone's business. All people need to understand the importance of customer satisfaction in any business transaction. They also need to know how their specific job can positively or negatively affect customers. They need to make sure that their daily deeds make keeping customers happy a top priority. That is not easy to do when your job is removed from direct contact with the customer. Most behind-the-scenes employees do not deal face-to-face with the definitive customer. Note that the *Wall Street Journal*'s list of irritations was almost exclusively aimed at frontline personnel. But paying attention to customers is an attitude that should pervade any organization. Many frontline irritations are caused by shoddy performance in the background. It's just not obvious to the patron that the real culprit is not the visible person being blamed. It is an anonymous person in the shadows isolated from the customer's reaction.

A customer-driven attitude is possible in anyone's job, whether or not they deal with the customer face-to-face. With all the recent attention and emphasis on service, why hasn't the quality of service improved? We believe there are two major reasons: (1) only frontline people are taught to focus on the customer, and (2) the definition of who customers are is too narrow.

Expanding Customer Service

The hidden cast is often left out of discussions about improving products or service. They don't hear the rhetoric and receive little or no information about the company's commitment. Most organizations usually direct their attention to the foreground people who deal directly with clients or consumers. This can leave up to 75 percent of employees tuned into their own private worlds—isolated from buyers.[3] Retail clerks, airline attendants, waiters, and other people on the organization's prow typically are the only ones who receive training and get the service message. Those astern are taught only to focus on the work immediately at hand. This narrow focus violates what top companies have learned. Wohlecke Hagglurd, president of Scandinavian Service School, contends, "Don't train frontline people alone. Service involves more than the frontline people who are visible to the public."[4]

The second reason why the needed emphasis on customer service is not paying off is that the term *customer* is usually too narrowly defined. Customers, or clients, are typically seen as the actual buyers of a certain product or service. The term needs to be expanded to encompass customers within an organization as well as the external recipients of whatever is being produced. Under this broader definition, employees provide goods and services to each other. Edward Fuchs, director of the Quality Excellence Center at AT&T Bell Laboratories, points out, "Whatever your job is, you've got a supplier and a customer."[5] The direct consumer for an unobtrusive worker's product or service is often someone in the forefront who deals with a customer face-to-face. But all goods and services flow through a series of internal suppliers and customers to the ultimate *moment of truth*.

For example, an accountant provides financial information for an organization's management team, as well as for operating departments such as personnel, purchasing, auxiliaries, facilities management, and acquisitions. Every person in each of these departments and areas is a potential customer. They, in turn, become the suppliers to others. Serving customers in this extended version takes on a new meaning. Good customer service requires paying attention to every link in the internal system of transactions that ultimately produces products or services for delivery. As an employee of Ben & Jerry's explained, "If one part of the system goes down, we all go down. . . . It's up to every individual to maintain 'the standard of product.' "[6]

Disney believes that their cast members (employees) should treat each other as guests and insists that everyone behave accordingly. All rearward people at Disney World or Disneyland, along with those in the foreground, see the same magic. This magic flows directly to paying guests. The formula for what Disney calls pixie dust is simple: Training + Communication + Care = Pride.[7] This pixie-dust mentality is evident throughout the entire Disney operation. The Disney management sees to it that each cast member, backstage or onstage, is treated as well as a paying Disney guest.

Ben & Jerry's, as a company, believes that if changes are made in the policies relating to employee concerns, its employees are treated with the same courtesy as its customers. According to Kathy Chaplin, personnel operations manager, Ben & Jerry's constantly looks for new ways to "improve employees' lives."[8] Chaplin continues by noting: "We want to make decisions that are based on looking at the customer— the employee. The entire quality movement rests on checking with customers and asking what they think."[9]

At the Dahlin Smith White advertising agency (cited recently in *INC* magazine as "one of the hottest small shops in the West"),[10] backroom employees are encouraged to focus on their entire agency as the customer. John Dahlin, president of Operations and Administration, actually calls himself "the backstage partner"[11]—and does not routinely interact with outside clients. John recognized early on that his fast-paced, ambitious ad agency is talent based and that satisfied employees are their greatest resource.

Always mindful of managing a creative environment, he stresses to his employees the importance of serving the client. And the client for his backstage employees is the agency itself. For support staff (accountants, runners, staff assistants, and directors of production, finance, and industry relations), the mission is to serve and satisfy the creative stars who produce ad campaigns and other materials for clients. It was not always this way. Artistic designers and other prima donnas often become emotional under deadline pressures and are well known for their penchant for screaming and yelling at anyone in close range. Support staff felt they were being treated poorly and unfairly. Dahlin noted that it took a mental shift, a flush of insight, for people in the background to adopt a good-sense philosophy that the agency—including even temperamental creative types—is the ultimate client and customer. Dahlin concluded by saying, "Sometimes customers are difficult. It is the responsibility of people in the agency's hinterland to deal with any difficulty in a satisfactory way. The agency is well on its way to expanding customer service, thereby improving its response to important people both inside and outside."[12]

Westinghouse has learned the same lesson. When its employees began to consider the guy down the hall as a customer, a profound attitude change helped employees become more sensitive to their own internal inner workings. The attitude change quickly extended to external customers. As author and well-known quality consultant Patrick Townsend says:

"A customer is a customer. By expanding the definition of 'customer,' you involve every employee—even those who never lay eyes on the paying customer—in your improvement efforts. The idea that *everyone* has a customer provides a framework for improvement. Without that focus you can end up just doing a lot of wheel spinning."[13]

Many organizations do spin their wheels when it comes to defining customer service. They get caught up in complex formulas and techniques, forgetting two fundamental maxims: "Do unto employees as you would have them do unto your customers," and "If you're not serving the customer, you'd better be serving someone who is." Extending the notion of service to people who have no face-to-face contact with paying customers and developing an inclusive definition of what service means can help focus efforts. But how does an organization make an expanded definition of service a reality? Our conversations with managers and employees suggest the following:

1. Make service a company-wide value.

One suggestion is to make customer service a formally stated value for the entire company. When serving the customer becomes a widely shared objective, employees will tune in, want to help, and bring forward ideas for needed improvements.

Backstage people at Service Merchandise have a definite service orientation and understand their role in providing top service. "We are here to serve," "We're proud to serve," and "We can make a difference with service"[14] are common phrases that pepper everyday conversation. This commitment to service is reflected in the company's name—Service Merchandise.

At Alexander and Alexander, an international insurance brokerage and risk management firm, the importance of satisfying the customer is detailed not only in a procedures manual but also reinforced in an annual stewardship report to the client. Their approach to customer service allows them to establish clear criteria for employee performance standards, evaluate individuals on a regular basis and communicate their performance to their clients. Senior Vice President Larry Shoaf emphatically says:

"Our philosophy on customer service is simple. We must, at all times, provide the highest quality, value-added service to our clients to ensure their satisfaction and to develop a long-term partnership. This means that all members of the service team, not just those individuals directly interfacing with the client, must perform at a level consistent with our corporate standards."[15]

The cornerstone of American Trantech's value statement is the customer.[16] The desire to understand and satisfy customer needs induced the company to organize around customers rather than functions. Utilizing a participative team approach and focusing one team on a single customer has improved the company's ability to know its customers' needs and provide individually tailored services. Empowered to operate in whatever way they think will best serve customers, the teams have been successful. This success has given American Trantech an unparalleled record of repeat business in spite of fierce competition from lower-price bidders.

2. Every department is vital.

The more connected a department feels to the core mission and the customer, the more value they will assign to their contribution. As Terrence Deal and Allen Kennedy state in *Corporate Cultures:* "People simply work a little harder because they are dedicated to a cause."[17]

Bill Boesch, American Airlines' vice president of Cargo, describes how he keeps cargo employees woven into the importance of their work. He contends that every piece of cargo is a box of money: "American Airlines could increase their profits by $100 million if they could put one more piece of cargo on every flight. When you carry a piece of cargo, you carry your client's business."[18]

Lt. Col. Jack Stevenson, a logistician in the military, knows it is of vital importance to keep every man and unit deeply entwined and aware of the significance of their contribution to the whole.[19] During Operation Desert Storm, logisticians (suppliers, transporters, and maintainers) routinely drove thirty hours, resting only six over a three-to-four-week period. It became standard practice because there was simply no other way to get the supplies to the Iraqi border in a timely way. Lieutenant Colonel Stevenson states his role is keeping his soldiers firmly connected to the mission:

"In my opinion the real heroes of Desert Storm were the truck drivers, the mechanics, and the soldiers trusted to move the ammunition.

Sometimes it was hard for them to realize how great their contribution was to the war effort because they could not always see the big picture. It was my responsibility to tell them what a critical part they played. The more they understood the total mission, the harder they seemed to work, regardless of their physical limitations."[20]

Laurie Shappert is Opryland's manager of Marketing Support. Guests are completely unaware that she or her department even exist. Shappert and her staff conduct statistical analysis and research on hotel occupancy. They try each day to create the perfect house, meaning "100 percent occupancy with no walks,"[21] she says. Although they are unseen, a mistake by Shappert and her group can create significant problems for the hotel and its guests. If their analysis is wrong in one direction, low occupancy results, causing income to fall. If their analysis is wrong in the other direction, guests with reservations will be turned away. Shappert knows the importance of her department: "Our function is vital to the bottom line and we clearly make a difference in the hotel's success."[22]

Each department at Opryland is convinced it makes a tremendous contribution to the success of the company. Imagine the impact if every single department and every single employee in America's organizations felt that way about their service, product, customer—and their bottom line.

3. Require training for everyone.

Few companies have customer service training

for all their employees—even though there is a direct relationship between training and satisfied customers. At Disney, all employees, including those behind the scenes, are required to complete a customer-service training program.[23] Last year, of the 33,000 Disney employees, 28,000 participated in various seminars.[24] As noted, they are trained to treat guests (customers) the way they want to be treated. Guests, as well, believe that cast members must receive the same kind of caring, friendly, and sincere attention. Disney's training shows people how to deal with fellow cast members as guests.

At American Airlines, President Robert Crandall stresses that the way to beat the competition is through superior service at all levels, across all areas of the company. A substantial commitment to training gives people the skills they need to provide the best. One example is their Committing to Leadership (CTL) Program.[25] The program was originally created for mid- and senior-level management and later was expanded to include backstage employees. American Airlines also broadened the scope of customer-service training to include mechanics, airport supervisors, airport ticket agents, and ramp service employees. The objective was to infuse the entire company with customer-service values and to provide supporting techniques. At last count, approximately twelve thousand senior-, mid-, and lower-management personnel, as well as rank-and-file employees, have been through the CTL program.

Yet another example is the Marriott Corporation. The company is training seventy thousand hotel workers, equipping them with both the knowledge and willingness to step outside their normal jobs and to solve a guest's problems.[26] The training appears to be working, as the following example will attest. While waiting for some friends at the Boston Copley Marriott property, a guest must have looked somewhat confused. In a five-minute period, five employees asked her if she needed some help. The last person to ask was an employee who was sifting cigarette butts out of a bronze ashtray and making sure that the Marriott logo was stamped in the sand in full view of its next customer.

Service training spawns imagination and creativity in backstage employees. They begin to think like the customer, walk in the customer's shoes, and infuse passion for customers throughout the organization. At Norco Windows, a leading manufacturer of windows and patio doors, all manufacturing managers are required to periodically spend a day with a salesperson to better understand their customers and their needs. Recently, a particular manufacturing manager spent a week answering telephone calls from customers and sales people.[27] These actions reinforced for backstage employees the idea that Norco expects everyone to better understand buyers' needs.

4. Find backstage role models.

Making serving the customer a shared company value is accentuated by finding heroes and heroines who exemplify this commitment through legendary or day-to-day actions. Summit Health, a for-profit health care system in Los Angeles with fifteen hospitals and twenty-four nursing homes, began a two-year program designed to improve customer service.[28] To reinforce the service value, they identified their most service-oriented employees. From these employees, they created a profile of effective customer service standards.

The classic service role model exists in AT&T's legendary Angus McDonald.[29] He epitomized the importance of Universal Service, AT&T's core value for over one hundred years. During the blizzard of 1891, he walked through the storm to restore telephone service on the lines between New York and Boston. His picture still hangs on the wall of many Bell employees. Ordinary people often give extraordinary service to customers. Communicating their exploits makes them feel special and also holds them up as role models for others.

5. **Use service as a performance criteria.**

Another way to reinforce the value of satisfying the buyer is to include it as a key criteria for performance standards and evaluation. When stressing customer service, "Don't expect what you don't inspect," as the saying goes.

Keeping buyers happy requires a commitment of the total organization, not just the frontline or the onstage players. Others in an organization must clearly see the entire organization's commitment to providing exceptional service. They need to understand that all layers and units within an organization ultimately depend on customers. For behind-the-scenes people, patrons in most instances will be onstage coworkers who have direct contact with the public. Successful companies stress and train all employees in service orientation, team efforts, and customer service attitudes. Robert A. Ferchat, president of Northern Telecom Canada, Ltd., a division of Northern Telecom, stated in a recent speech:

> "If customer service is to be the priority of an organization and the focus of organizational productivity, then conceivably we should be applying an inverted pyramid. In other words, a pyramid that sees the functions immediately involved with customer service on top, while support staff and senior management are positioned as resources tasked to aid the customer-service tier."[30]

6. Put backstage people at center stage.

Another way to get people in the background to think about serving the customer is to periodically bring them onstage. Basking in the limelight can be a meaningful occasion for anyone. For behind-the-scenes employees especially, public recognition for a job well done spotlights them, making everyone aware of their important indirect contributions to success with customers. This spotlighting can be done in several ways.

Randall Food Markets, Inc., now the leader in Houston's $5 billion grocery competition, believes in placing the hidden cast in starring roles.[31] At their newest stores, employees who normally ice cakes, trim meat, wrap strawberries, and juice oranges in the back rooms do it in full view of the customers. These employees are expected not only to do their work but also to respond to customers' inquiries. By bringing background people front and center, the company emphasizes freshness while simultaneously extending its direct customer-service force.

When the Opryland theme park hit its highest attendance day (forty thousand plus), many people in backwater jobs were enlisted for frontline duty to help make the event enjoyable for the visitors.[32] Engineers sold popcorn, while accountants emptied trash bins. The following day, the entire complex was buzzing with excitement. Everyone had enjoyed the camaraderie and team spirit of pulling together. People enjoyed the opportunity to deal with the customer directly for a change.

Bringing people into direct customer contact, if only for a moment, creates a sensitivity and emotional bond hard to duplicate in any other way. As the old adage goes, "I hear and I forget, I see and I remember, I do and I understand."

To echo the main point of the chapter a final time: every organization needs to find ways to focus everyone's attention on the consumer. Services and products need buyers. Unless services and products can be delivered to satisfaction, financial success is a fleeting pipe dream. America has a long way to go in eliminating irritations that drive customers either crazy or away. But if the companies above can, so can others.

Diagnostic Questions

1. Would most of our behind-the-scenes employees cite serving the customer as one of the key values?
2. Does our definition of service include internal customers?

3. How do we emphasize customer satisfaction to all people? Are service training, role models, performance criteria, and opportunities for occasional onstage experiences a part of our company fabric?
4. Do all employees have the authority to serve atypical needs of patrons?
5. Does our backstage cast have firsthand awareness of its impact on customer service?

■ Chapter 8
Broadening the Base of Ideas

The Cost of Ignoring Good Ideas

A frustrated executive described his company's futile efforts to reduce costs:

> "The managers come to our cost-cutting meeting rattling tin cups. No one wants to give up anything. They always want more resources, but they want them from somebody else's budget. They remind me of a bunch of chipmunks, crying 'Poor me' with their cheeks stuffed full."[1]

Without a doubt every organization has its excess budgetary blubber. Trimming the fat is typically a rigorous line-item search led by people at the strategic apex. While the top dogs search, underlings invariably hoard resources. Their parochial interests, rather than the company's overall welfare, take priority.

As a result cutting costs or improving quality leaves many

executives feeling like the one quoted above. Although they don't always have the poetic flair to portray the problem quite so succinctly, they know viscerally how hard it is to get anyone to reduce excess overheads. Typically they are unable to solve the problem themselves but unwilling to ask others for their ideas. Many executives are trapped this way. They assume sole responsibility for generating ideas and solving problems. They overlook the creativity of others who may be able to look at the problem differently or help to develop novel solutions.

Everyone who works in an organization has ideas. They know how to do their own job better and more efficiently than it is currently being done. They also have opinions about how things might be improved overall. The chief barrier to their thoughts getting anywhere is the all-too-common assumption that genius resides in the theoretical insights of great minds at the summit. As a result the direct, commonsense experience of "grunts" at the bottom is discounted or ignored.

Many organizations lack an organic conduit encouraging a free flow of ideas across levels and functions. Some have suggestion boxes, but too often they are stuffed with pornographic suggestions of various ways executives themselves can stuff it. In such unwelcome climates good ideas initiated from the trenches are pushed aside, while people passively conform to organizational policies and procedures that are often counterproductive. As one disgruntled employee of a well-known corporation told us:

> "We have an employee suggestions program, but our suggestions are never considered. That is why we are not better. I see several ways to improve our company, but I've given up. Top management is interested in only profits, not in making improvements or providing better services."[2]

There are companies that realize the potential of untapped ideas. These organizations have learned that the best cost-saving ideas come from those closest to the action. Jack Welch, CEO of General Electric Corporation (GE), summed it up best:

> Not every idea is a capital *I* idea. A breakthrough in biotech, that's the wrong view of an idea. An idea is an error-free billing system. An idea is taking a process that requires six days and getting it done in one. Everyone can contribute, every single person. The people who process the work in general have better ideas than those in the office, far better ideas. The key is to give them respect, dignity. When you spend three days in a room with people mapping a process, the ideas just about bubble up inside. Just give them respect, everybody in the organization, and the improvement is enormous.[3]

Consider these small *i* ideas that bubbled up from behind-the-scenes people at Ben & Jerry's:[4]

- Originally, nuts used in the ice cream were mixed by hand, contributing to a time-consuming process and to a potentially harmful repetitive hand movement. Some workers suggested a stainless steel barrel to spin the nuts, which ultimately led to another employee innovation, a motor to turn the barrel.
- A cherry press eliminated most of the hand movement associated with draining cherries.
- A glue chute was installed onto the cartoner where previously an electronic-eye safety guard required that the machine be shut down when the glue emptied. Downtime is eliminated now.
- On the same cartoner, boxes came off the line flat,

requiring workers to manually flip them to facilitate packaging. A mechanical finger was designed through the maintenance department to automatically flip the container to avoid this potentially harmful repetitive motion.
- Workers initially hand-scooped chocolate to touch up the chocolate coating on Ben & Jerry's Peace Pops. A hose now aids the process.

Maybe each idea is not that significant when viewed separately. But in aggregate, they really begin to add up. Other companies are discovering the same benefits of looking widely for good ideas.

American Airlines' Brainstorm

Robert Crandall and other executives at American Airlines realized in 1986 that their own cost-cutting measures were not working well enough. Despite the fact that American's leadership team is one of the best in the world, their executives' collective wisdom was not yielding enough new creative ways to reduce costs. Many of the airline's expenses, such as fueling an aircraft, were outside their control. In addition, American has established a long-term commitment to high quality and safety. Their dilemma was one facing most contemporary organizations: how do we maintain high quality while also lowering costs?

American decided to turn its idea-churning procedures upside down. By creating its IdeAAs in Action Program, all the company's sixty thousand employees became idea generators.[5] Backstage employees along with frontline people were able to share their thoughts about cutting costs and improving quality. Robert Stoltz, the program's manager, outlined the goals of the program:[6]

- Generate profits from employee ideas
- Promote a sense of involvement
- Develop an entrepreneurial attitude among employees
- Support the corporate program that enhances the quality of work life

The IdeAAs program was introduced in 1986 with the appropriate hoopla and publicity.[7] Each employee received a box with party favors, hats, and a proclamation that "the party is just about to begin." The goal for the program's first year was $12 million in savings. Instead, vigilant employees spotted $50 million of fat that could be cut without jeopardizing American's high standards of safety and service. The employee response to the program has been so great that at last count a staff of fifty people were required to evaluate the constant flow of ideas. In 1988 alone there were 12,116 suggestions; nearly a quarter of them were approved, with a cost savings of $31,408,000.

Both individuals and groups submit ideas. Two groups in the airline's Chicago offices submitted an idea for a personal-computer–based communications and inventory-tracking system that saved the company $241,000.[8] A group of alert flight attendants noticed that passengers rarely ate the olive on their salad. Eliminating the olive reportedly saved the company $57,000.[9] An employee cleaning the restrooms between flights observed that when passengers washed their hands, they used a bar of soap and then tossed it away. Soap dispensers in American's lavatories now save the company untold dollars.

But it is not just the company that profits from employees'

ideas. The employees themselves are awarded prizes that range from $75 to $37,500.[10] Many of American's employees have nearly furnished their homes with prizes from the ideas they have submitted. The top prize each year is a run through the warehouse at the headquarters of Maritz Corporation (the company that operates the Ide*AA*s program in conjunction with American) outside St. Louis, Missouri. The warehouse is stocked with all kinds of prizes and products. A one-minute run through the warehouse can earn an American employee over $20,000 in goods. Done in a highly ceremonial way, the warehouse run also earns the employee the respect of his or her peers and supervisors. American's faith in its employees has paid mutual dividends. Crandall, who himself took a run through the warehouse because of a good idea, remarked, "You need a constant message from the top that we want an open door and a participative management so that we can get the full scope of ideas from workers."[11]

Of the workers profiting from American's Ide*AA*s in Action Program, many work behind the scenes. Knowing that their ideas are important and worthwhile provides them a sense of pride and belonging. Unfortunately, this feeling is absent in many organizations today.

TJ International's Approach to Ideas

TJ International long ago realized the value of employee generated ideas. Walt Minnick, president and CEO, observed that employees are "key in keeping technically current and actively improving the product and/or process."[12] Through programs such as Innovator of the Month, employees are encouraged to look for new ways to improve TJI's production processes. The Innovator of the Month Program solicits and recognizes ideas on a continuing basis.[13] When an employee is caught "doing something good," he or she is written up by a manager. Once the idea is formally submitted, the employee receives (a) a congratulations letter from Mr. Minnick and (b) a featured write-up in the company's newsletter, *TJI Today*.

The accolades do not stop here for many TJI "innovators." At year's end, the company's managers pour over the submitted ideas, looking for those that will allow one of their owners to be named Innovator of the Year.[14] The criteria for selection is based on how well the TJI employee's idea affected the company's production process. The Innovator of the Year receives a distinguished title. In addition, the honoree receives shares of TJI stock, induction into the Innovator's Hall of Fame, a catalog gift, and a full-length feature in the company's news digest, *TJI Dimensions*. Alexander MacDonald, TJI's all-time leader in nominations for the Innovator's Hall of Fame, described how he feels about the programs in a recent *Dimensions* article:

> "I was asked the other day if there is any difference between an inventor and an innovator. I answered, after much thought, that an inventor creates for profit and an innovator creates for self-satisfaction and pride in job performance."[15]

Other TJI associates echo his sentiments:[16]

> "A good ideas program is far more than a lottery—it's a backstage worker's empowerment to affect positive change. For example, the Innovators' Hall of Fame is excellent recognition, but don't mistake it as the reason why our associates are motivated to generate ideas. They generate ideas because they want to have a positive impact. They appreciate the fact that every suggestion gets management attention. They know they are linked to our performance—*that's* motivating."

"The exciting aspect of TJ's program for me is to see production workers backstage participate in a fact-based analysis of the impact of an idea on the company's performance. It's motivating for them to see the scale with which they affect the company, and it helps them allocate their efforts better by understanding what factors have the greatest impact. It's one way to make the invisible person's efforts more visible to us."

Bell Atlantic's Champion Program

At Bell Atlantic, employees at any level can submit revenue-producing ideas to the Champion Program.[17] If an idea is accepted, the employees are permitted to devote five hours per week of company time, in addition to their own, to putting their idea into action. To assure a safe and effective incubation period for the project, employees are trained in market analysis and entrepreneurial techniques. They are given start-up money, up to a thousand dollars. After three months, ideas are further screened by a committee of senior managers. At this point, employees can receive additional funding if their projects are supported by solid marketing research.

If an idea passes this initial screening, employees are put on loan to the Business Development Group for six months. There they are trained to develop a business case for their innovation. They also test its market potential. If a product is launched successfully, the employees see it through as its project managers. They also share in potential benefits. They may invest 10 percent of their wages in exchange for 5 percent of their innovation's revenues.

During the program's first years, thirty to forty products and services per year were put into the pipeline for commercialization. Many of the creative ideas came from people in the background. Some of their projects include Creative Connections, a line of designer phone jacks; Emerg-Alert, prerecorded emergency messages targeted to latch-key children; and CommGuard, a package of backup phone services. The most noteworthy success is Thinx, an intelligent graphics program integrating data with images to help users explore relationships visually and apply data or calculations automatically. This idea was developed by Jack Copley, a behind-the-scenes budget manager of Network Services.

The Champion Program has become so successful that the revenue generated has become a permanent part of the Bell Atlantic planning and budgeting process. In five years, they expect to realize at least $100 million from various projects. Sharing up to 5 percent of these new revenues, many of the company's employees also have profited from the program.

As all these organizations have discovered, good ideas come from all employees, not just from executives, managers, or those on the front line.

Training Generates Ideas

For some organizations, employee-generated suggestion programs require simultaneous efforts to retrain and reeducate employees. Donald Weiss, CEO of White Storage, a manufacturer of automated factory-retrieval systems, commented, "There is a growing realization that if you don't empower workers, if you don't educate them, [then you cannot teach] them to pay attention to quality, or to generate new innovative ideas."[18] Because of this belief, Weiss invested heavily in programs emphasizing literacy, math skills, and the proper uses of tools and machinery. In 1991 the company offered over seven thousand hours of training in math, blueprint reading, Japanese manufacturing techniques, quality, English, and how to use small tools properly.[19]

Through these programs, White Storage has reduced employee turnovers (from 25 percent to 10 percent) and on-site accidents (from 180 to 30), in addition to realizing a tremendous increase in employee-generated ideas. Providing training and education for employees is nothing new. What is new is the manner in which companies choose to exploit the employees' newfound knowledge. White Storage encourages employees to believe in themselves and what they know. In return, they generate innovative suggestions for the company. Weiss summarizes: "You unlock the power [of ideas] by educating employees and by giving them an opportunity to develop their skills."[20]

Ideas Mean Dollars

During World War II, a shortage of professionals left U.S. factories with few engineers, scientists, or foremen. As an indirect result of the shortage, management experts discovered that workers really did not need so much supervision.[21] They were not dumb, immature, or maladjusted. They were treated as though they were—and responded in kind. Many companies are just now rediscovering this principle: employees know a great deal about their work and have good ideas about how to improve how things are done. Modern managers need to listen to these line workers. They very often know exactly how the job can be done better or what might be changed to create higher-quality products or services.

Creating an incubator for good ideas encourages people to become reflective and creative. When people put their minds to it, there is no limit to the novel ideas they can create.

For example, meter readers at Florida Power and Light in Boca Raton suffered more on-the-job injuries than any other group.[22] This was due to a large number of nasty dog bites. The meter readers formed a team to study the problem and came up with a new system. A group of ten employees pinpointed which houses had dogs and then programmed handheld computers to beep when the meter reader approached the property. Dog bites and employee absenteeism among the readers decreased; morale and service improved.

There are other examples:

- Dahlin Smith White, the ad agency mentioned earlier, has used electronic mail to encourage ideas from all employees—including their runners and part-time assistants.[23] They have found that their hinterland employees see the business from a different perspective and therefore can often generate suggestions with significant dollar savings.
- A new product from Becton Dickinson, a maker of high-tech medical diagnostic systems, was launched 25 percent faster than previous products.[24] A team of engineers, marketers, and suppliers worked together to develop it.
- Xerox saved $200 million in inventory costs because of the work of an adaptive, flexible team that included both backstage and frontline people: accountants, salespersons, distributors, and administrators.[25]
- By organizing assemblers into self-directed teams on the pilot production line of their new 400E, Mercedes Benz reduced defects by 50 percent. Line workers contributed many of the best ideas.[26]

Managers need to learn how to say "Why not" rather than "You cannot." Billions of dollars are wasted each year by management neglecting sound ideas from people everywhere—especially those behind the scenes. Through innovative programs, managers and executives learn to appreciate the value of employee suggestions as well as the collective camaraderie that sharing and creating together always produce.

Some Final Considerations

- Everyone has valid ideas, regardless of their level in the organization, their experience, or their education.
- Ideas do not have to always be major breakthroughs. Minor adjustments in work processes can literally save thousands and millions of dollars.
- For most companies, a planned, defined program on new ideas generates huge dollar savings and service improvements.
- Given that the hidden organization is 75 percent of most companies, ideas from backstage employees hold tremendous dollar and service potential.

Diagnostic Questions

1. How important are new ideas to our success?
2. When we solicit ideas, do we engage all employees—especially those who actually are doing the work?
3. How might we implement a formal program to generate more ideas?

■ CHAPTER 9
Trusting While Helping

Seeing the Chips Fly

There is a story about a man who was hired by a psychologist for an experiment. The psychologist took his newly acquired subject to a pile of wood and gave him an ax.

> "Do you see that log lying there?" he asked.
> The man nodded.
> The psychologist continued, "I want you to make like you're chopping wood; only I want you to use the back side of the ax—not the blade. I'll give you ten dollars per hour."
> The man looked at the psychologist, thinking to himself that this must be some sort of joke. Either that or the psychologist was crazy. But since the pay was good and he needed the money, he started to work. After a couple of hours, he returned to the psychologist's office and knocked at the door. The psychologist asked him what he wanted.
> "Mister, I'm quitting this job!"

"What's the matter, don't you like the pay you're getting? If it isn't enough, I'll raise your wages."

"No, mister, the pay is good enough—but when I chop wood, I've got to see the chips fly!"[1]

People operating behind the curtain often don't see the "chips fly." In many companies, they are told what to do and are compensated in return. But they are not trusted to do a decent job. Managers believe they need constantly to look over the shoulders of employees and review their performances at regular intervals. To most employees such supervision is not helpful. It is seen as "snoopervision"—just another indication that management has little faith in them. Supervisors who talk a helping game while snooping around create what well-known leadership guru Warren Bennis describes as a trust gap.[2] Usually this gap is portrayed as a one-sided affair where employees are distrustful of management. But the other side of the equation is equally important. Do managers trust employees, especially those whose work is hidden from public view?

Trusting While Critiquing

Lack of trust creates a difficult managerial dilemma. On one hand, trusting people allows them an opportunity to deal with everyday problems without relying too heavily on their managers. On the other hand, how do managers give people constructive feedback without having them feel invaded and controlled? Giving people their head and trusting them to do good things can backfire. It can create a feeling of isolation and undermine learning and growth. But tight supervision can create suspiciousness and feelings of dependency or powerlessness. The dilemma rests on whether trusting and help-

ing can coexist in effective management practices. We think
they can. Consider the following example:

> "I think my boss is wonderful. She lets us work; do
> anything. She reviews it, but we can create. Some people
> are spoon-fed, but Kim doesn't do that. She offers you
> suggestions. Constructive criticism. And that was true
> from the beginning. So, it's good."[3]

This supervisor obviously trusts her people, yet also reviews
and critiques their work. She listens but feels free to offer
constructive criticism. Her supervision is welcomed and
viewed as a source of positive feedback and learning. As Jack
Welch of GE said, "We've got to take out the boss element."[4]
By this he meant eliminating the distrusting, controlling person who believes there's only one way to get people to do
things: tell them what to do and then look over their shoulder
to make certain that it is done. Instead, management must
believe that people are trustworthy. They need to be seen as
human beings who need encouragement, not as objects to be
manipulated or controlled.

There are very few of us who awake each morning, yawn,
stretch, and announce, "I want to do a really bad job today."
Yet, treatment of people in rearward positions often suggests
that management believes this to be the case. Fortunately,
some employers are beginning to realize that trusting people
while helping them to do better work is a sensible way to get
people to work hard.

At Kodak, assembly workers who make X-ray cassettes
and film spools, canisters, and cartons arrange their own hours
and keep track of their individual production.[5] They fix their
own machines. They do not require someone telling them
what to do or how to do it. Nor do they need to be reminded
to inspect to see whether or not it has been done right.

At Chaparral Steel, employees do not punch a time clock.[6] Instead, they set their own lunch hours and breaks. Their salaries and bonuses are based on three things: profits, performance, and new skills they learn. In exchange, workers are expected to use their heads as well as their hands. As a result, Chaparral steel is produced at 1.6 hours of labor per ton. The industry averages range from 2.4 hours to 4.9 hours per ton.

Tangible Feedback

When employees do a good job, it is important to let them know in tangible ways. Seeing the chips fly is important, but when a cord of wood is chopped for someone else, some form of economic recognition is also appropriate. Stars in the limelight benefit from sales contests, profit sharing, and special incentives. Few such incentives or performance rewards typically are extended to the cast backstage. Imagine a director who gave feedback and rewards only to those in starring roles. She would never be able to create an exemplary dramatic production. The same is true for managers trying to create organizations capable of producing an exemplary product or service. People backstage need to know when they are doing well. They need to see some link between doing a good job and being rewarded, while simultaneously learning how they can do their job better. Employees need to know what is expected of them and how to do their job the right way. Once they know what to do, they can pick up the ball and run without tight supervision or interference. Like any onstage employee, people working behind the scenes need to know how to do the job, be given sufficient authority and autonomy to do it, and receive regular feedback on how well they are doing. When people feel entrusted to do a job, there is a good chance that they will do it well.

Gary Sasser, CEO of Averitt Express, a freight transportation company, puts this enlightened philosophy to work. His company goes to great lengths to avoid conventional labeling of employees or workers. Employees are called associates and treated as such:

> "We work hard to give our associates feedback so they know how they are doing. Then we try to reinforce them by finding and pointing out what they do right. We expect performance from our people, but we also want them to share in the results of that performance. Each person has specific pinpoints to work on. In offices, in meeting rooms, in the cabs of our trucks, you'll see measuring sticks people are using to gauge performance. We establish those pinpoints collectively and share them constantly. Those keys are for everybody."[7]

People in the hidden cast often cannot relate the quality of their performance to a company's bottom line. Data entry operators do not receive a commission for entering information correctly. It is difficult for accountants to see how balancing the books affects annual performance. They need some other method of evaluating their performance. Faye Wattleton, former national director of Planned Parenthood, requires her employees to write yearly goals for themselves.[8] Instead of basing pay increases on sales volume, which few nonprofit organizations have, she bases raises on how well performance measures up to stated goals. This provides a benchmark for evaluating performance and allocating rewards in a just and equitable way. For Planned Parenthood, the key is the feedback and evaluation of the employees' own goals.

At Square D, indicators of performance are prominently

displayed in their plants.[9] Under slogans such as "Together we will outrun the competition," "Dedicated to growth," and "Committed to quality," employees post their daily and monthly progress on wall charts that are scattered throughout the manufacturing floor. On the floor the assembling of Square D's electrical distribution products is divided into four main teams. Within each main team, several smaller, specialized teams operate. Both the main and smaller teams keep wall charts that examine first pass yield, defects, cycle time, on-time, productivity, safety, and inventory. In addition to these individualized progress charts, Square D has an overall company productivity chart that lines the wall leading to the employee cafeteria. Such displays are clearly posted for everyone to see and help connect the plant's production to Square D's overall operation and financial performance.

First Union Georgia Servicecenter, a back-room processing operation, credits much of its phenomenal success to providing performance data and statistics daily.[10] Employees know how they are measuring up on suspense (pending) account entries, checking account statements, staff levels, or service levels. Employees themselves set and meet these quantitative goals; but they also constantly look for improvement. Their results are impressive. Suspense account entries have been reduced from 6,000 to 126, operational losses cut from $1.1 million to $4,026, and total employees on the payroll slimmed from over 600 to 315. Answering 75 percent of customer calls within a month has been reduced to answering 99 percent of calls within twenty-four hours.

Ben & Jerry's is another company that gives feedback to employees while going to great lengths to seek their feedback.[11] In a new manufacturing plant in St. Albans, Vermont, each Wednesday afternoon and evening, two team "beatings" (meetings) are held to accommodate workers on various "phases" (shifts). Employees themselves humorously relabeled their meetings. They prefer the term *phases* to *shifts* as a means to avoid feelings of superiority or inferiority according to the hours one works. A Ben & Jerry's team leader attends both meetings to provide continuity between the two groups and to act as facilitator. Employees are given the opportunity to facilitate team beatings as a means of enhancing their skills while also receiving guidance from the team leader.

Problems to be discussed at the team beatings originate from employees. They write their concerns on the "parking lot," a dry-erase board located in the employee break room. Each individual concern is initialed and becomes a formal part of a meeting's agenda. As issues are discussed, consensus is reached around a greater understanding of the conditions affecting particular issues. As one employee explained:

> "Decision-making empowers you. You have an idea and they listen. We are all trained to do each others' jobs, so we have a better understanding of what is involved on the production line. There is mutual respect for each other. No hierarchy exists here. You know if something goes wrong, it's like dominos. It's up to the individual to maintain the standards of the products."[12]

Recognition and Incentives

Not all feedback to backstage employees needs to be statistical or financial in nature. There are other ways for people to know how well they are doing and how important they are. Opryland relies heavily on personal recognition. Jennifer Martin, park operations supervisor, said:

> "I try to give personal recognition to my employees. This used to be the easiest form of recognition for me to give,

but now it has become the hardest. I guess because I worked in the phone center for so long and wasn't dealing with people face-to-face. Now that I'm a supervisor, though, I really try to give that personal recognition. I especially try to use the employees' names a lot when I talk to them or say hello. Everyone likes to be recognized and hear their name. The employees love it as much as anyone, and I try to remember that.[13]

In addition to lots of personal feedback, Opryland uses other strategies to spread recognition and feedback to all parts of their large organization. Kathy Roadarmel, employee relations manager, related:

"We really try to negate any differences between onstage and backstage. We try to recognize equally as best we can. We know that the onstage people get more applause and feedback from the guests, but we try to spread the recognition around. We have comment boards in various areas, where any comment related to that area is posted for all to see."[14]

Consistent recognition and feedback instills a sense of belonging for people in obscure positions. It is a feeling that is often lacking in most organizations. It is important to spread incentives around. Though many companies acknowledge the need for incentives for frontline employees, few know how to create incentives for people in the wings.

American Airlines instituted the innovative You're Someone Special Incentive Program.[15] Each month frequent fliers receive You're Someone Special coupons, which they award to any American employee who gives an exemplary performance. The coupons are good for one thousand miles free travel for the employees. But as one flight attendant said,

"The real value of these coupons is instant recognition for a job well done."[16]

Unfortunately, American's onstage employees are usually the ones recognized by passengers. Occasionally, a reservation person or someone less visible will receive an award; but as it turns out, the You're Someone Special program's primary recipients are those who work directly with passengers. Recognizing this, American is considering other programs for those working behind the scenes. Crandall's push for a national Golden Wrench Award (best maintenance) is one way to provide recognition for American's mechanics.[17] Even though passengers rarely see them, no one would dispute their importance.

Other companies also have begun incentive programs that include the cast behind the scenes. Remington has a unique incentive plan.[18] Only 65 percent of factory employees' paychecks are in salary and the remainder is based on incentives. The incentive plan, based on measurable goals, resulted in a 17 percent increase in productivity over four years. At MBNA America Bank, N.A., a leading credit card company, recognition and incentives were combined with tangible feedback to improve quality.[19] Seventy little things that matter to customer service are measured daily with the fourteen most important posted visibly in the hallways. All employees are on incentive programs geared to the fourteen customer-service indicators. By meeting these customer-service goals, MBNA's five thousand employees have earned bonuses as high as 20 percent of their annual salaries.

Avis takes another approach.[20] Employees now own the company. Several benefits have resulted from this significant proprietary shift. A shop steward who had previously protected marginal employees, gave them two weeks to improve. Employees themselves initiated cost-saving measures once they began to see how the company's performance affected their paycheck. They check to make sure the gasoline tanks of returned cars are actually full. They watch that people do not swap cheap baby seats for the high-quality ones Avis supplies. They have reduced phone costs by looking up phone numbers rather than calling information.

These formal incentive programs have found success, in part, because most people in backstage roles are usually left out of recognition and reward programs. Therefore, almost anything to demonstrate sincere appreciation for a job well done is very well received. Joann DeMott, author and well-known consultant for Total Quality Management, recently asked a group of backstage employees, "In what way do you like to be recognized for your exceptional efforts?"[21] Their answers included

- to be told in person about the great job I did
- ice cream sodas
- new opportunities to do tasks that no one wants to do
- verbal thank-you's
- future opportunities to be creative and try something new
- comments on my annual evaluation, especially written in my supervisor's own handwriting
- M&Ms

DeMott observed:

What seemed to matter was having their work be seen by someone who mattered to them and hearing that their work made a positive difference. For some members of this group, doing exceptional work added to their own sense of accomplishment and was a reward in itself. Each employee knows how he/she likes to be recognized and the manager must find out what each person prefers in order to be able to provide that satisfaction.[22]

Some Final Thoughts

Trusting and helping while recognizing a job well done undoubtedly will bring some welcome sunlight into the lives of people who often operate in the dark. Consider the following as guidelines for simultaneously turning people loose, giving them feedback, and recognizing their accomplishments:

- Trust people to do what is right. Booker T. Washington said, "Few less things can help an individual more than to place responsibility on him and let him know you trust him."[23]
- Find a way to provide constant feedback (formal/informal) to all employees.
- Review your organization's incentives. Consider simple, meaningful incentives. However, make sure they are continual and constant.
- If possible, link all compensation to performance and results; backstage people perform better with merit increases.

Constant feedback, continual improvement, and rewards for good performance are especially important for people behind the scenes. Regular evaluations, informal coaching, and incentives provide direction, encouragement, and improvement. Under this system, autonomy, attention, and incentives are not at odds. They are effectively integrated into better ways of managing people who are rarely seen or rarely see the results of their work.

Diagnostic Questions

1. What is the current level of trust between management and employees?

2. Are feedback mechanisms satisfactory from the employees' view?
3. Do managers make decisions on the advice of subordinates, or do subordinates make decisions subject to the approval of managers?
4. Are the company incentives meaningful and understood by employees? Do incentives invoke employee participation?

◼ CHAPTER 10
Avoiding the "That's Not My Job" Syndrome

The Myopic View

There is nothing more frustrating than asking someone for help and having them shrug their shoulders and state empathically, "Love to help, but that's not my job." People sometimes think of their job as an end in itself rather than as one link in a means-to-end chain that ultimately delivers a top-quality service or product to a customer. This is a very parochial view of a job. Quality is not the sole purpose of a corporate quality-assurance team; it is a collective state of mind. It is woven day-in and day-out into everything people do. As Total Quality Management is defined: "Quality is everyone's responsibility."

For many years, American industry emphasized specialization and accountability. Companies assumed that by giving people a straightforward, well-defined, compartmentalized task and having them do it over and over, they would become highly proficient. By routinizing work, they believed, relationships between specialized activities could be tightly pre-scribed and vertically managed.

The main problem with this line of thinking is that as people become highly skilled at a particular task, they quickly become extremely bored. Tight regulations and micromanage-ment do not motivate people. Nor do they keep people from finding ingenious ways of covering up mistakes and passing them down the line. As an assembly line worker at an automo-bile plant commented, "If the car's engine breaks down, it's not my fault. I put on the fenders."[1] Or as a ticket agent for an airline retorted recently to a passenger's complaint about lost bags, "Look, that's not my problem. Wasn't your ticket OK? Wasn't your mileage duly entered? You have a baggage problem. I do tickets. Go talk to the people in baggage claim."[2]

These people see their responsibility as doing their job, not serving the customer, or making a contribution to the company. As long as they focus myopically on their specific responsibilities, they consider themselves successful. While individually this may be true, collectively it can spell disaster.

The Broader View

Fortunately, U.S. organizations and employees are waking up to the fact that simply doing one's job is not enough. They are beginning to realize that the all-too-common "That's not my responsibility" mind-set has its costs. Ignoring the big picture often results in bankruptcies or loss of market share to foreign countries where all employees do take responsibility for the overall quality of products or services. Striving for an environ-ment where each employee can share responsibility outside his or her job description for a larger good pays substantial rewards. Consider these dramatic examples of people going well beyond the call of duty:

- A reservation agent for Delta Airlines received a call from a woman in her nineties who wanted to book a flight to California. In helping her make the reservation, the agent discovered this was the woman's first plane trip and probably her last. She had just sold her house of many years and was flying to California to enter a nursing home. In choosing the home, the family's obligations evidently had ended. None of them had the time to accompany her, even though the woman was very apprehensive about making the trip. After booking the woman's reservation, the agent booked himself on the same flight. On his day off, he accompanied the woman to her destination.[3]
- Upstart Kiwi International Airlines sees its future and competitive edge as going beyond the "That's not my responsibility" syndrome. Trying to hold operating costs 20 percent below United, Kiwi's strategy is for its owners/employees to avoid the structured, cumbersome, and nonsensical work rules that have afflicted their competitors. As CEO Robert Iverson describes the competition, "It's not unusual to have two people sitting around all day whose sole purpose is to move the jetway. Those people cannot load bags. The people who load bags cannot change a tire." Iverson expects his employees to have a broader view—a view that includes stepping out of the job description whenever it is necessary.[4]

While these examples are exceptional, more routine actions outside one's formal job requirements occur every day. More than ever before, responsibility for overseeing total quality is being spread across the board. For example, a woman at Anheuser-Busch reportedly pulled an emergency lever to stop the bottling operation because she realized that the labels on the Budweiser bottles were slightly crooked.[5] At Nissan of America, anyone on the assembly line can stop production if they notice anything amiss on any part of a pickup truck or Sentra car.[6] And at Ericsson GE Mobile Communications, all employees on any of the fifty-eight teams are authorized to shut down a production line if they are not satisfied with the quality.[7] Ericsson's average employee is forty-seven years old and has been with the company for twenty-two years. Since Ericsson started involving their backstage employees in 1987, it is no wonder that the coordinator of the program, Sam Hedrick, voices some surprise: "To see a fifty-five-year-old worker now stopping a production line because it is not up to quality, well, that's a sea change."[8]

Encouraging More Responsibility

How does a company encourage people to enlarge their assigned scope of work? First, top management models the concern for quality. At Anheuser-Busch, the action described above probably was influenced by a widely shared story that August Busch III himself had done the very same thing several months before.[9] Through watching him directly or hearing the story from someone else, the employee recognized that maintaining the perfection of a bottle of Budweiser is a shared responsibility.

Second, companies need to recognize that most employees want more responsibility. Chuck Raper, director of Administration at McKinsey and Company in Atlanta, tells how backstage employees want to be included:

"A business analyst at McKinsey is often a behind-the-scenes number cruncher—usually a person who plans to later pursue an undergraduate degree. About seven or eight years ago, we had a minor revolt from the business analysts. This revolt seemed to be springing up in many offices across the country simultaneously. They were saying, 'We are not very happy. We don't like to just crunch numbers.'

"At the same time, these employees were beginning to be recognized by McKinsey as a great source of recruitment for associates and partners. So the firm decided to have a series of meetings with analysts to discuss their role.

"At one of the meetings, I remember saying to one of the best and most brilliant analysts, 'Jean, somebody has to crunch the numbers!'

"She said, 'Chuck, I know that, and I do not mind doing it. I just want to be included as a member of the team. When there are meetings of the associates and partners about a project or client or final report, we [the analysts] would like to be there. And once in a while we would like to have some direct contact. We do not want to just be a backstage person sitting in front of a PC crunching numbers.'

"Today, throughout our firm, business analysts have gravitated toward becoming full team members. While they still crunch numbers, they also are in on team meetings and often have client contact, especially the second year."[10]

Chuck Raper's story is one of mutual discovery. Most employees want more responsibility. Giving them what they want improves performance plus offers people more opportunities to broaden their repertoire of skills. They then assume even more responsibility.

Third, good companies infuse a concern for quality into everyday operations. Opryland, in particular, provides a host of excellent examples:[11]

- In the Opryland Theme Park, there is a large sign proclaiming "Caring is contagious, pass it on." The sign represents the tip of the iceberg in the park's We Care Program. The program empowers all employees to do whatever possible to assure that guests enjoy their visit. Any employee can give a guest a full refund if something goes amiss. Every employee is given the responsibility of helping guests. If they cannot help, they go to a nearby phone and dial C-A-R-E, and a supervisor comes immediately to provide assistance.
- Any reservations agent can book a special room for someone celebrating a wedding or anniversary.
- Once a year Opryland puts lead people into supervisory positions for a day to broaden their perspectives.
- Employees are cross-trained. That way, in the evening when there are a limited number of housekeepers on duty, a portion of the work can be given to someone else, on short notice if necessary, taking full advantage of the cross-training that has been done.
- Employees are encouraged to get involved in something unrelated to their job. For example, Mary Beth, who is a communications specialist, took a basic sanitation class and loved it. It is refreshing to her because it is totally unrelated to anything in her work, but it helps familiarize her with the total operation.
- A quality assurance supervisor on her way to a meeting passed some men standing in the hotel's lobby holding tuxedos on hangers and looking lost. She located their intended destination and asked the front desk for a room where they could change before making a guest appearance at an important function.
- Two supervisors pitched in to help an overworked group

in food and beverage. As one said, "I served mashed potatoes and loved it. I was covered in them from head to toe. But it didn't matter. I worked with people. The other supervisor related the serving of mashed potatoes back to my early experiences of rolling up my sleeves and doing what is needed. These experiences are good. They make the employees feel special and needed."

Fourth, consider the possibility of self-managed teams. Though such arrangements are highly controversial, the controversy usually originates from managers who don't want to give up their control—or employees who don't want to think for themselves. Self-managed teams typically include both onstage and backstage employees. A synergy develops because people bring different perspectives, have different skills, and represent different functions. Ideally, participation on teams broadens the employees' responsibilities and horizons and offers them a chance to step beyond their normal work boundaries. The results can be impressive:

- A group of Federal Express clerks spotted and solved a billing problem that was costing the company $2.1 million per year. Other teams have cut service glitches, such as lost packages, by 13 percent.[12]
- A team of blue-collar workers at Johnsonville Food, a maker of sausage, helped make the decision to proceed with a major plant expansion. Since that time, productivity has increased 50 percent.[13]
- General Mills claims its plants with self-managed teams can be as much as 40 percent more productive than those without such teams.[14] To date, some 60 percent of their plants converted to self-managed teams, with the intent to spread the concept to all of its operations.[15]
- A team of five steel workers from U.S. Steel, Gary (winner of the USA 1992 Quality Award), reduced the reject rate

from automotive customers from 2.6 percent to 0.6 percent.[16]

- An agricultural chemical plant of the Plant Protection Division of Ciba-Geigy Canada, Ltd., switched to a boss-less organization and found its productivity increased by 20 to 30 percent. The company took away the traditional management hierarchy and empowered workers to set schedules, manage costs, develop job descriptions, interview for new hires, and make what were once known as management decisions, including planning their own downsizing. One consultant ranks the Cambridge Canada plant as the best example of participative management he has seen.[17]

- Lechmere, Inc., a twenty-seven-store retail chain, believes a multiskilled work force enhances employee performance and relations. At the Sarasota, Florida, outlet, pay raises are based on the number of jobs employees learn. Cashiers are encouraged also to sell products. Sporting goods staff members receive training in how to operate forklifts. As a result of multiskills training, Lechmere, Inc., can adjust staffing needs by rerouting employees, thereby creating a more stable work force.[18]

These companies have learned that putting people into a rigid slot and asking them simply to do their job is counterproductive. Charlie Wilson, a successful team leader at GE in Decatur, Alabama, describes the syndrome very clearly: "They used to come to work, leave their brains at the door, put in their hours and get their paychecks."[19] Everyone needs to realize that his or her job is much broader in scope and that each person is responsible for making customers and clients happy. This spirit can be woven into everyday activity in successful organizations. It is important for people backstage to perform their specific tasks. It is equally important for them to step across the formal boundaries to serve both external and internal customers. Doing whatever is required to enhance customer service is everyone's responsibility. Doing only one's own job well is simply not good enough.

Diagnostic Questions

1. Are our people too specialized?
2. Are there ways we can encourage people in the hidden cast to expand their scope of responsibilities?
3. What have been the results for departments that have extended or blurred work boundaries?

■ CHAPTER 11
Right Things, Not Tight Rules

Rule Breakers and Rule Followers

People who make transatlantic telephone calls have probably never heard of Linn Mollenauer. But whenever they make an inexpensive, error-free overseas call, they are able to enjoy his creation. He developed perfect light pulses that are capable of sending overseas messages quickly and cheaply with a near-zero failure rate. His success, however, involved short-term insubordination.

Mollenauer had been working on a new optical fiber for several years.[1] In 1988, at Bell Laboratories in Holmdel, New Jersey, his team demonstrated their ability to transmit light pulses 4,000 kilometers without degeneration. While 4,000 kilometers can transmit a message between New York and Los Angeles, it takes 7,500 kilometers to carry a message between New York and London, and 9,000 kilometers for a transpacific communication. Because of this, his superiors did not feel that Linn's soliton wave idea would be feasible for use in overseas cables. For his close-but-no-cigar accomplishment, his boss gave him a congratulatory pat on the back and a bonus. Enough work had been done on the soliton project, and Mollenauer was given six months to wrap it up and look for something new.

At this point, most of us probably would have accepted the pat and the bonus and then set our sights on new horizons. But Linn Mollenauer was not about to stop. Infuriated, he went ahead with his experiments anyway, thinking and hoping management would back down. They eventually did. He knew he was right. He just needed some proof to change their minds.

A similar, well-known example comes from 3M. Early in its history, a scientist came up with a revolutionary idea for a see-through tape that would adhere to most surfaces. His superiors didn't think much of the item and reassigned him to another project. The next day, he went back to work on his tape. Angered by his insubordination, his superiors fired him. Again, the next day he showed up to work on his tape idea. His frustrated superiors, not wanting to incur the negative publicity of forcibly removing someone, threw up their hands. They permitted him to proceed—as long as he didn't bother anyone else. Ultimately, his idea resulted in one of 3M's most well-known products—Scotch tape.

Scientists like these two are not the only ones who are frustrated by rules and policies that overly constrain initiative and creativity. While no one would argue that anarchy should replace bureaucracy, following rules to the letter often leads to outcomes that are less than desirable. Consider the following story about janitor Garth Peterson. He worked at the same university as did Dr. Albert Einstein. Mr. Peterson once stated, "Most of the professors appreciated it when you washed off the blackboard. But Dr. Einstein did not. Every morning the doctor burst into tears. But the way I saw it, my job was to wash the blackboards and I was bound and determined to do my job."[2]

In both the Mollenauer and the Einstein episodes, following the rules was not necessarily the right thing to do. Breaking the rules allowed Linn and his 3M counterpart to succeed, while sticking to the rules may have erased some of Einstein's most important scientific equations. Mindlessly adhering to policies or slavishly following questionable rules often undermines the quality of products or services. Created with the intention of helping organizations succeed, policies and rules can just as easily play a major role in causing them to falter or fail.

There is absolutely no doubt that policies and rules are important. Without them, organizations would be chaotic and unpredictable. McDonald's assures the quality and consistency of its products through highly standardized rules and procedures. But when following the rules interferes with quality performance, other options need to be made available. Under certain conditions, people need to feel that they can break the rules without being chewed out, demoted, or dismissed. One of the navy's most well-known rule breakers was Hyman George Rickover, father of America's nuclear submarine fleet. Rickover's disdain for rules was expressed with the fervor of an evangelist:

> I never read the rules. Someone brought a book of Navy Regulations into my office and I told them to get the hell out and burn it. I didn't need a book of regulations to tell me what to do, I did the things I thought were right. . . . Any rule that I agree with I like.[3]

While some people may fault Rickover for his unabashed irreverence, it is hard to minimize his unparalleled accomplishments. He broke the rules in order to get things done. In the end the navy dismissed Rickover, but not before he built a nuclear submarine fleet that gave America a strategic edge over the former Soviet Union's nuclear capabilities. His trouble-making helped keep the U.S. Navy afloat and ahead of the game.

Very often it is not rule breakers who get organizations in trouble. It is the bureaucratic rule followers who adhere mindlessly to outdated policies and regulations. Consider this scenario:

> A newly commissioned officer, well versed in military policies and regulations, attempted to command "by the book." Ignoring repeated warnings from his well-seasoned sergeant that there were faster and more efficient avenues through which paperwork could be processed, the officer chose to adhere religiously to the more bureaucratic rules. After two weeks of filling out triplicates, filing and refiling, and obtaining signatures, the officer became so inundated with paper that his frustration level rose and his productivity plummeted. Finally, in desperation, he called for his sergeant and humbly suggested, "Uh, Sergeant, why don't we start handling these matters informally".[4]

Going by the book can divert people's minds from the real task of satisfying customers or producing high-quality products and services. When Jerre Stead joined Square D as CEO in the late eighties, he was handed four thick manuals of official policies and procedures.[5] In total, the manual prescribed 760 different rules to be followed. Many of these governed who could talk with whom in the company. Several specified who could talk with customers and when. Stead replaced these rigid rules with 11 general policy statements. He believed that common sense about the right thing to do should take precedence over tight specifications about how it should be done. By hiding behind unproductive rules, people will either offer marginal work performance or become alienated from their organization's mission. Either way, they tend not to care anymore.

Like Square D, other organizations must decide between rigid rules that inhibit creativity and general guidelines that allow their people to make money, save money, invent new things, and help others succeed. Spartan Express, a freight company with a 90 percent on-time record, encourages employees to go beyond the formal rules to satisfy customers with its WITS (Whatever It Takes) Program.[6] All employees at Spartan are encouraged to use their WITS. For example, Account Manager Robbie Dudley learned of a misdirected shipment on its way to a new customer. Knowing that this error could severely damage or even ruin the emerging relationship, he personally reloaded the freight and, using his own truck, delivered the shipment correctly.

Good organizations have learned that people should be empowered to make decisions rather than programmed to follow rules. In a 1989 speech, Robert A. Ferchat, president of Northern Telecom Canada, Ltd., stated his company's philosophy:

"Rules and controls from some central sources don't work. At Northern Telecom, we have books and books of policies and procedures. But our progress is always, always, driven by individuals or small teams who take on problems and solve them, given enough support. To enlist volunteers in support of your enterprise, you must be willing to give them more freedom—freedom to create, to make decisions, to challenge the status quo, to contribute, to participate fully in the business, freedom to make mistakes. And freedom to take ownership of the business, if not materially, at least in their gut."[7]

Encouraging ownership involves giving people discretion, rather than demanding their compliance. Management of travel expenses is a typical area where companies tend to dictate rigid rules. Employees consequently manipulate the system to find ways around the procedures. There are better alternatives. At McKinsey, employees are expected to make decisions as if they were top management—to minimize costs for clients while retaining the goodwill of employees. As an entry-level staff member described: "The firm told me to manage my expenses so that I could stand before the client and justify any item. Consequently, I was free to creatively solve the needs of myself and the client."[8]

United Electric Controls recently developed a Valued Employee Program, encouraging employees to participate in "problem-solving action centers."[9] It also implemented a Valued Ideas Program, realizing that if the company was going to improve its manufacturing process, the involvement of its employees was critical. All of these impressive companies want to empower people to make decisions and to assume responsibility for results—even at the lowest level. Doing what's right is more important than following rules. As a result, their employees are constantly thinking about doing what is right, not trying to avoid doing something wrong.

YEGA: The Ultimate Strategy

Tim Firnstahl operates a chain of highly successful restaurants in Seattle. One reason behind his success is an absolute guarantee that customers will be highly satisfied with every aspect of their dining experience. Any customer who complains about the quality of service or food is given a free dessert, meal, or other recompense. But initially Firnstahl's foolproof system of guarantees didn't work very well.

> Our procedures for responding seemed all wrong. Giving
> out that free dessert required approval from a manager.
> Getting a suit cleaned [e.g., because of spilled soup]
> meant filling out a form and getting a manager to sign it.
> We were on a treadmill, getting nowhere.[10]

His first response to the problem was to write Ten Tenets of Excellence as a philosophical guide for employees. One day, when an employee asked what the sixth tenet was, Firnstahl couldn't remember. So he streamlined the philosophy into a simple slogan: "YEGA—Your Enjoyment Guaranteed, Always."

Despite this new slogan, the same complaints arose again and again. Even though customers were given freebies, employees always were trying to pin the responsibility for poor service or food on someone else:

> They tried to bury mistakes or blame others. I saw it
> every time we tried to track down a complaint. The food
> servers blamed the kitchen for late meals. The kitchen
> blamed food servers for placing orders incorrectly.[11]

His solution was to give *every* employee the power to guarantee customer enjoyment. Although general guidelines were provided, employees could now give customers a free dessert, free meal, or anything to make good on the restaurant's promise. They were not required to fill out a form, check with a supervisor, or make a phone call. Anyone could do whatever was required to make good on the guarantee—on the spot:

> In one case, a customer wanted a margarita made the
> way a competitor made it. So our bartender called the
> bartender at the other restaurant and, bartender-to-

bartender, learned the special recipe. In another case, an elderly woman who had not been in our restaurant for years, ordered breakfast, which we no longer served. The waiter and the chef sent someone to the market for bacon and eggs and served the breakfast she wanted.[12]

The restaurant chain's guarantee is not time bound or dependent on customer initiative. Each month, a group of employees using available records calls several hundred customers and asks them to evaluate their dining experience. Even an OK response earns a customer a letter of apology, a free meal, or a follow-up phone call.

To keep guarantee costs down, systems, not people, are blamed when problems occur, according to Firnstahl:

> Our search for the culprit in a string of complaints about slow food service in one restaurant led just to the kitchen and then to one cook. But pushing the search one step further revealed several unrealistically complex dishes, that no one could have prepared swiftly. . . . In another case, our kitchens were turning out wrong orders at a rate that was costing us thousands of dollars a month in wasted food. The cooks insisted that the food servers were punching incorrect orders into the kitchen print-out computer. In times past, we might have ended our search right there, accused the food servers of sloppiness and asked everyone to be more careful. But now adhering to the principle of system failure, not people failure, we looked beyond the symptoms and found a flaw in our training.[13]

In many organizations a problem such as a large number of returned dishes would have triggered the typical knee-jerk response: create new rules to govern either the waiters' behavior, the cooks' behavior, or both. But in Tim Firnstahl's restaurants, employees are given freedom to operate within the boundary of a simple philosophy. When problems arise, reviewing the system, rather than blaming people or writing new rules, is the preferred response.

Doing What's Right

The importance of having well-defined policies as a way to ensure compliance and motivation has been ingrained in managers. Many employees have become accustomed to following rules rather than thinking for themselves. Lessons from top-performing companies suggest the following guidelines for empowering people behind the scenes and focusing their attention on doing what is right for the business:

- **Give authority to make decisions.**

  At American Airlines, cargo loading dock employees have the authority to decide the tonnage of cargo allowed on a flight. Since each cargo price directly affects the company's bottom line, cargo workers can make on-the-spot decisions to add or not add each piece without going through multiple checkpoints or jumping through a series of formal hoops. American also gives more discretion to its dispatchers than do other airlines. Decentralized flight planning makes every flight a legal contract between the captain and the dispatcher. They, not the higher-ups, sign off on the final plan.

- **Consider values in place of rules.**

  Replacing rules and policies with organizational values is not easy. Having a short, well-known set of values may be a much better guide for everyday decisions than a long list of specific and inflexible rules. Governments at our local, state, and federal levels are infamous for their tight rules and regulations. A state employee in North Carolina told us, "For years I tried to do the right thing and use my imagination and creativity, but eventually I was usurped by the system. Now, I am looking forward to an early retirement."[14] Values, not rules, should shape the way that employees do business. With the YEGA philosophy, Tim Firnstahl may have provided us with the ultimate in simplifying values so they are widely shared and uniformly understood.

- **Balance flexibility with standards.**

   Empowered employees still need parameters for making decisions. Employees at Microsoft Corporation operate in an environment that encourages creativity, flexibility, and self-motivation. They also are expected to adhere to guiding principles that set the company apart from the rest of the software industry. Surrounded by a forest, playing fields, hiking trails, and a pond, Microsoft believes that a corporate environment must be "as employee-friendly as possible."[15] It must also provide a philosophical guide for its employees.

   Microsoft's values are not constricting; they leave room for creativity. The company refers to a lot of its employees as "wild ducks"[16] (people who live by different rules). But their values also encourage teamwork. Through balancing individual initiative and teamwork, Microsoft achieves togetherness and a level of intimacy, something CEO Bill Gates believes is often missing in large bureaucratic organizations.

   Tom Corbett, a developer at Microsoft, describes this paradoxical working environment: "The company trusts them [developers] to do what they already know how to do, turns them loose to solve problems and helps them when they get stuck."[17]

   While it is not easy to create an environment through trust and employee empowerment as Microsoft has done, organizations may find that rigid rules sometimes need to be broken—in order for the business to grow.

- **Tolerate mistakes and reward creative rule-breaking.**

    One way to stress customer service is to empower employees to make changes when the situation demands. Employees should be given authority to make certain decisions on the spot when the options affect service, the budget, or the customer. While people may not always make the right decisions, management needs to trust their ability to make them. There is nothing more demoralizing than to be encouraged to take risks and then have your head handed to you on a plate following your first mistake. Employees are naturally suspicious of discretion that may lead to punishment. In many organizations, it is well-known that following the rules and staying within specified boundaries is the safest thing to do. People may not do the best possible individual work, but at least they keep their jobs. They keep working even though the company's overall performance keeps getting worse.

    During the landing of aircraft on a navy carrier, even the lowliest deckhand can halt the operation if that person feels something is wrong.[18] Even if the judgment was in error, the individual still receives praise for exercising discretion in the interest of safety.

    At Hewlett-Packard, employees are encouraged to make their own judgment calls when it comes to matters of productivity. CEO John Young believes that his employees should "rethink every process from product development to distribution."[19] Creating teams that include people from all disciplines helps to decide how best to develop products for Hewlett-Packard. The teamwork allows employees to have a greater degree of control over company decision-making. By making their own decisions, team members can "develop products faster than the company's formal organization."[20] During the last two years, results from this effort have spawned leading-edge products, allowing HP to gain ground in the work station market and in microcomputer sales.

Encouraging discretion and tolerating mistakes is not enough. Creative rule-breaking needs to be publicly rewarded. The managers of Four Seasons, one of America's best-run hotel chains, provide a vivid example of rewarding creative rule-breaking:[21] Roy Dyment, a doorman at Toronto's Four Seasons, forgot to load a guest's briefcase into the taxi. When Dyment called the guest and found out he desperately needed his briefcase, the doorman jumped on a plane to return the case before receiving any approval for his actions. Even though the doorman's actions definitely did not follow procedure, the Four Seasons approved of his actions. The company named Dyment Employee of the Year.

There will always be a necessary tension between individual judgment and established company rules. The best backstage people we have observed have little tolerance for filling out forms and excessive red tape. They want the latitude to do the right things. When they do, morale, performance, and customer service improves. Employees, as well as the company, prosper.

Trends for the Future

There appear to be at least four major trends regarding company rules. While several organizations are struggling with how to loosen up, the more progressive companies are moving aggressively in these directions:

• Some companies search for rule-breakers. Many times

these mavericks can break the ruts and serve as examples for others.

- Many companies are making a substantial effort to eliminate and alleviate rules.
- Values rather than rules may be a better way of defining the playing field for employees.
- People at all levels are allowed to break the rules if it makes sense in terms of the big picture.

Diagnostic Questions

1. Do our employees feel empowered to make sensible decisions that may technically break a rule?
2. Do values, rather than our rules, shape the way we do business?
3. Do we reward good decisions rather than just positive results?
4. How do we treat our mavericks?

■ CHAPTER 12
Don't Steal
the Show

All the world's a stage,
And all the men and women merely players:
They have their exits and their entrances;
And one man in his time plays many parts. . . .
                As You Like It, William Shakespeare

The Unwelcomed Ovation

Many years ago, a production of *Lute Song* in a small college
auditorium created a major stir. In this oriental drama, the
curtain never closes. Two Chinese people dressed in black
costumes rearrange the set between acts in full view of the
audience. But as is true with any member of the backstage
crew, the audience is not supposed to notice them. It is as if
the curtain is closed while they do their thing of moving sets,
scenery, and props. At one point in the play, the set movers
actually assume acting roles onstage. During an especially
gripping scene, they are cast officially as guards blocking the
exit of the hero. Other than that, the two set movers are meant

to be unseen and unheard. They have behind-the-scenes responsibilities but are asked to perform their jobs in front of the curtain.

In this particular collegiate performance, an unexpected deviation from the script caught the entire cast and director off guard. A misguided personnel decision cast two undergraduate "hams" as the Chinese set movers. Their supposedly obscure between-set roles were done with such dramatic flair that changing the scenes came to be more appreciated by the audience than the drama onstage. The intended melodrama became an engaging, rib-splitting comedy. At the play's end, an appreciative audience gave the set movers a standing ovation. The audience's applause and appreciation was not shared by the play's faculty director. She summarily dismissed the two from the play and threatened to have them expelled from school. Her on-the-spot decision was short-lived.

At the very moment it was announced, the president of the college approached the director. He praised her genius for devising such a creative interpretation of a work and informed her that he would be bringing some trustees to the play's next performance. The two set movers were immediately reinstated to their backstage roles and asked to be at the next performance. Although later that year they were admitted to the school's Thespian Club, they were never forgiven by the play's stars or supporting cast. Neither set mover was asked again to be in one of the school's dramatic performances. Star performers do not like being upstaged—whether the play itself is successful or not. The same principle applies when organizations begin to recognize and appreciate the efforts of people in backstage roles.

Stars Want the Stage

Upstaging is not even appreciated onstage. Stars often do not welcome sharing the limelight even with other members of the onstage cast. Jerry West, one of the best guards in basketball history and later general manager of the Los Angeles Lakers, tells how a supporting player can cause trouble by trying to steal the show.[1] Pat Riley, former coach of the Lakers and now with the New York Knickerbockers, was, by most accounts, a mediocre professional basketball player. Early in his career, Riley realized his role was as a member of the supporting cast—making the stars look good and forgoing personal publicity and rewards. In 1972, Jerry West and Wilt Chamberlain were the Laker's stars. An unwritten rule mandated that if a final shot was needed to tie or win the game, the ball went to either West or Chamberlain. Pat's role was to get them the ball. They got the glory—or the blame—if the crucial shot was missed.

In one particularly close game with three seconds left, the Lakers trailed by one point. The ball was passed to Riley. He was wide open. Seeing a chance to shine, he took the shot and missed. The Lakers lost the game. Riley felt bad about his missed opportunity. He felt even worse when he got to the locker room. Wilt Chamberlain minced no words. "Riley, you should have passed the ball to West, that is your role." Trying to save face, Riley retorted quickly, "But, Wilt, I was wide open!" Wilt replied, "Riley, there's a *reason* why nobody guards you!"[2]

Stealing the show is a long-standing taboo, a violation of the basic rules of theater. Entertainers are accustomed to and thrive on pressure and applause. When upstaging occurs, stars feel betrayed and audiences become confused and upset. Within organizations, stealing the show from the stars can be just as disruptive as it is in the theater or on the basketball court.

Upstaging Happens Anywhere

After several recognition programs and celebrations honoring clerical staff, groundskeepers, and others of the hidden cast, certain faculty members raised questions about how much the events were costing their university. While they cited financial constraints as the reason for their concern, cost wasn't the real issue. Their real problem was that the backstage operations were receiving a disproportionate share of recognition and attention. Disgruntled faculty pooh-poohed efforts at delivering support service with enthusiasm. The vice chancellor of Administration was nicknamed the vice chancellor for Pine Needles because of the widespread and visible use of pine needles manicuring the university's grounds. Despite the fact that the university's landscaping had achieved arboretum status in 1988 from the American Association of Botanical Gardens and Arboreta, faculty resented the attention and resources being focused away from the primary educational and research mission of the institution. In the faculty's view, instruction and research are the university's onstage events and deserve the lion's share of the recognition and applause.

A similar issue arose in a manufacturing corporation that was trying to recognize and involve its backstage crew in making key decisions. The CEO spent a considerable amount of time on the factory floor and talked regularly with workers. While they were thrilled with the attention, some supervisors and middle managers became resentful. Privately they remarked that the best way to get the CEO's ear was to "tell an employee."[3] Over time, the ruffled feathers of ignored onstage people can cause morale problems and create unwanted rifts.

The commitment of both onstage and behind-the-scenes people is important. Cooperation among everyone is what makes a theater or an organization work well.

Upstaging Unions

There is an additional area where recognizing backstage workers can create problems. In some organizations, many of the backstage employees are members of labor unions. The unions exist to represent the interests of their members to management. When management begins to recognize employees and ask them to participate in technical and managerial decisions, it is possible for union leaders to feel like someone else is stealing their show. That is probably why the union leader at Saturn has his office in the executive suite. He is the backstage champion of the on-the-line workers, and having him as a participating member of the executive team helps to prevent anyone from feeling upstaged.

Preventing Upstaging

There are several other ways to prevent upstaging. The first is to actively encourage the sense of ensemble—a theatrical term that means being united in a common quest. An ensemble is a group where everyone—the onstage and backstage players—*play off each other*. The former *Late Night with David Letterman* show and the final *Tonight* show with Johnny Carson provide excellent examples of how the spirit of ensemble works. Backstage employees are featured regularly on Letterman's evening performances. In fact, an entire show was devoted to exploring how the show's backstage operates. Cameras moved from place to place, introducing the audience to people they had never seen or even thought were an important part of the show. As a result, David Letterman's show belongs to the entire enterprise. The viewer gets the impression that Letterman himself enjoys sharing the limelight—at least occasionally.

The *Tonight* show's final broadcast provides another example. After a thirty-year reign onstage, Carson shared the limelight with the hidden cast in order to "thank them all."[4] After observing with a national TV audience a four-minute video of his support staff in action, Johnny remarked, "If I had known the staff had worked that hard, I would have given them a raise—NOT!"[5] In Carson's own way, he recognized employees who undoubtedly take pride in what they do and who enjoy the added status of appearing on national television. Both shows created a sense of ensemble, a family of players in which people seemed to enjoy each other while delighting the audience.

Is the sense of ensemble reserved only for the theater? We think not. Saturn has incorporated the notion of ensemble into their management philosophy. There is a connection between retailers and plant workers. The assembly line is frequently toured by retail partners. Assembly-line team members regularly visit Saturn's retail outlets. The retailers are in a genuine partnership with the people on the line. The retailers are not the stars, nor are those who assemble the cars. Both share in the final performance: a pleased customer who appreciates his or her car. (More will be said about Saturn in a later chapter.)

Separate but Equal Attention

McKinsey and Company provides another alternative for how to spread recognition around. For many years, the consulting team of one of the firm's offices went on an annual retreat.

No administrative or support staff were invited. The office's management realized that they were creating two separate groups: an inner circle that received all the attention, and a group of outsiders that were virtually excluded. The second group was becoming more and more isolated, even though it included people who were an important part of the operation.

After much discussion, the powers-that-be realized that asking support staff to join the annual retreat could upstage associates and partners. Nor were support staff members high on becoming part of the consulting team's event. They were not that interested in discussing the latest business theories. Their focus was more on how they could better serve the consulting staff. McKinsey decided to add a retreat for the support staff, making it equivalent in duration and style to the consultant retreat. It was to be held over a long weekend at an out-of-state resort. The staff invited two consultants on their retreat. Instead of focusing on business or economic theory, the topic of discussion emphasized how to improve services to the consultants. From the retreats have come a list of do's and don'ts for both support and consulting staffs. The support group developed its own mission statement, which covers how its clients, the consultants, should be treated so they could serve the ultimate client as well as possible.

Support staff retreats are now part of this McKinsey office's culture and generate their own interesting stories. The retreats pay attention to the support staff without upstaging the stars. Separate but equal attention may be a compromise when joint events, for whatever reason, are not desirable.

Everyone Onstage

Some companies encourage backstage workers to think of themselves as part of the performing cast. Quality Food Center (QFC) in Seattle encourages behind-the-scenes workers to take an active role onstage.[6] QFC has an operating margin 70 percent higher than the industry average. Sales have increased from $135 million in 1985 to $400 million today. All employees understand they can be called onstage at any time. In fact, QFC has a rule that if more than three customers are waiting in a checkout line, another register is immediately opened—even if someone has to be pulled from another department. If a customer asks an employee about the location of any grocery item, the person is expected to take them there, not just point them in the right direction.

When duty calls, backstage employees are expected to provide the individualized high-quality service on which QFC thrives. They are motivated by liberally awarded stock options, performance bonuses, and an employee stock purchase plan for both full- and part-timers. They are aware of the company's mission and willingly go the extra mile when they are cast into the spotlight in front of a customer.

Terry Warren, president and CEO of MedTrac, Inc., a medical and disability cost management firm, vividly described the importance of bringing backstage onstage on rare occasions. MedTrac employs nurses who evaluate medical claims to determine whether or not the treatment prescribed is medically appropriate and necessary.

"At times we take a backstage person, one of our clinical evaluators, on a sales call when we think it is important for customers to meet the employees who are backstage and to hear what they do straight from the horse's mouth. Taking backstage people to meet customers once in a while does a couple of things: One, it does not upstage the salesperson, and two, it gives customers a greater appreciation for the nurse's professionalism. It also gives the nurse the opportunity to get feedback from customers and hear a customer say, 'I think you guys do a great job,' or 'I wouldn't buy that service if it were the last thing on earth,' or 'Man, this is wonderful.'

"A great example is one of our nurses who went on a sales call with us and afterward said, 'Well, you know, those of us who are nurses are kind of depressed about this new service we're offering because it seems we have some days where everyone is behind us and cooperative and other days medical providers and clients are fighting us.'

"I replied, 'I know you are. And that salesperson sitting right beside you faces the same thing every day out on the road. They'll go in to a customer today who thinks we hung the moon, and tomorrow they'll hang up on you.'

"Our onstage personnel are trained to deal with the ups and downs. If the nurse were to move onstage on a regular basis, her being depressed—to use her word— would certainly be picked up by the customer, and we'd probably lose the sale. So the best approach is to sparingly move backstage to the forefront. They support the frontstage—it is not intended that they take over."[7]

Working Together

Companies with successful behind-the-scenes operations usually pay equal attention to the visible performers. Backstage champions who recognize the efforts of their workers need to encourage onstage managers to follow their example. Stars onstage need at least as much recognition as those in the wings. Otherwise, tension arises between the two groups, jeopardizing overall company performance. From our study, a few final observations are worth noting:

• Upstaging creates problems for many organizations.

- Notwithstanding our attention to hidden employees, it is important to remember the stars are whom the audience come to see.
- The concept of ensemble holds much potential for many companies that make a distinction between onstage and backstage.
- Occasionally putting behind-the-scenes workers onstage has a positive and lasting impact with minimal cost.

Diagnostic Questions

1. When we recognize the crew, do our stars feel upstaged?
2. Do we have programs to ensure that all employees receive appropriate attention?
3. Does our recognition of the efforts of those in background positions ever distract from our core mission?

■ Part IV

Caring about the Hidden Cast

■ CHAPTER 13
Appropriate Tools Guarantee Top Efforts

A Key to Competitiveness

Will America remain competitive in an expanding and changing international market? The following facts raise some real doubts:[1]

- During the 1980s, the United States imported almost $1 trillion ($1,000,000,000,000) in goods more than it exported.
- American electronics and auto industries lost market share to the Japanese.
- In 1980, the two largest banks in the world were in the United States; today our biggest bank, Citicorp, ranks eleventh.
- America's share of the computer market has dropped almost 40 percent, and semiconductors have lost over 20 percent in that sector.
- The percentage of patents granted to U.S. corporations and citizens has fallen almost 10 percent over the last ten years.

- The Council on Competitiveness recently identified ninety-four technologies as critical to the future of most industries. The United States was weak or losing badly in 33.

Tom Stewart, senior editor of *Fortune*, recently stated:

> There are no mysteries about what America must do.
> Topping the agenda is the need to lift investment, bolster
> the competitiveness of small manufacturers and service
> companies, strengthen U.S. technology and increase
> workers' skill at applying it.[2]

If technology and training are key to America's competitiveness, we need to do more than motivate our work force. Author Jay Jackuma noted that companies need to use technology to remove walls, not to raise them, enabling people in every job to do their best.[3] In short, employees need up-to-date equipment in order to do the job right. Many echo Churchill's plea during World War II: "Give us the tools and we shall do the work." Without appropriate tools, modern equipment, and proper technical training, America's work force will not be able to compete in a modernly outfitted global market. W. Edwards Deming (guru of statistical quality control) and J. M. Juran (pioneer of total quality control) estimate that 85 percent of all quality problems are management's doing.[4] One of the common errors is saddling workers with inferior machines. These problems are compounded by the low wage rates of several foreign countries. South Korea, Taiwan, and Thailand can produce high-quality goods at lower costs without a sizable investment in technology or worker skills. America no longer enjoys the luxury of cheap labor; therefore it must make its higher-paid workers more productive.

Equipping the Backstage

According to *Webster's*, tools are a "means to an end."[5] Well-suited tools include more than wrenches, computers, or machines. They include any item, skill, or opportunity enabling a worker to improve job performance, increase production, raise profitability, or expand customer-service capabilities. State-of-the-art equipment, such as telephones, pagers, mowers, or vacuums, provide up-to-date tools that are an important source of employee motivation, morale and pride. Top-flight equipment even helps organizations attract and retain employees, especially those working behind the scenes. Through providing excellent equipment, management offers an alternate source of recognition and applause people otherwise infrequently enjoy.

As Courtney Reynolds, former corporate planner for Morrison Knudsen (MK), points out:

> We [MK] found that giving employees proper and modern tools, be it computers, rigging equipment, power tools, or whatever they need, not only increases our employees' productivity but also has a direct impact on their morale and motivation. People at all levels want to have the best equipment because it signals they are the best.[6]

Chuck Raper, director of Administration at McKinsey and Company, puts it this way: "Support staff are turned on to up-to-date equipment. The new stuff. We never scrimp on equipment. To some, it is more important than our business strategy."[7]

Federal Express, a few years ago, changed our time-worn concept of mail delivery. A key component to their success is their extensive use of technology. Federal Express is committed to leading the industry in automation and training. Larry W. McMahan, vice president of their Human Resources Development Group, reflects on their commitment: "Because we expect our employees to know a lot and to keep up with a lot of changes, we have to equip them with enough tools to give them a good running chance at satisfying our customers."[8]

American Airlines also stays in the lead by investing in the best technology possible.[9] The company installs state-of-the-art equipment as a matter of policy. Their ambitious office automation path, for example, is one that is more creative than cautious. They are currently in the process of updating their office computing by investing in AT&T, IBM, and Tandy Corporation's 386 and 386/sx workstations—the intelligent desktop devices. The company expects the system to provide major gains in productivity that eluded previous generations of office systems. It expects productivity of management and clerical workers to increase by 7 percent. Another 2 percent improvement is expected as a result of offering people more timely and accurate access to the company's data base.

American provides superior resources to help employees achieve their best results. The airline involves employees in the process of updating equipment, rather than leaving the decision to managers who may never use it. A visit to the new systems-operating control room at the Dallas/Fort Worth airport provides a spectacular example of American's commitment to providing top-of-the-line tools. The company has installed the most modern computer equipment available in the world. Employees participated in the selection of the equipment and helped to design the working space.

Management at Carlisle Plastics, Inc., a trash bag manufacturer in Victoria, Texas, understands the important role equipment and capital improvements play in the welfare of their employees as well as the financial welfare of the company.[10] Since 1989 the company has spent $75 million on capital improvements. Forklifts move automatically through the plant, tracked by wires embedded in the floor. Carlisle purchased a $2 million computer system in order to centralize the ordering processes, production scheduling, and warehousing. Appropriately equipped backstage employees play a large role in sales-per-employee. Sales have doubled since 1990. William Binnie, the boss of Carlisle Plastics, makes no bones about his commitment to maintaining the backstage employees' morale and productivity: "The first thing I do whenever I visit a plant is use the hourly workers' bathroom so I can see how the company's treating them."[11]

New technology enables workers to serve more people effectively. Computers provide accurate market research data and distribution patterns needed for precision marketing. Suppliers better accommodate the customer and provide superior service. Employees are pleased with their enhanced ability to serve. Customers are pleased with the product or service they receive. Many organizations recount stories of how investing money in technology improves the attitude and productivity of employees. For example, Sulzer Brothers, Ltd., a Zurich-based heavy machinery manufacturer, increased the service-derived revenue of their heating and air-conditioning equipment operators from 10 to 25 percent.[12] Management credits this improvement to the use of more high-tech products and systems in heating and air-conditioning operations.

A company's commitment to advanced technology also helps to attract and retain well-qualified and confident people. In 1988, Federal Express modified their classroom training programs with a computer-based training system that uses interactive videos on workstation screens.[13] Through this new employee training program, the company expects to show higher profits as well as improved productivity and performance from its workers. Savings are estimated at $150 million.

Selecting Equipment

A commitment to providing appropriate tools and equipment is only a beginning. Once a company is committed, exhausting investigative work begins. Employees' desire for whatever is in fashion must be balanced against studies of what is currently available and will not become quickly obsolete. Top organizations read and explore the latest technological advances in the industry. High-level analyses determine whether an investment in technology will be cost-effective. Stanley, a maker of tools and hardware, decided to automate its factories when faced with stiff competition from Asia.[14] It provided its employees with appropriate tools and proper training. It also listened to what its employees wanted. The investment has apparently paid off. Stanley's profits and revenues have doubled since 1980.

Employees who use equipment and technology are the logical ones to provide specifications for new purchases. Regular operators know what is best, what is needed and what are the most important pieces to acquire first. Asking employees what equipment will suit their needs or what they might like is a first step in assuring that resources will be wisely invested. Asking for employee opinions and responses helps generate wise decisions and increases employees' involvement and interest. Recognizing and responding to employee ideas about needed equipment acknowledges their ability and know-how. Rollie Boreham, chairman and CEO of Baldor Electric Company, remarked, "Most companies have all the management guys talking about what to do and don't ask a great resource just 100 feet away—the line employee."[15]

Training: A Step beyond Equipment

Cutting-edge equipment induces employees to stay aboard and also improves their self-esteem. But new equipment almost always makes old skills obsolete. Any new technology requires a commensurate investment in employee training. It takes time for employees to become familiar and comfortable with new equipment. Only after new skills are mastered will employees be able to get the most from potentially superior technology. Operated properly, a new computer system can become a great asset to a company. But when computers are operated by people who cling to old ways, the potential is severely undercut.

During the training process an initial slowdown in productivity may be necessary to ensure proper learning. Employees need to be encouraged to tinker and experiment. When they are asked to maintain current production levels while learning new techniques or equipment, opportunities are missed to discover more efficient methods. To illustrate:

> Suppose you were to come upon someone in the woods working feverishly to saw down a tree. "What are you doing?" you ask. "Can't you see?" comes the impatient reply. "I'm sawing down this tree." "You look exhausted!" you exclaim. "How long have you been at it?" "Over five hours," he returns, "and I'm beat! This is hard work." "Well, why don't you take a break for a few minutes and sharpen that saw?" you inquire. "I'm sure it would go a lot faster." "I don't have time to sharpen the saw," the man says emphatically. "I'm too busy sawing!"[16]

Many employees are kept too busy to have time for creative reflection. Getting the most from investments in new resources entails both training and equipment. When both are attended to, investments evoke employee trust and a sense of company pride. Kim Igoe, director of Museum Assessment Programs at the American Association of Museums, stated, "I have been on my soapbox to computerize this place and it was six years coming, but it's wonderful!"[17] Such an investment obviously gives her new zest for her job.

Investing in people, whether in terms of training or equipment, conveys a sense of faith and trust. Giving them the advantages of modern equipment also demonstrates their importance. As competition increases, people need every advantage they can get. They need suitable equipment. They also need more training. Training clearly offers rewards for both employers and employees. Motorola claims it has saved almost $1.5 billion because of improvements that resulted from investments in employee training.[18] It got a return of thirty-three dollars for every dollar spent. Even if the training had yielded a return of only three to one—the normal payoff cited by the American Society for Training and Development, you still have substantial argument in favor of investing in training.[19]

Some Final Points

- Employees, especially those out of the limelight, want the best equipment. It signals their jobs are important.
- Equipment and technology are just as important behind the scenes as they are in the customer's view.
- Backstage employees can be extremely helpful in assessing, selecting, and purchasing equipment and technology.
- Forward-looking companies are moving away from seeking more employees and adequate equipment to obtaining the best employees and providing them with the best equipment.

- Training is becoming more critical to both employee morale and performance.

Diagnostic Questions

1. What is the current state of our equipment and technology?
2. Do we utilize the talents and knowledge of backstage employees when selecting and purchasing new equipment?
3. Have we added enough training programs to make sure we maximize the potential of our new equipment?

■ CHAPTER 14

Dressing the Hidden Cast

The Disney Model

The name Disney has become synonymous with entertainment. Visions of Mickey Mouse, Donald Duck, immaculate, sculptured grounds, and grand exhibits dance in everyone's head when they hear the magical name. Disney's make-believe world, made real, brings out anyone's hidden child. Whatever their chronological age, visitors find happiness and joy at Disney properties. The magic is everywhere. Part of it comes from the easily recognizable characters roaming the streets and performing in parades. Disney appropriately uses the term "cast members" to describe all its employees.[1] Each cast member is dressed in a costume appropriate to an assigned identity: Cinderella, Goofy, Tinker Bell, and others. These employees obviously are onstage. Their performance is part of what the guests pay to see. Their costumes are an essential part of their act. Without a costume the magic would be gone.

Costumes are a vital part of any onstage performance.

Movie stars worry even about what they wear offstage.[2] When actress Demi Moore appeared in public for the first time after the birth of her baby sporting a whole new wardrobe, it wasn't just a maternal whim. It was the work of stylist Jane Ross, a former *Vogue* staffer. When Jodie Foster appeared on TV promoting her latest movie, her classy elegance wasn't entirely homegrown. Before interviews in advance of the debut of *The Accused*, Foster's mother reportedly called celebrity stylist Sharon Simonaire and asked her to find Jodie something to wear—besides her customary gym clothes. Visible people are painfully aware that both their private identity and public persona are highly influenced by what they wear. The style of their wardrobe determines the image portrayed in the public eye. Among celebrities, decisions about costumes are often approached with unspoken paranoia. One bad choice could mar a person's public image or ruin their career. That's life for those onstage.

But what about people backstage? A visit to one of Disney's seminars reveals another dimension of its astute organizational savvy.[3] There you meet legions of employees the typical guest never sees. Because they are an integral part of the cast, they also have an official Disney uniform. Depending on the position, the uniform might include a blazer with a name tag, or just pants and a shirt, or a dress and apron. Each ensemble is color coordinated. Each is individually designed for a particular area, making it instantly apparent where someone works. Disney realizes that the identity and public image of its hidden cast are just as important as its visible cast and makes sure behind-the-scenes people are dressed appropriately.

Dressing the Invisible Cast

As we have already seen, behind-the-scenes people play an essential role in how well an organization performs. Their invisibility does not reduce for them the importance of titles, office space, or appropriate attire. Symbols and costumes are just as important to those who work in the wings as they are to people in the lights. Organizational symbols create a sense of pride and belonging among all employees, whether they are visible to the customer or not. Backstage uniforms are just as symbolic as the costumes of key actors in front of the audience.

For almost every company, uniforms are usually an issue. Should they be worn or not? Do employees like to wear them? Should a uniform code be enforced? What should the uniform dress code look like? Who, if anyone, should select the uniform? Conventional wisdom often assumes that people want their costumes to reflect their individual whims or tastes. But that's not always the case. Uniforms can have a positive effect on employee morale, pride, and productivity.

Companies use uniforms in a number of different ways. Uniforms hold substantial symbolic importance and are often used for marketing and recognition purposes. They instill a sense of pride and are often used to boost employee morale and develop prestige. They can make a difference in building a well-connected, solid team and infusing the team with spirit. Uniforms represent authority and identification in addition to practical purposes of comfort or protection.

Horace Small Apparel Company is the producer and distributor of uniforms and accessories.[4] Its major clients include the National Park Service, the U.S. Army Corps of Engineers, the U.S. Postal Service, Federal Express, Commonwealth Edison, and American Airlines. Doug Small, the company's CEO, believes that uniforms have come out of the dark ages of repressive conformity and are now widely accepted by employees, employers, and customers as symbols of function and status. With new technologies in fabrics, design, and fit, uniforms can be stylish as well as functional. Small views the importance of uniforms in this way:

> I think uniforms provide an alternative method for a company to develop a competitive advantage in today's marketplace. Service being our most important product, it is easy to equate that whatever a company can do to increase employee morale, to enhance their efficiency and upgrade their appearance makes for a more competitive company.[5]

Mechanics often are notorious for greeting customers in oil-stained shirts and grimy, torn jeans. For Amoco Oil, this questionable public appearance represented a problem that needed to be changed.[6] In the late 1980s, Amoco initiated an expensive career apparel program. It was designed to improve the company's image with the public and create a better, cleaner working environment for employees. For Amoco, the move toward worker uniforms made perfect business sense. Done properly, it had a dramatic and positive impact on employee morale.

Ameriscribe Corporation is a back-room mail-room operation and copying service with over two thousand employees.[7] Sales have tripled in the last three years. This year, the company expects to exceed $115 million in transactions. Operating in an environment of high confidentiality, where time and information is extremely valuable, it is of absolute importance that Ameriscribe employees are carefully selected, highly trained, and professionally attired. Crisp blue shirts, maroon ties, dark slacks/skirts—the uniform of the day—immediately identifies and sets apart these service providers. CEO Bill Shaw commented:

"In terms of our operation needs, uniforms are very important to our staff and to their self-esteem. The uniforms give them a sense of value, they feel a part of the organization. These feelings manifest themselves in improved performance. The customer reaps the benefits and we grow our business."[8]

The 110-year-old Cabot Corporation is one of the world's leading industrial companies.[9] It is the largest manufacturer of carbon black, a material used to improve the quality of industrial rubber products, specialty inks, plastics, and cable coatings. Cabot's sales in fiscal 1992 totaled $1.5 billion, and the company now sits on a wealth of assets. It wasn't always that way. Working with carbon black requires special considerations. In simple terms, carbon black is made by burning heavy fuel oil with too little oxygen to allow for efficient combustion. The fine black powder residue is called carbon black. All this is to say that the process of making the product is a very dirty job. In the mid eighties, employee morale mirrored the task they were asked to do.

CEO Samuel Bodman, hired in 1987, recognized early on the necessity for restoring employee morale. A clean plant, he reasoned, is one where employees take pride in their work. As one way of meeting this cleanliness challenge, employees in Cabot's plants are outfitted each day in freshly laundered uniforms. While the business may be downright grimy, the employees are sparkling clean.

The company's clean plants are an indication of newfound pride. Bodman himself conducts a ritual to ensure Cabot's uniformed men and women are keeping their plants spotless. He dons a pair of white slacks and strolls through each one of the facilities. It's not enough that his pants remain pure white. Bodman says the plants must pass the more formidable ankle test. "Sometimes the white pants will look fine," he said.

"Then you roll down your socks and you'll be filthy. It's called the ankle test."[10] Bodman is pleased that, more often than not, Cabot plants pass his rigorous lower extremity exam.

A group of Opryland employees work in what is called Costume Production. They are responsible for making costumes for Opryland's entertainers. Their job is to keep the performers looking good. Laboring over their sewing machines, they take pride in producing first-rate garments. At Opryland, however, it is not just the stars whose appearances receive top priority. Located directly below Costume Production is Wardrobe, the name given to Opryland's laundry facility. The operation cleans thirty thousand pounds of laundry each day—including all employee uniforms.[11] The huge building looks like a barn from the outside. Inside, it is a large, commercial dry-cleaning operation. At the beginning of each day, employees pick up their clean uniforms. At the end of their shift, they drop them off to be cleaned.

Not only are employee uniforms cleaned, they are tailored and custom fitted. No pull-it-off-the-racks-and-throw-it-on approach to uniforms at Opryland. If regular sizes cannot be altered, special orders ensure that each employee will look his or her best. Opryland wants its employees to look nice and feel comfortable while working. Management knows that it's not just the entertainers who are concerned with how they appear—all employees are. As one employee remarked: "All employees are fitted for their uniform, whether they are wearing a two-hundred-dollar jacket at the front desk or a forty-dollar white smock and pants in housekeeping."[12]

A variation to uniforms is the trend of occasionally "dressing down." A recent poll indicated more and more companies are permitting their employees to wear casual clothes on specified occasions.[13] About two-thirds of those surveyed felt that allowing employees to wear casual clothing instead of formal dress improves morale. Many also believe that casual clothing reduces status distinction among employees.

At Jewish Hospital, backstage employees create their own costumes on a monthly "blue jeans day."[14] This practice provides a comfortable sense of team building and identification at no cost to performance. Management views the design-your-own-costume opportunity as a way to respond and reward the individuals and departments for service beyond the norm. At Health Management Professionals (HMP), a Nashville company, recently merged with Quorum, that provides management assistance for a group of hospitals nationwide, casual dress is the order of the day—unless clients are paying the corporate headquarters a visit.[15] Then, Shelly Kriselman and his colleagues look like a Brook's Brothers ad. They realize the impact of costumes and have encouraged a work culture that benefits from both casualness and carefulness in uniform wear. Even more interesting, no one ever wrote down or enforced the different-costume-for-different-occasions policy. It's part of HMP's way of life.

The Use of Symbols

When employees of Diamond International Corporation, a fibers product manufacturing unit, achieve membership in the 100 Club,[16] they are given a jacket embroidered with the company's logo and a 100 Club designation. The 100 Club and its symbols are part of a recognition program rather than a financial incentive program. The jacket demonstrates that employees are performing their jobs well. Points are accumulated for attendance, punctuality, safety, commitment to quality, goal attainment, and accurate paperwork. The 100 Club, started in the company's Palmer, Massachusetts, plant, has now expanded to other Diamond Plants in Natchez, Mississippi; Red Bluff, California; Plattsburg, New York; and Cincinnati, Ohio. The club has not only become a strong internal symbol for Diamond employees; it also has reaped dividends for the company. The financial savings associated with the program are staggering. An independent consultant estimates that the club has generated in excess of $1.6 million in the Palmer plant alone due to improved attendance, a 14 percent productivity increase, and a decrease of 40 percent in quality-related mistakes. In addition, formal grievances have dropped 72 percent at Palmer. Other plants participating in the program show a 57 percent reduction. Overall, 86 percent of the company's employees echo the following statement: "They feel that the company and management now believes me to be 'very important' or 'important.' "[17]

Symbols are a low- to moderate-cost item not requiring a substantial monetary investment. But properly done, the return can be sizable when symbols represent things of shared meaning and pride. Much of what motivates people is intangible. People like to work for a company that stands for something special. They like to see how their individual job links to the company's overall purpose and values. If an organization can translate purpose into symbolic gestures of appreciation and recognition, "specialness" can be grounded in tangible ways.

As mentioned previously, American's Cargo Group is reminded of their purpose: "Think CAArgo."[18] The double AAs in the slogan shows that the division is a part of the American family. Despite their backstage role, cargo workers are taught that air packages are passengers, actual paying customers of the airlines. They treat "CAArgo" with the same special care given to American's other passengers.

The importance of an organization's purpose can be exhibited to employees through any number of ways. At one company, an exemplary housekeeping employee was given a

In paying attention to organizational costumes or symbols, keep several guidelines in mind:

- Costumes, such as uniforms, are extremely important to the backstage crew. Looking their best can help transform alienated workers into proud members of a working team.
- Symbols, such as name tags and recognition, are probably more important to backstage employees than to onstage performers. Unseen people need a sense of belonging. They want to know that they add value to the company and are an important part of the company's success.
- Name tags are an inexpensive way of adding recognition and team spirit. Many companies have used the name tag to show achievement, special assignments, and even length of service. Name tags can help to reinforce values prevalent and important to a company.

Costumes and symbols provide immediate identification and recognition for all employees. What a costume or symbol represents—either by association, resemblance, or convention—is what counts. Keep in mind the power of an academic ceremony. Caps, tassels, and gowns are the costumes—the regalia—that administrators, faculty, and anticipating graduates don at thousands of universities and colleges each year for graduation exercises. Some students choose not to participate in the ceremony and tradition. They get their diplomas through the mail. Those who attend the event bask in the pride and glory of the occasion. In either case, the graduate comes away with the degree. But those who are there to observe and share in the first trumpet fanfare, the array of colors and banners, the conferring of degrees, and all the symbols of the institution's history will always remember the ties that bind them to their classmates and alma mater. The institution will be part of their hearts and, hopefully, their future donations. Costumes make an occasion special.

Diagnostic Questions

1. Do we consciously think about how our rearward crew looks? Where we have used uniforms in behind-the-scenes operations, does there seem to be improved performance and morale?
2. Have we capitalized on the possible use of low cost symbols, such as name tags and nameplates?
3. What kind of office space do people in our hidden cast have?

CHAPTER 15
Celebrating Hidden Achievements

Tennessee's answer to New York's Off Broadway is the Tennessee Repertory Theatre (TRT). Located in Nashville, the company does several productions each year. Mac Pirkle, the theater's director, is aware that to produce top-flight performances, the entire company must work together: "The hardest task in our business is to maintain the spirit of the show among all people involved."[1]

This requires, to revisit a concept from previous chapters, the creation of ensemble. Pirkle describes it as a shared understanding that "roles that everyone fulfills onstage and off are done for the good of the whole as opposed to doing one's thing for individual achievement."[2] To create the spirit of ensemble in TRT, Pirkle relies heavily on ceremony.

> "When TRT started, we took everyone out to camp. We did a variation of the 'green corn' ceremony used by the Indians to celebrate the beginning of a New Year. Everyone was to bring something to share, something to consume, something to get rid of. We also invented a

ritual song to use in the ceremony. This turned into an extremely emotional and inspiring event. People really dug down deep and came up with things that were very important to them. In the prop room, we now display a blanket that is made up of squares everyone at camp signed in any way they wanted. The signed squares are arranged around a large middle sector with our mission statement."[3]

The ceremonial commitment of TRT does not stop at a once-a-year retreat. Each production is marked by a series of important events:[4]

- "Load-in" provides a solidifying event for the backstage crew. It is an extended all-nighter, with the technical crew working around the clock for three or four days. The sets, built off location, are brought to the theater and set up. "With problem solving acting as glue, the event is a bonding session as well," says Pirkle. "The bond is formed when trying to work everything out."
- "Dress parade" is another event organized around the time when all costumes are tried on. Costume designers see the results of their work. Dressers practice getting the cast into costume. The stars begin to feel their role.
- "Blocking" is the time when the director, actors, and actresses decide where they will be positioned onstage, and when and where they will move during the performance. The event is usually attended only by the performers.
- "Dry-tech" is the backstage rehearsal when only the technical aspects are enacted. Lighting, set changes, and other technical aspects of the performance are practiced without the presence of the onstage cast.
- "Opening night" is where it all comes together, and the audience either applauds or pans the performance. This

often provides an occasion for a cast party, which usually includes all people—onstage and backstage.

Whether visible or not, each person at TRT has a stake in the outcome. While the audience may not actually see TRT's celebratory backside, it will either be felt or missed in the actual performance.

Every organization needs some form of ritual and ceremony to build a common spirit among diverse functions and interests. Bill Boesch of American Airlines summarizes the company's philosophy:

> "The secret of leadership is to stand behind people and try to catch them doing things right. The old way of thinking about leadership was to try and find people doing things wrong and get on them about it. That's easy to do compared to trying to stand behind people and trying to find things they are doing right and help them celebrate."[5]

His insightful words reinforce the theme of Chapter 9: Trusting While Helping. But in this succinct paragraph he also reinforces the need for celebrations. Celebrating people who do the right thing is important whether you catch them in the act or not.

Ceremonial occasions not only recognize an individual for a job well done, but also let others know what is valued and encourages them to try for their opportunity in the spotlight. Annie Hayes, a backstage worker at Service Merchandise's oldest outlet in downtown Nashville, exemplifies both the joy of being recognized and the longing for even more:

> "Service Merchandise has an Associate of the Month Award. The employee, selected by management, is

honored and given a gift certificate. At the end of the
year, management selects a Superstar from all the
monthly awards. I've been chosen for Associate of the
Month a few times, but never a Superstar. It is a goal of
mine to get there someday."[6]

Being recognized publicly for a superb performance is
especially important for hardworking people behind the
scenes. One supervisor remarked, "One problem with managing backstage is that sometimes backstage people see those
onstage as not making as much of a contribution as they do,
but getting all the limelight."[7]

Hard work is an important ingredient for success anywhere. Equally important is working hard on those things that
add value to an organization's core product or service. The
crucial challenge is how to motivate people to work hard and
do the job right when their important contributions are invisible. That is where celebrations come in.

In our modern world, it is very easy to conclude that
working for an organization is almost entirely a rational economic exchange. Unfortunately, this perception often leads to
an "I do what you ask; you give me a paycheck" attitude that
casts employees in the role of organizational prostitutes. One
computer programmer summed it up: "I'll go through the
motions but you'll never get my commitment or love. I'm
always available to the next highest bidder."[8]

Celebration as Bonding

Another way to think about what really motivates people is to
focus on commitment and meaning. From this vantage point,
work becomes a relationship. People feel part of the organization and want to build or deliver something of great pride. As

in TRT, they work as much for the joy and meaning as for the money. Being a part of a productive community causes people to work hard and help customers because they want to—not because they have to. As in any community, celebrations are a way to bond people to one another, to reaffirm shared values, and to anoint the heroes and heroines whose deeds exemplify what the company stands for. Rob Beltramo, a business consultant from Boise, Idaho, describes an important celebration story:[9]

> "It all happened back in 'eighty-two, when I had been working with Morrison Knudsen a couple of years and working in Keith Price's part of the organization. Keith was then the vice president in charge of the Power Group, the organization that handled major energy projects, such as nuclear power plant construction and modification, and design and construction of cogeneration facilities.
>
> "I had been with the Power Group a couple of years doing financial planning and marketing analysis—all backstage stuff. I had an inside office with no windows and was certainly not a frontline or an important player. Anyway, we were pursuing contracts with the Department of Energy for a $500 million project. The project team worked hard to get the contract. On the date the award was announced, it was a day of great celebration internally. Keith Price came around to each and every employee in the Boise headquarters of Power Group, whether or not the employee had been directly involved in pursuing the DOE contract. He shook every single person's hand in the building—including all the backstage players.
>
> "He said, 'Congratulations and thank you for all your good work. We are taking the rest of the day off, and you are invited to a Power Group party at Lucky Peak

Reservoir. I will bring the goodies—if you have a boat or something, bring it along, we are going to celebrate.'

"I told Keith that I appreciated the invitation, but that I was not personally part of the project team. Keith replied, 'You are part of my team. You helped by carrying on with your work. We all work together.' "

Keith Price obviously knew the power of celebration and its positive impact on employees. He had the foresight to include the backstage crew in the total mission and success of the company. As a result, there were very few things all employees would not do for him. He evoked the kind of loyalty that one would "march into hell" for him and the company. His story helps to bolster the theme of celebrating hidden achievement.

Terry Jackson, manager of First Union Georgia Servicenter, also understands the power of celebration. He proudly states:

"Today, we stopped and applauded ourselves for reporting improvement in Items Processing. We have many ways we celebrate. There is a customer service wall of honor where every commendation, thank-you, comment, note, statistic, and performance graph is hung for all to see. We also bring in pizza, have ice cream parties, and have casual-dress days when we reach new goals. You do not have to do elaborate things. Celebration is a way to bond. It doesn't take a rocket scientist to think of ways to celebrate, but most managers fall short in this area."[10]

Celebrations take a number of forms. Events—staff meetings, quarterly reports, and training seminars—provide daily, weekly, and monthly symbolic parentheses in the work day. Events, such as loading in or blocking, provide a special time for people to relate to one another in a different way. Ceremonies provide a less-frequent symbolic benchmark. In a very special way ceremonies acknowledge deep cultural roots and values. TRT's beginning was a ceremonial event, not just a matter of getting together and starting to work. Without ceremonies, organizations would be hollow, mechanical, and spiritually bankrupt. As David Campbell, a consultant for the Center for Creative Leadership, poetically summarized:

> "[Ceremonies] serve useful functions: they act as a cohesive glue, giving expression to common beliefs; they provide a source of stability by marking calendar events; they provide mileposts in our lives by setting aside noteworthy occasions and enlightening special accomplishments. A leader who ignores or impedes organizational ceremonies and considers them as 'frivolous' or 'not cost-effective' is ignoring the rhythms of history and our collective conditioning. [They] are the punctuation marks that make sense of the passage of time; without them, there are no beginnings and endings. Life becomes an endless series of Wednesdays."[11]

For people who work in an organization's hinterland, it is all too easy for every day to seem like Wednesday. As in the theater the visible people onstage bathe in the regular applause they receive for a job well done. Recognition of extraordinary performances behind the scenes awaits the much less frequent hoopla of a cast party. Because of their infrequency, cast parties are more important to those in the backstage crew than to those who are constantly in the limelight.

For economically disadvantaged people in Rio de Janeiro,

Carnival is one of the few events they can look forward to each year. People from all walks of life save their money to splurge on new clothes and wonderful food. Carnival provides the rush of joy that encourages Brazilians through another year. Stories of the festivities are frequently told and retold. For people in backstage roles, the company picnic, holiday office party, or yearly gathering plays a similar role. For many, the annual event is the highlight of the year, something special they can share with family and friends.

Ceremonial Profiles

What forms do celebrations take? That depends entirely on the values and traditions of a particular organization.

American Airlines

Celebrations take various forms at American Airlines. Robert Crandall appears each year at twenty-one sites for his annual presidential conferences. At each site, all employees—onstage and off—gather to ask questions and find out what's going on in the company. These are no-holds-barred, ask-the-tough-questions occasions.

Recently, at one site, the first question asked of Mr. Crandall was "How did you find the terminal when you arrived?"

Mr. Crandall replied, "What do you mean?"

The man repeated his question, adding, "I'm in charge of the custodial staff and I hoped you noticed how clean the facility is." He got a standing ovation as well as Crandall's public approval.[12]

An example of how much a part of life celebrations are at

American Airlines is illustrated by the following. Al Becker, director of Public Relations, went to Miami for a news conference.[13] As he got off the plane, General Manager Don O'Hare and a divisional vice president were coming off a cargo ramp. They had just been to a hot dog party with all the workers on the ramp and the flight service attendants to celebrate their cargo achievement award. They had celebrated the achievements with each shift.

As mentioned in a preceding chapter, Robert Crandall proposed the concept of the Golden Wrench Award as an incentive for airlines to strive for excellence in their aircraft maintenance programs. An excerpt from his remarks at the company's 1989 annual meeting in Dallas reveals the motivation for the award:

> "To reach its full potential, our industry must also come to grips with the public's growing concerns about safety. Let the Department of Transportation give out the annual award to the U.S. airline that does the most outstanding maintenance job. I'd call it the 'Golden Wrench'—and I'd give silver wrenches to other carriers that did an excellent job but didn't quite make the gold—and not say anything at all about the rest."[14]

Bill Boesch told us, "I spend 10 percent of my time in cargo telling people how good they are."[15] The night following our interview, he was taking his employees to a world-famous barbecue restaurant. He also had invited the spouses. It was a celebration of CAArgo's accomplishments. Bill praised each employee in front of his or her spouse. Celebrations of this type are held at least once a quarter.

In 1987, American Airlines initiated the American Achievers Program.[16] This program recognizes employees for anything special they may have done or for consistently just doing a good job. Managers, lead agents, and other supervisors can award Achiever points at any time to any employee in the company. The points are presented as certificates to be cashed in for travel benefits or merchandise from a catalog compiled specially for the program. Millions of dollars in such awards have already been given publicly to American employees.

Morrison Knudsen

Recently, Morrison Knudsen (MK) completed an especially tough job for the city of San Diego.[17] A ruptured pipeline in the city garnered national headlines for spewing millions of gallons of treated effluent into the ocean daily. Morrison Knudsen was called in on an emergency basis and charged with fixing the underwater breaks within two months. Most everyone said it couldn't be done, but dedicated and determined MK employees worked seven days a week, around the clock, to meet the nearly impossible deadline. While this tremendous effort resulted in public accolades for MK management, the real heroes were the people who, working long shifts under terrible circumstances, saw the project through to its successful completion. To recognize these invisible contributions, the mayor of San Diego arrived at 4:00 A.M. on the day the project was completed. He shook hands and congratulated each person who had helped with this remarkable feat. The thanks and appreciation of the city of San Diego were evident in the mayor's gesture. For those few moments, MK's hidden troupe found itself at center stage to take a quick bow before the next challenging assignment.

While not always as dramatic as the event above, Morrison Knudsen regularly recognizes contributions of employees who work quietly and conscientiously to move the company forward. These *can-do* employees are located around the globe and are called on whenever a contract estimate is made or a bid is submitted. Diligent people are typical of MK employees at work everywhere; on tunnels under the streets of Chicago; at igneous mines in Sarpy Creek, Montana; on the magnet development and test labs at the Superconducting Supercollider site in Texas; on rail cars in Hornell, New York; at a power plant in Georgia; at an air base in Kuwait; and in accounting offices at headquarters in Boise, Idaho.

In addition to ceremonial events at the time when a contract is won or a project is completed, Morrison Knudsen honors employees annually with service awards for those with five years or more with the company. Biannual service award dinners recognize those who have served the company ten years or more. These are small but important symbolic events, public pats on the back for people whose invisible efforts are just as crucial as the folks who are running the onstage show.

Ben & Jerry's

Ben Cohen and Jerry Greenfield seemed destined for the ice cream business.[18] After all, both received perfect scores on their tests given through Penn State's ice-cream-making correspondence course. Cohen and Greenfield opened their first ice cream shop in a Burlington, Vermont, renovated gas station in 1978. Three years later, *Time* magazine heralded their ice cream as the best in the world. Since then, Ben & Jerry's has seen sales skyrocket as its unique ice cream has cornered America's frozen dessert market. The two entrepreneurs seem to know what America's taste buds want. In 1991, Ben & Jerry's did over $100 million in revenues, employed over four hundred people and operated three ice cream plants in Vermont.

What accounts for the company's meteoric rise? Obviously the quality of the ice cream has had something to do with it. More important, the founders subscribe to a business ethic that includes not only employee empowerment and generous employee bonuses and benefits, but also a strong and sincere belief in what Greenfield says: "If it's not fun, why do it?"[19]

Greenfield is the "self-proclaimed minister of joy" for all of Ben & Jerry's employees.[20] In 1988, he formed the "Joy Gang." The gang, "a roving band of merrymakers, who, at any given moment, may be seen celebrating lesser known holidays," includes people from several of the company's departments. The Joy Gang's written mission is "the relentless pursuit of joy in the workplace, leaving a trail of deliriously happy employees wherever it goes."[21] The gang's antics have ranged from celebrating the national clash-dressing day, which gave awards to employees for the best mismatch in costume colors, to cooking a complete Italian meal for the third-phase workers (11:30 P.M. to 8:00 A.M.) and bringing in a disc jockey to play tunes on request. As Mitch Curren, a public relations officer, noted, "It's energizing. They help put the fun into coming to work."[22]

There are also other ways Ben & Jerry's employees celebrate.[23] At their annual meeting—attended by all employees—everyone completing his or her first year of service with the company is presented a Ben & Jerry's hat from the founders themselves. For each additional year, workers receive an ice cream cone pin to adorn the hat. At first glance everyone knows how long a fellow employee has been with the company.

The winter party is given each December to celebrate what the company is all about.[24] The party extends over a period of time to accommodate different work schedules.

Child care is provided until 1:00 A.M. Music, food, libations, games, and door prizes enhance the celebration.

Other annual festivities include the One World, One Heart Festival in Waitsfield, Vermont, and similar festivals in Chicago and San Francisco.[25] Plant operations shut down and employees offer their services as part of their regular work schedule. Ben & Jerry's provides regular opportunities for the celebration of backstage workers. They receive public recognition and enjoy the festivities. In addition, festival-goers receive a warm welcome that captures the spirit of Ben & Jerry's:

> We had such a great time last year, we're doing it again. There's nothing quite like throwing a party for thousands of your closest friends. We're thrilled to be able to celebrate and frolic and continue our efforts with you to create a more caring world. We invite you to join all of us at Ben & Jerry's in opening our hearts and minds to the possibilities of what can be. Enjoy![26]

It is no wonder that Ben & Jerry's recently received the *Personnel Journal* Optimas Award in the "quality of life" category.[27] Its supportive employee environment has resulted in its phenomenal financial success.

Celebration: A Company Way of Life

The attention to ceremony is not confined to the examples above. Dahlin Smith White pushes the celebratory limits of our traditional management thinking. The ad agency's motto, "Do something wild," incorporates flexible employee celebrations into the daily working schedule.[28] Backstage personnel participate equally in the open-style festivities, according to

John Dahlin: "If people want to play music loud—every office has a company-bought boom box—or dance in the hallways, they can. If they want to go skiing or go to a movie in the middle of the day, they can. If they want to play pool, the company has a pool room. People have even been known to bowl down the corridors."[29]

For Dahlin Smith White, the key to the company's success is the celebratory working environment it has created for its employees. The company doesn't have to wait for a reason to celebrate; it believes that, "when people are having fun, they're encouraged to work harder,"[30] as Dahlin commented. He added: "I worry whether the staff are happy. Are they motivated and compensated well enough? We want people to have fun, to be stimulated, to do something wild."[31]

In response to our request for the company's "wildest celebration story," two were mentioned—one spontaneous, the other more organized. The spontaneous event occurred one Thursday in 1992. In order to relieve mounting pressures, an employee suggested that since the next day would be Friday the thirteenth, an impromptu party should happen. An observer described the event:

"We were all in a party mood—had a hard time. In the late afternoon on the thirteenth, the party began with the showing of rented horror films, a menu of gooey, tomato (bloody) pizza, and lots of stupid jokes. There was a real sense of relief, a sense of spirit and a concept behind it which made it playful and fun. Everyone had a chance to be clever and stupid all at the same time."[32]

On the more organized side, the company has an annual bowling party on Halloween. Again, a firsthand account:

"This time was a 'biker' theme. The costumes followed suit—the agency staff became tough looking folks—completely out of character. The company rented out an entire bowling alley, brought in a Harley, which served as a backdrop for employee photos, and we gave away gifts. As the evening progressed, the group proceeded outdoors for one big company photo shoot. As it happened, passing cars began slowing down to rubber-neck, and then a very nervous police officer drove in to see just what was happening. In the spirit of playfulness, the employees cajoled the officer into posing with them in the photograph for posterity. These were great fun and go down in my memory as hard-to-beat company mixers and celebrations."[33]

Dahlin Smith White believes that daily celebration en-courages employee productivity and creativity, the lifeblood of their industry.

Yet, interesting celebrations are not confined to the cre-ative environment of an ad agency. They arise also in the routine of manufacturing tangible products. Workers in a man-ufacturing facility can easily become removed from the prod-ucts of their work. They are often not connected to the triumph of getting a large order or receiving satisfaction first-hand from a happy customer. Excitement for the production worker often comes in the form of negative stress—the rush to get product out the door, the crises of quality errors, the struggle to plan never-perfect sales forecasts. Without a con-scious effort to create positive excitement, morale in such organizations can easily get worn down.

In Marenisco, a small town on the upper peninsula of Michigan, a sixty-person plant makes patio doors for Norco Windows.[34] Without a doubt, this is entirely a backstage facil-ity. But the deliberate effort of plant management to promote a celebrative atmosphere shows what simple efforts can do. The plant's efforts spawn local celebrative events rather than focus on company-wide occasions. Each department is encouraged to organize its own celebrations: Bear Feeds, Elk Feeds, and other luncheons occur on a monthly basis. (Some of these are jokingly referred to as Road-Kill Parties.) Periodic pancake and wild blueberry breakfasts bring workers in early for their 6:00 A.M. shift.

After one long winter, the entire Marenisco facility decided to bring in spring with a Hawaiian party. The maintenance crew rolled out the barbecue pit they had built and cut palm trees out of cardboard. Everyone dressed for the occasion. Even the UPS man making a delivery jumped out of his truck and unloaded packages in a wig and bikini.

These events are clearly fun, but what do they do for the plant? Plant Manager Jerry Lukach says:

> "They break down barriers, particularly between departments. The events remove people from their cast roles at the plant and cause them to relate to each other in new manners. Celebrations do not solve problems, but a celebrative atmosphere washes away some of the stress and bitterness that surrounds those problems. The positive atmosphere at the plant makes people more positive about managing the day-to-day challenges of working in a manufacturing facility."[35]

Celebration takes many forms depending on the company and the occasion. One of the more unusual was a joint event between Stevens Aviation and Southwest Airlines. The explicit purpose was to settle a dispute between the two companies over an ad slogan, "Plane Smart," claimed by both. Stevens chairman Kurt Herwald challenged Southwest chairman Herb Kelleher to an arm-wrestling contest to determine which claim would prevail.[36] In March 1992, three thousand employees from both companies, most of them behind-the-scenes workers, were bused to Dallas to witness the event.

Over seven hundred of the employees were designated as cheerleaders and equipped with pom-poms. The event also caught the attention of the media. After Herwald beat Kelleher, he announced that Stevens would allow Southwest to continue to use the slogan.

The event had several important payoffs. Besides saving an estimated $500,000 in lawyer fees, both companies received about $5 million worth of free publicity. The event was reported in approximately 400 newspapers, over 150 radio stations, 15 business magazines, and all major TV networks—including over twenty times on CNN. Even more important, the celebratory rally boosted the morale and spirit of both sets of employees. Steve Townes, executive vice president at Stevens, succinctly captures the less obvious symbolic benefits of the occasion:

> "Not only did we solve the slogan question creatively, but it gave us a chance to let the backstage employees celebrate, cheer and become more linked to their company. It was a zany, wonderful moment that actually boosted our collective self-esteem as a company and put an extra bounce in our step."[37]

Halfhearted Celebrations

Whatever form they take, whenever they are held, rituals and ceremonies must be meaningful, authentic, and heartfelt; not regimented, overly planned, or mandated. As one frustrated executive remarked, "I know I need to recognize employees, but it doesn't work for me. I tried a wine and cheese party at 4:30 P.M. on Friday, but after one or two times no one seemed interested."[38] Professor Mark Pastin of Arizona State University says, "Company picnics don't mean a damn unless other factors are present such as honest communications, respectful treatment, and equitable standards of gain and sacrifice."[39]

Awards and recognitions at rituals can also symbolize management's appreciation. Unfortunately, many companies make halfhearted attempts to show appreciation, especially for those who are not the key performers. At one company, an employee did not become aware of her Employee of the Month award until weeks later:

> "Earlier this fiscal year I got this pat-on-the-head memo from someone very unconnected to what I do and my hierarchical structure. I thought this most puzzling, so I took it to a friend who was an associate of the memo's author and asked what it meant. My friend said, "Does this have anything to do with your being Employee of the Month?" I was dumbfounded; I had never heard of that. When were they going to tell me? My friend said the award was made three weeks ago. Not even my supervisor had come to me. Everyone I told thought it was hilarious. The award totally lost its meaning. It was an honest attempt that miserably failed.[40]

This employee recognition program was viewed as phony, hollow, and shallow. It backfired even though management's plan was initially well intended. Employees can easily see when a thank you is halfhearted. It is management's responsibility to instill meaning into recognition events.

No employee wants to be part of a time-consuming, unauthentic occasion. Hollow or shallow events demotivate people and cheapen the value of their accomplishments. But in many of today's organizations, celebration is often undervalued. Author and theologian Harvey Cox observes:

> We have pressed [modern man] so hard toward useful work and rational calculation that he has all but forgotten

the joy of ecstatic celebration, antic play and free imagination. His shrunken psyche is just as much a victim of industrialization as were the bent bodies of those, back as children, once confined to English factories from dawn to dusk. Western industrial man . . . must learn again to dance and dream.[41]

This is especially true for people behind the scenes who may find celebration an especially important source of joy and recognition. As Bill Boesch of American Airlines aptly observed in the chapter's beginning, we need "to stand behind people . . . and help them celebrate."[42] Organizations need to encourage festival as a way of reconnecting people to what the business is all about.

Some Final Considerations

- The power of ceremony, while difficult to quantify, leaves a permanent mark on employees.
- Celebrations can take many forms, from routine meetings to extravaganzas.
- Celebration is most important for hidden employees because they are not recognized as often as those on the front line. It provides employees a way of bonding to the company.
- Most important, ceremonies need to be authentic and supported by top management.

Diagnostic Questions

1. Do our ceremonies draw enough attention to people in backstage positions?
2. Do people consider celebrations an important part

of our company's culture? Would they say there are too many celebrations, or not enough?

3. Within our organization, is there a difference between those departments that have celebratory events and those that do not?

PART V

Pitfalls and Promises of Backstage Management

■ CHAPTER 16
The Hidden Cast Speaks

An employee described a possibly overburdened supervisor who would not listen and appears not to care:

> "It's not the patients that cause me trouble, it's the supervisors over me. I've been here seven or eight years, but the people over me don't know a single patient. . . . We had one patient who wasn't acting right. We kept telling the charge nurse. She said she'd check the patient but told us to keep watching her. Then the patient died that night."[1]

Another employee voiced her basic needs in equally simple and straightforward terms:

> "I want my supervisor to be fair, have respect, be aware and helpful, alert, friendly—not harsh—keep a confidence, and sometimes take my side with others when they expect miracles outside of company policy."

Why can't supervisors cultivate more-supportive, satisfying relationships and better represent employee interests
with higher-ups? Typically, managers assume or demand support from subordinates. Less often do they take into account
the law of reciprocity: "You have to give something to get
something."

Training the Manager

In deciding what kinds of training employees need, executives
and managers are heavily involved and highly influential.
When it comes to determining training for managers, employees are seldom asked for their opinions. Usually, professors
and organizational consultants shape the form and content of
management training. They make sure that training reflects
new developments in management or organizational theory.
At the best M.B.A. programs, course titles include Management Statistics, Operations Management, Management Information Systems, and Managerial Finance.[2] At even the best
companies, managers are usually trained in how to use the
latest management techniques: strategic planning, problem
solving, and quality assurance. Employees who will be the
firsthand recipients of many of these techniques are rarely
polled about their views of the working situation. They are
almost never solicited about the promising targets for management training or what skills managers need to help employees
perform better and more efficiently.

What happens when you ask directly and listen carefully
to what people have to say about how their managers could
improve? We decided to find out. We convened focus groups
of professional (exempt employees), hourly workers (nonex-
empt), and union workers in behind-the-scenes positions.
When asked for their opinions, people responded with little

hesitation and great relish. From what they had to say, we began to see some pronounced trends and clear patterns. Most of their suggestions differed significantly from traditional management ideas and thinking. These people were more than eager to suggest ways in which their managers could be trained. This was a marvelous reversal of how "things" are typically done.

Employee Focus Groups

Ten focus groups, each composed of three to five backstage employees selected from three different companies, responded to several questions:

- If your manager asked you what things he or she could do better concerning his or her job, what would you say?
- If you were given an opportunity to train your manager, what would you do or suggest?
- Does management acknowledge the contribution of people in roles behind the scenes? If so, how? If not, what would you suggest to management regarding their acknowledgment?
- Do you feel listened to by your manager? If so, how do you know? If not, how would you train your manager to be more sensitive and open to your concerns and suggestions?

Responses to these basic questions suggested these people may be working from a very different mental map in determining what is really going on or deciding what kind of training managers actually need. The discrepancy is important because mental maps are essential in charting the terrain of human organizations, as author Stephen Covey pointed out:

The fundamental problem has nothing to do with your behavior or your attitude. It has everything to do with having a wrong map. We simply assume that the way we see things is the way they really are or the way they should be.[3]

Employees' maps point to some unique and promising directions for management development. Theirs is a decidedly humanistic view with some simple basic requests:

- We'd like managers to listen.
- We want to be kept informed.
- We'd like managers to be trustworthy.
- We'd like managers to know what we do.
- We need to be acknowledged.

Please Listen to Me

According to Calvin Coolidge, "Nobody has ever listened himself out of a job." Despite this, the ability to listen effectively continues to be a fading art. Listening is a critical leadership factor and a sure way to demonstrate to employees and co-workers that they have value. People in backstage positions repeatedly expressed that listening implies caring, motivating, and showing gratitude. They want to be heard but often feel shut out:

"He would do well to listen. He seems to start answering before he listens. That makes one feel invalidated and makes it very easy to become discouraged and float down the river barely getting by."

"My managers are very busy. They forget to listen and hear what I have to say. I have been a professional server for over ten years. I know my job. I know what to do."

"It is amazing to me that the managers have no idea what we are thinking. They do not know what the troops are thinking."

"There are two sides to every story, and the manager may not know the whole story. The manager needs to hear both sides."

It is clear that people feel they are not being heard. Their managers are thereby deprived of information, and the employees themselves feel out of the loop. The reverse is also true. Listening patiently shows special attention and allows good things to happen.

"My manager listens well. He gives understanding and empathy. It's there. He does talk to us and has an open-door policy."

"In follow-up conversations, there is recognition of the previous conversations. That's the way I know my supervisor is listening."

"When I go to see my manager, I usually get results and I always get feedback. She listens."

"They get back to you on things. You know they listened."

Yet, even with managers who listen well, there is always room for improvement:

"My manager is very good about listening and taking suggestions, but he does not ask far enough down the chain. He needs to ask the people who have to deal with the issue and the decisions that are made."

"Even when there is a problem, she will listen and we can talk it out. However, sometimes her door is open physically but closed mentally."

"She listened to me about the problem, but observed only part of it. She normally listens. I give her credit for that."

Employees simply want to be heard. The most pervasive training need that they see is to get managers to close their mouths and lend their ears:

"To listen. To take the ideas. To listen to what you have to say."

"They need to listen."

"We need them to listen, be patient, understand what is going on."

"First thing would be a willingness to listen and hear all the news—good and bad."

"They should listen to hear new ideas, keep an open mind when it comes to an employee. They should be honest."

Most management training emphasizes presentation skills—communicating ideas clearly and forcefully. Listening skills are only briefly touched on in most university courses or company training programs. As a consequence, listening skills—the ability to hear what others are presenting—continues to be one of the most neglected aspects of communication. Improving listening skills will require a shift from a management attitude of knowing it all to a belief in the value of cooperation. In the minds of employees, a first step would be to have managers think about the following questions:

Manager's Checklist

- What would my employees say about my listening skills?
- Do I have an open-door policy?
- How can I systematically improve my listening abilities?
- If I begin to practice active listening, could we improve the department? Would morale and productivity increase?

Share Information

Keeping informed means being included and considered an integral part of the communication network. Many employees feel isolated because their managers do not communicate or share information with them—including information that is meant for general consumption but which impacts each employee's ability to carry out his or her specific job responsibilities. Being up-to-date and in the know is also a status symbol. It is demeaning and embarrassing to always be the last to hear what is really going on.

> "There are few managers who do keep things close to their chest. I heard about our recent expansion from a client. The managers just assume you know."

> "I would like to be more informed directly, instead of through a third party."

> "Some employees pick up the newspaper and read about something that affects their areas and was never communicated to them."

> "I read in the paper things that affect me and my life. There is a lack of communication. They should hire someone to let us know what we are doing and where we are going and why."

Employees also want to know what other departments are doing. Otherwise, they start to work at cross-purposes with people with whom they should be cooperative. Even if the manager has the big picture, when employees are working in information-tight compartments, snafus occur. Necessary information needs to be widely shared. Everyone needs some idea about what everyone else is doing. Their right to know is often overlooked.

"We need to know what is going on with other areas that will affect us."

"I would like to know what to do—get a better understanding. I need to know what others are responsible for."

"The department is very diversified. I have no idea what others are doing, what projects they are working on. We do have the right to know."

How can a manager ensure that people have a clear understanding of global guidelines, policies, and benefits? This knowledge is essential if they are to serve both the general welfare and best interests of customers. Employees are clear about how they expect the boss to communicate with them.

"The manager should give a better interpretation of company policy."

"I want the manager to go over certain policies and learn how to enforce the policies."

"Sometimes you are just told to do something without a reason. It is the bosses' right not to tell, but it would be nice to know why. Sometimes I just think, 'God, why am I doing this?'"

People want and need to be appropriately informed in order to do their job to the best of their ability. *Information is power*; but it is more than that: *information is empowerment*. Empowered employees make contributions far and above those that wait for managerial dictates. How can managers know how effectively they are sharing information? The following questions provide a start.

Manager's Checklist

- What is my policy for keeping employees informed on major decisions and changes within our company?
- How well do I disseminate information about what is going on in other departments?
- Do I include junior employees in meetings that affect them?
- How often do I revisit policies, guidelines, and rules with employees? Do I solicit questions and opinions?

Trust Is a Two-Way Street

Trust is basic to any healthy, productive human relationship. As we saw in a previous chapter, a trusting manager shows confidence in employees and recognizes their ability to do a good job. However, trust is a two-way street. It is equally important for an employee to trust his or her manager. The employees want to believe that actions serve the best interests of the employees, the company, and customer, not just parochial management interests. Unfortunately, many people wonder whether trusting and being trusted are illusory managerial qualities:

"Talk about trust. They all make you feel as if you are not valued. My immediate supervisor is so insecure, incomplete as a person, and all this personal stuff filters downward instead of upward."

"Trust is what pops into my mind. I'm not sure you can be taught that."

"Trust? If you go above your immediate supervisor to resolve certain issues, your performance evaluation would be at risk. You wonder why people even care. It's better to just do the best you can—you really have no one to go to."

A major factor in trust is consistency. Unfair or inconsistent treatment is spotted easily by employees and always undermines trust:

"One employee gets by with murder, and the supervisor will just deny a problem exists."

"The situation is clear and blatant. Everyone weighs their words carefully. It's like walking on eggshells. Managers in our department are politically motivated but not smart enough to realize that people can see through this."

"One time during a snowstorm, I came in on the weekend. I had to walk in knee-high snow to another department to get the data, just because I knew the payroll had to go out. It did. I got no thanks. Then not long ago, a secretary stayed late one night in accounting, and she immediately got a letter from the controller thanking her for staying over. I was happy for her, but I didn't feel good about not getting the same treatment."

In a trusting environment, employees go the extra mile. Trust and productivity go hand in hand:

"I trust that they will be fair and will want what is best for the department. That encourages me to come out with the product. They see that in me. You have to develop the trust factor, and it comes gradually."

"All the trust he puts into me is the absolute compliment. It means more than anything he could do. He is extremely complimentary and always says 'Everything will be all right.' The amount of trust is better than a raise."

"My manager trusts me both professionally and personally, and I trust my manager—she has earned it and so have I. I call that personal power."

"We have empowerment to stand on our feet to make decisions, trusted not to abuse the power we are given. Many times in a large organization, you must have trust. If there is no trust or support, you have no flexibility whatsoever."

"I work in printing and on a recent job, I knew the color was not right. I did what we call a 'double bump' on my own. It made a tremendous difference although it took more time. I used my own judgment because my supervisor trusts me."

Old managerial practices such as standing over employees while they work, keeping count of how many times employees leave their desk to go to the bathroom, or reviewing all completed work in fine-grained detail are no longer part of a workable managerial map. Establishing and maintaining trust in the workplace is hard for anyone, especially for managers. But it can be done if people take the time to think about how they are doing and what might be done. How can you evaluate the trust factor in an organization? Asking some basic questions is a good place to begin:

Manager's Checklist

- Do I trust my employees? If not, is it my problem or theirs? How can we establish a more trusting relationship?
- Do I treat my employees as decision makers, or as advisers to me?
- When I am able to trust my employees, does more work get accomplished?
- Am I consistent in my behavior and actions? Do I feel that employees trust me?
- Are my employees held responsible for executing requests or for the end results of their decisions and actions?
- Should I talk to my employees about trust?

Know What I Do

People want management to be able to walk in their shoes, to understand what they do and what they are up against. In the navy, this is sometimes referred to as "bulkhead knowledge," a reference to officers who get off the bridge and know what each seaman is doing. Knowing the environment, the players, workloads, required skills, and the complexities involved in an employee's tasks provides valuable information in any organization. Taking an interest in people's work instills a sense of connection and camaraderie, rather than a feeling of bitter anger or apathy:

> "My direct supervisor and the others would not have the foggiest idea what I do for a living. It is most humiliating—it is really degrading—I could slap them into next week—could spit in their eye—it makes me really angry. They have no idea and could care less."

When anyone actually experiences a task or situation, they come to know it better because of that. Employees want managers to roll up their sleeves and get their hands and minds into a job. Only then can they appreciate the multitude of tasks involved in an employee's work:

> "I would have them do my job for a day or two."

> "He should understand my job and what I do."

> "Need to know the job. Some supervisors are not familiar with what a worker is doing. It is frustrating when they don't know what you do."

With an increased understanding of the pressures employees face, more realistic planning and production schedules can evolve.

> "Put them in my shoes. If they would walk through the process, they would have a better understanding that things take time. Some things cannot always be done accurately and hurriedly."

Strategic planning, cost-benefit analysis, and other top-level bureaucratic tasks often absorb managers' time, leaving them little time for understanding of the operational details.

> "In my area, my manager needs to spend at least a week within the department in every area of purchasing to find out how each works and how they work together."

> "From a previous manager, her favorite saying was 'Just make it go away.' She didn't even know how to reconcile the registers at the end of the day. If you are managing an area, you need to know how to do it."

Will tomorrow's manager be a person who actually rolls up his or her sleeves, gets in the trenches, and works alongside the employees? Their subordinates makes a sound case for that possibility:

> "If I have a question, I cannot get much help. If you are a manager, you ought to have an idea of how things work."

> "They are not out there on the floor. They do not know what is going on. They are not there to roll up their sleeves, which would mean a lot. It says you are going to be there, not just dictate."

Associating directly and personally with employees is not always easy. The potential for dividends and payoffs is there, but only if managers check their maps out against the actual territory once in a while. Check your knowledge of what employees do as you work through the following questions:

Manager's Checklist

- Are you perceived to have understanding and appreciation for your employees' work?
- Can you explain the operational details of your department?
- From time to time, do you actually do an employee's job? Do your employees see you as a working manager?

Acknowledge Us Once in a While

Throughout this book a theme comes up time and again: all employees want to be praised for a job well done. People want to know when they do a good job or be acknowledged by "higher-ups" when they make that extra effort. This is especially true for those who rarely get to stand in the limelight.

> "Backstage employees want more positive motivation
> from their managers, i.e., not just what went wrong, but
> how to do it better. On days when things go right, the
> manager should say 'Thank you, it has been a great
> day.'"

> "It is important for everybody to know that they are
> doing a good job. They can say 'Thank you' or 'Hey, good
> job, it looks great' more often."

> "Everyone needs to feel important, everyone deserves
> recognition."

Recognition by management takes so little time but offers so much to the working environment. When employees are recognized, it makes a profound, lasting impression on them. Thanks and praise encourage people to do their jobs better.

> "During preshift, our supervisor tells the guys what is
> going on the next day, how great a job they did today
> and shakes their hands. He finds as many people as he
> can."

> "My manager is very, very complimentary. He always
> makes a special point to thank you when you have done
> something out of the ordinary. He is conscientious.
> When he says something, he means it and you know
> because of the honesty and integrity of his everyday life.
> He is a great example—he follows what he preaches."

It's important to reiterate that expectations for praise are often minimal, but they have a disproportional impact on motivation:

"My boss doesn't mind saying 'Thank you,' and he sincerely means it. It makes you go that extra mile to want to make him feel good."

"Pats on the back make you go out and work ten times harder. It makes you feel good about yourself."

"In the year-end report, it was written that we had experienced the lowest percentage of chargebacks ever. My manager left on my voice mail: 'You are the one who makes me look good.' That encourages me to do even better. The first quarter of this year, the figure was even lower—a compliment will keep people pushing to better themselves."

To some managers, constant praise and recognition may seem unimportant or inappropriate. Assuming that employees will just know when "I think they have done a great job" doesn't work anymore. A simple thank-you can go a long way in boosting worker morale and productivity. Managers need to learn to shift from assumptions to acknowledgments. The following questions will help determine if you have started to make such a shift:

Manager's Checklist

- How many times today have you offered a sincere thanks or acknowledgment to your employees for their contribution to the company?
- Do you take the time to recognize an extra effort by an employee?
- Do you, at times, publicly acknowledge your appreciation for the efforts put forth by your employees?

The Humanistic Side of Management

Not surprisingly, the mental maps of employees present a unique view of management training terrain. To them, training is not needed in the quantitative, theoretical business areas, but in the human aspects of managing people. Sharing information, listening, trusting, understanding employees' jobs, and praising work are not complicated concepts. Yet these are the very areas in which many managers today are seen as needing help. By learning how to affirm, exhibit fair treatment, listen, and view situations accurately and by recognizing employees as responsible people, managers may find new potential in people. Their new management maps might provide better guides for getting along in a territory that employees often see very differently.

■ CHAPTER 17
Saturn: A Look to America's Future

America's automobile industry did not fare well in the opening chapters of this book. In fact, what was once America's showpiece industry received a barrage of criticism. Many of the horror stories of indifference and sabotage on the part of workers behind the scenes came directly from the automotive assembly line. People seemed more interested in finding ways to avoid work or to gum things up than to build quality cars. In particular, General Motors stood out as an example of mismanagement at its worst. It seems both ironic and uplifting that our closing example of what the future holds would come from the same company.

Saturn is General Motors' fresh attempt to restore America's ability to compete successfully in the automobile industry. Technologically, Saturn does things once thought to be impossible. Computers are used extensively throughout the plant and robotics are employed in jobs where there could be potential harm or injury. Ninety percent of the car's bulk and 65 percent of its parts are built on-site, which includes stamping and welding of the parts.[1] Workers on skillets (slow-moving floors) ride along with the car bodies as they are assembled.[2] Parts are delivered "just in time" for the next production step instead of being stockpiled in inventory. This allows for lower inventory costs, and it helps the company monitor the quality of its parts more carefully.[3] Engine components are produced by lost-foam casting, a process eliminating a significant amount of machining, processes, and materials.[4] Automatic and manual transmissions are built on the same assembly lines.[5] The factory has 101 delivery docks, making it easy for parts to be delivered to the assembly line quickly.[6] The plant has only 300 outside suppliers, whereas another GM plant might use 1,500 to 2,000.[7]

Despite its allure, this design and technological dazzle is not the real miracle of Saturn. How the company organizes and leads (not "manages") people is the real breakthrough.[8] For example, Saturn's three hundred suppliers were all chosen by a consensus of workers and managers. The car is assembled by one hundred production teams of eight to fifteen interdependent people per shift, rather than by the sequential efforts of isolated, individual workers. All employees are salaried team members, not hourly workers. All decisions must be reached by consensus. Team members are taught conflict-resolution skills and trained to work cooperatively in close-knit groups.[9] Five percent of a working year is devoted to training. There is also incentive to keep one's skills current. A portion of everyone's salary is held back. If everyone receives the allotted amount of training, everyone earns back the portion of their salaries that was put at risk.[10]

Unlike most backstage people, Saturn team members are well connected to the consumers. Retail partners visit the plant to talk with team members. Team members on vacation often visit the dealerships. If any Saturn employee sees one of their cars on the side of the road, they stop to find out what might be wrong or to ask how they can help.[11] All of this, in the words of a Saturn employee, "is nothing like things were in the 'Old World,' "[12] with reference to practices at GM. The three main streets at the plant are Handshake, Venture, and Quality,[13] summing up Saturn's revolutionary turnaround in how people can work together to produce a top-quality product.

The stakes are high. Lester Thurow, dean of MIT's Sloan School, put into words what many Saturn employees feel:

"If Saturn is successful, it will prove that it's possible to junk the old bureaucracies, change the corporate culture, change the adversarial relationship between union and management and put it all back together right. If they succeed, it will be a big positive for America. If not, it will be a huge downer."[14]

By most statistics, the company is succeeding. In fact, 1992 may be viewed as the year Saturn turned the corner. The company scored some notable successes:

- For the second consecutive year, Saturn was named the third-best nameplate and the best domestic in customer satisfaction in the J. D. Power Customer Satisfaction Index. It is the highest ranking for any domestic carmaker since Power began publishing the index six years ago.[15]
- Saturn shot into the top of several J. D. Power surveys, including number 2 behind Lexus in dealer's attitude, number 6 in overall sales satisfaction, number 3 on delivery condition of the car, number 5 on delivery process. In all cases, Saturn was surpassed only by luxury cars, not by the Japanese middle market. These surveys also show that Saturn owners recommended their cars to other people more often than owners of any other car.[16]
- Surveys now show 65 percent of the Saturn buyers would have bought imports.[17]

- In a spring 1992 survey of owners, Saturn ranked number 1 among domestic cars in fewest consumer complaints.[18]
- The plant now is producing over a thousand cars a day, with demand still exceeding supply. Since January 1992, sales have increased 77 percent.[19]
- Saturn began an export program to Taiwan and is presently shipping two to four hundred cars per month.[20]
- While no other GM division posted a sales increase in 1991–92, Saturn's sales shot up 182 percent.[21]
- A recent survey by *Popular Mechanics* found that 83.4% of Saturn owners would buy another Saturn.[22]
- Saturn dealers sell more cars per showroom than any other dealer in the United States. This high rate of sales leaves dealers with only a seventeen-day supply of cars compared to a sixty-day supply for all other dealers. In August 1992 that seventeen-day supply dropped to thirteen—the lowest reported in the industry.[23]
- More than a month before the 1992 model year ended on September 30, Saturn sold out of its 1992 cars.[24]

Whether Saturn can produce high-quality cars and well-satisfied customers and still yield a profit to shareholders will not become apparent for some time. However, it is off to a fabulous start and continuing its business in a fashion consistent with many of the principles of this book. It has even taken a step beyond our original premise by virtually eliminating the distinction between people in onstage and backstage roles. Everyone at Saturn is a star and all share the limelight. Saturn represents a profound change in the way a company runs its business and deals with its people and customers.

Hoping to learn Saturn's auto-manufacturing philosophy, teams from Oldsmobile, Ford, and Chrysler, as well as officials from Nissan, Suzuki, Mazda, Land Rover, and Renault are flocking to Saturn's headquarters and showrooms. One of Saturn's first retail partners, John Campbell, pointed out,

"They're all looking for the answer but I'm not sure there is an answer. It's a whole bunch of things . . . a whole new culture."[25]

Whatever Saturn's answer is, the company has definitely created a new look in the American business world. Donald Ephlin, a retired UAW vice president and coauthor of the Saturn–UAW agreement, noted that "in the mid 1980s, Chrysler's Lee Iacocca called the [Saturn] plan 'a lot of nonsense,' and a Ford Motor executive called it 'Ephlin's fantasy.' Today, both are studying the 'Saturn concept.' "[26]

Yet Saturn's reputation goes far beyond the automotive and business worlds. Recently, Lamar Alexander, U.S. education secretary in the Bush administration, declared: "America's education system [could use] an overhaul much like the one GM's new Saturn subsidiary [is giving to the world's automotive industry]."[27] He noted that Saturn "rethought the process of making cars. . . . And now it's an American car that can compete with any car in the world."[28] To Alexander's thinking, America's education system, in addition to its business world, could learn a thing or two from Saturn.

Saturn's Roots

Prior to Saturn, most people had their favorite GM story, very few of which were favorable. Janan Stortie's story is just one of many that led GM executives to conclude that survival sometimes requires radical change. Stortie drove a Honda Civic. Her husband commuted to his job in a 1984 Chevy Camaro, which yielded four factory recalls, mediocre gas mileage, and many visits to the repair shop. "I am sure he would not want me to say this, but it was a piece of junk,"[29] she said. The interesting twist to the story is that Stortie herself worked for GM.

With comparisons like that from GM employees, it is easy to understand why Japan's share of the automobile market was increasing while America was losing ground. This slip became even more worrisome when Chevrolet lost substantial market share to Japanese competitors. It was obvious that something needed to be done. Then GM's chairman Roger Smith responded with a bold challenge: "Our game is not to pull even, but to pull ahead. If Saturn works out, it will bring a lot of buyers back to American cars."[30]

With that global mission as a general guide, Saturn's founders rolled up their sleeves and went to work.

Their first job was to determine how the company would be organized. The task was assigned to the "Group of 99," which visited over 160 successful companies worldwide in search of new ideas and promising practices.[31] Three common themes emerged. For GM and most American organizations the ideas were radical:

- Give employees a sense of ownership.
- Have few and flexible guidelines.
- Impose no job-defining rules.

Radical ideas meant radical manufacturing changes, including moving away from the traditional assembly line and adopting production teams. Among the Group of 99 there was a conviction from the start that Saturn would not be a remake of the other GM models. Nor would the manufacturing facility or the use of human resources resemble much from the past. Saturn was to be *a different kind of a company. A different kind of car.*[32]

While the organization was being designed, the management–union relationship at Saturn itself underwent a significant overhaul. The agreement signed in 1985 by the United Auto Workers stood labor relations on its head. "While the rest of GM and the UAW measure their operating relationship against a 597-page contract expiring every three years, Saturn and the union use a 28-page contract that the company and the union refer to as a living constitution."[33] As Robert Boruff, vice president of Manufacturing Operations, noted: "The power of our contract at Saturn is its very simplicity. It is intentionally general to allow us all the flexibility needed to address specific issues when they come up."[34]

The contract included permanent job security "barring unforeseen events or severe economic conditions,"[35] full participation in daily decision-making, and salaries 20 percent below other GM workers (the 20 percent to be earned back through production performance and quality incentives.)[36] In addition, the contractual agreement specifies participation of union employees in executive decisions about strategic matters such as selecting suppliers, ad agencies, and dealers.[37]

Building the plant was not cheap[38]—it cost GM $1.9 billion. A 4-million-square-foot facility located on twenty-four hundred acres of beautiful rolling hills, it required new construction of eighteen miles of roadway. It's currently building a new 310,000-square-foot warehouse for $10 million to accommodate the increased demand for sedans and their new Saturn wagon. At the same time, Saturn is determined to be a good neighbor in their Spring Hill community. Special attention paid to the surrounding rural environment reserved eight hundred acres for cultivation of hay, barley, and soybeans.[39] A series of birdhouses were constructed to attract bluebirds.[40] When a dilapidated burial ground was unearthed, the remains were moved to a beautiful spot on the site. All markers were restored to their original condition.[41]

In 1988, the most important step in the company's development was taken.[42] Saturn began recruiting people willing to adopt a philosophy of team management and employee participation. UAW members transferring to Saturn forfeited their seniority rights. There was no turning back. It was either going to be a success under a different working philosophy or a change of career if the experiment did not pan out.

After making the decision to join the new company, all team members went through extensive training. Most training focused on people skills and how to make decisions and deal with conflict. Team members collectively refined assembly procedures. On July 30, 1990, Roger Smith, only a few days away from retirement, drove the first Saturn car off the production line.[43] An emotional ceremony marked the possibility that a new age in the American automobile industry had begun.

The next two years were filled with vexing challenges.[44] Production in 1991 lagged behind projection because team members themselves would not relax demands for high quality. Dealership openings were delayed. In February and May 1991, the first recalls were announced: faulty backseat latches and contaminated coolants. On an October 1991 visit to Saturn, former GM chairman Robert Stempel was confronted by team members wearing black-and-orange arm bands. The actual motive behind the demonstration, however, signaled new hope. Team members were not asking for higher pay. They were demanding that management pay more attention to quality.

How Saturn dealt with these adversities provided even more evidence that a new age was under way.[45] When production was delayed, Saturn gave its retail partners an average of $100,000 as recompense for the lack of product. Faulty seat latches were fixed by Saturn team members who went directly to some customer homes to make the repairs. The 1,836 cars mistakenly filled with bad coolant from a supplier were replaced with new Saturns. These unconventional responses caught consumers' attention and raised their confidence. Some retail partners reported increased sales because Saturn was replacing defective cars rather than just repairing them.[46] One month after Stempel's visit, a new labor agreement was signed tying 20 percent of the team members' pay, the reward portion, to quality and productivity, while reducing the daily production schedule.[47] All this provided additional evidence that an old mold had been broken and a new one was being cast.

Saturn's People Policies

The secret of Saturn's success is the way it organizes and manages its people. In fact, it is something of an error to apply the term *management* to Saturn's approach. In reality, they have created a work environment where people provide leadership for themselves and for others. It is cooperation and self- and team management that makes Saturn tick. Problems are solved by people working together—they are not kicked upstairs for someone else to solve. Saturn has a shared, well-thought-out set of principles and policies. In fact, theirs fit many of the principles outlined in this book. In our view, Saturn is enjoying the fruits of putting these principles into practice.

Champions

Saturn management assumes the responsibility for being an advocate for the accomplishments of the line worker. President Skip LeFauve and UAW president Mike Bennett share the same executive office suite and set the tone for a cooperative approach.[48] LeFauve says, "When people come and say, 'How did you do that?' we say we did it through the people."[49] Managers do not consider line workers as backstage employees. In fact, they are seen as the heart and soul of the company—the stars. Advertisements feature Saturn employees describing their decision to join Saturn. As one employee put it, "Our leaders recognize who makes things happen here."[50]

Core Mission

At Saturn, team members have internalized the company's mission: "Market vehicles developed and manufactured in the United States that are world leaders in quality, cost and customer satisfaction through the integration of people, technology and business systems and to transfer knowledge, technology and experience throughout General Motors" to "make a better car."[51] As an employee in the chassis department explains, "It's almost like a religion here, it is a way of life. It's in our hearts, and we all either win or we all lose."[52]

Saturn demonstrates that when employees understand mission and direction, they make better decisions and are more productive. They know what they are working for and they care about what they do. An employee described the pride in watching the first Saturn roll off the assembly line. There is clearly a part of her in that first car:

"When the first Saturn rolled off the assembly line, it was a moment I'll never forget. Roger came down from Detroit to drive the first car off the line. He had been so embattled that I think the manner in which the Saturn workers greeted him threw him. Anyhow, it was so moving, people had tears streaming down their faces. I remember someone telling later that up in Detroit, they had shown it live on TV, and those Detroit people saw us down here crying, and they were skeptical about the sincerity, until they looked around the room at those Saturn people who were in Detroit and saw tears coming down from them as well. It was a very emotional day. We had worked so hard and to actually see the final product was just overwhelming. What was even more special was that team members from various areas in the factory were the ones that pulled the tarps off the new cars, not top management."[53]

Hiring

Hiring the best person for *all* positions is more than a philo-sophical principle at Saturn, it is an iron-clad practice. Saturn's search for new employees in 1988 was rigorous. Prospects were told up front they would have to discard old habits and work as members of a team. Recruiters emphasized that the new Saturn environment would not be desirable for everyone. They selected people who wanted to be part of a challenging new venture. Newly hired people had to be flexible enough to cope with ambiguity, consider challenging new ideas, and change their behavior. Since that initial selection phase, hiring has continued as a thorough, leave-no-stone-unturned pro-cess. The details were described by a team member on the rear-body assembly line:[54]

- A person must first apply.
- There is an initial phone interview, usually an hour in length. In some cases, members of the team sit in on the call.
- The team reviews the conversation and discusses the application to decide whether or not to invite the person for an interview.
- If invited, the person takes a series of assessment tests that examine personal as well as technical skills.
- The person is interviewed by the team and is introduced to work on the assembly line.
- After the team interview, union members and manage-ment discuss the candidate and examine the test scores. The team writes up an assessment of the person. One member can block the hiring but must state exactly why he or she would not want the person on the team.
- It has to be a real good reason! *Overall*, the team is looking at the skills the person has, any key elements. It is an intense process, but Saturn wants high-caliber people. Throughout the entire process, interviewers are

continually instilling Saturn's mission, philosophy and values, so that if an individual does not agree with them, he or she can get out before the individual starts.

Because of its intense selection process, Saturn makes few mistakes in hiring. If made, the mistakes are corrected, but in a humane way. In the summer of 1991, Saturn surveyed team members. Although very few were unhappy, Saturn offered separation packages ranging from $15,000 to $50,000 to any employee who was not satisfied with his or her work.[55] Management and labor agreed that they do not want hiring mistakes to undermine their company.

Customer Service

Customers, both internal and external, are foremost in every person's mind. This strong customer commitment is part of Saturn's mission and is reinforced by continuous training. Team members have both direct and indirect contact with customers through a number of novel practices:[56]

- Saturn asks all employees to be part of the overnight-drive program. Employees drive a new car overnight and evaluate it. The person leaves a note for the new owners telling them about their evaluation. In some cases, the employee actually calls new owners to see how satisfied they are with their new automobile.
- One customer sent her picture with the order for a new Saturn. Team members created a certificate telling her how glad they were to have her as a customer. It, as well as her car, were received with great delight.
- An employee summed up Saturn's attitude toward internal customers: "Our view is the next customer [fellow workers] to the ultimate customer [the buyer] are all im-

portant to me. We consider the other teams our customers. If they aren't happy with our work, then we aren't happy. They have that right."

- Informal traditions have every Saturn employee looking out for the customer: stopping if they see a Saturn in distress on the highway, asking people in Saturn cars how they like their car, and while on vacation, stopping at retail partner dealerships to see if the cars they are building are satisfying customers.

- Because of their pride, Saturn line workers double as marketing agents. They feel a personal responsibility to "tell and sell" their neighbors and relatives on the merits of their automobile. They are often successful: "The company let us bring the family in to show them the plant and how things are done. I convinced my parents and sister to buy a Saturn car. I am that proud." If not successful, they are still tenacious. "I tried to sell a Saturn to my sis up in Kentucky, but she ended up buying something else. I think the Saturn dealer was too far away for her to go. But I'm proud of my work and the car. I'll keep trying, and the next time she'll buy my car."

Ideas

Saturn has taken employee empowerment to a new level. They own the company—both figuratively and literally. Everyone is looking for ways to do things better and more efficiently. At Saturn there is no official program for soliciting ideas from employees. Coming up with new ideas is part of doing the job. When an employee was asked about a new idea program, she said, "New ideas are expected, and it is part of my job. No incentives are expected or need to be given."[57]

Consider an example. An interior design team itself eliminated sixteen team member jobs. While looking for ways to cut costs, the team found a glaringly inefficient practice: walking unnecessary distances to pick up parts. Bringing the parts closer eliminated the extra walking. It also made some positions unnecessary. The entire team, including those whose jobs were in danger, agreed the positions were unnecessary. However, eliminating a position does not mean the end of an employee's career at Saturn. Displaced employees were relocated within the company.[58]

Continuous improvement is an important part of the Saturn culture. Employees are never satisfied. They are hard on themselves and constantly looking for ways to improve the quality of their car.

Trust

The Saturn labor agreement explicitly states that "adversarial relationships that existed between labor, management and contractors must end and be replaced by cooperation and mutual respect and understanding."[59] Further evidence of trusting relationships can be found in the fact that all people at Saturn are salaried, eat in the same cafeteria, and use the same parking lots and spaces. "Whoever arrives first, parks closest to the plant" is a rule that applies to both management and labor.

Employees are trusted to do what is right. An employee in the body system's team explains: "There are nine different jobs and everyone in the team rotates. The working conditions are like running your own business. We decide when shifts are, who starts where, break and eating times, and vacation schedules."[60]

Another employee notes how team members depend on one another: "Either we are interdependent or else everyone will fail."[61]

Commitment and trust by management has eliminated the

need for supervisors and inspectors. Trust did not happen automatically at Saturn, especially for those who had never been trusted before. As one worker said: "You have to be able to do away with the old-world mentality that dictates worker tasks and visualize your own empowerment as a team worker. It's hard sometimes."[62]

Trust to do the right thing is balanced with feedback on how to do things better. Numbers of defects and other statistics are posted daily and provide public evidence of team performance. There is even a list of the ten best- and ten worst-performing suppliers posted near the cafeteria.[63] How well the teams at Saturn are doing is public knowledge. So is the quality of their suppliers. Rather than treat the statistics as a final score, Saturn works with its people and suppliers to bring less than desirable performance up to par.

Broad Responsibilities

Bipolars in Saturn's language are people who want to make cars all day and nothing else. "Bipolars will fail to make it here at Saturn; they just want to do the same thing over and over. They do not want to take risks or change jobs. They do not want to get involved in the decision-making process. Bipolars are miserable,"[64] says one of the employees. At Saturn, workers learn as many team functions as possible. In one body-systems team, there are nine different jobs that each member learns. This enables them to fill in for fellow team members. Doing one job is not good enough at Saturn. "That's not my job" is not a phrase used at Saturn. All employees, while knowledgeable of their own tasks, learn others and take responsibility for the overall operation.

No Tight Rules

Saturn requires employees to use their brains, not just their hands. The company has a penchant for keeping rules to a minimum. Rule-bound people don't fare very well:

> "We had this one manager. He was new and was accustomed to ordering the workers around and following the rules. He was walking the line and noticed one worker standing around with some parts, and he asked why the worker wasn't using the parts. The worker replied that they weren't any good, they didn't meet his standards. The manager grabbed the parts and shoved them together, and he turned to the worker and said, "run it." The worker wouldn't. Very quickly, the UAW president and a top manager came to the scene. They flat-out told him [the manager] that things aren't done that way here at Saturn and that he'd better learn his job. To which, the manager replied, 'What is my job?' and the union president retorted, 'That's for you to discover.' "[65]

Saturn employees do not accept rules and orders as a substitute for quality. The mentality that *conflict is not bad* ensures that issues will be confronted on the spot. Blindly following rules is not an acceptable part of Saturn's ways.

Upstaging

The attention lavished on team members at Saturn would lead a naïve observer to the logical conclusion that there is potential for the dealers and top managers to feel neglected. Within the plant, however, the concept of upstaging is foreign. Every employee is a player and Saturn has gone to great lengths to eliminate the distinction between backstage and onstage work. When we asked one of the Saturn executives if she ever felt upstaged, she responded:

"Never. My commitment comes from the value placed on the workplace and involvement. Upstaging goes against the whole Saturn mission. If someone tried to do that, they would be confronted by their peers. Any manager accustomed to the applause hasn't been brought into the Saturn mission. It rarely, if ever, happens here."[66]

A gesture of waving to visitors has become a tradition by the production workers. When we asked a line employee why this was the case, he replied: "It's not something managers started or company policy. It just means that the workers are happy to see you, proud of their car and their company. It gives us a chance to be onstage."[67]

There is evidence, however, that some people outside the Saturn troupe resent the attention that the plant receives. Saturn's huge investment and public success has alienated many within GM and in other parts of the American auto industry. Early in Saturn's history, UAW president Douglas A. Fraser remarked, "They need that car like they need a hole in the head."[68] Some GM workers have greeted the project with suspicion and continue to cling to the old system of rigid rules, adversarial relations, and little flexibility in job functions. Some employees at the GM plant level have been heard to say, "Screw Saturn."[69] A GM manufacturing consultant remarked, "We could do that too if we had $5 billion."[70] Too much limelight can become a significant problem, since Saturn was created as an example for reform at GM. There is an element of the Old World that will try to avoid change and resent those who are receiving widespread applause for doing things differently.

Technology and Training

The Saturn plant reflects the latest in manufacturing technology. Both state-of-the-art equipment and extensive training are obviously an important factor in employees' high morale and productivity.[71]

- Saturn is one of the most integrated automotive plants in the world. Unlike most car assembly plants, a Saturn car can begin assembly and be completed within the same plant.
- Saturn uses simultaneous engineering. A large group—marketers, engineers, suppliers, workers, accountants, salesmen, and service representatives—meet with the aid of computer-based design tools to develop new products that are buildable and will eventually be profitable.
- Saturn is the only auto manufacturer using a lost-foam casting method at high production levels. The technique produces a higher-quality engine and components with less machining, manpower, and energy.
- Rather than walking along the line, Saturn developed plywood skillets that employees ride on to assemble the car.
- They are the first company in North America to build automatic and manual transmission on the same line, eliminating inventory buildup and lowering cost.
- Their vertical side panels are made of plastic, thereby eliminating dents. Running over the side panel with a tram renders no damage to the panel.
- Saturn is becoming a paperless company with a checkless, all-electronic ordering, inventory, and financial system.
- New workers receive 100 to 750 hours of training. Current employees must have 92 hours of training a year or lose a portion of their pay.
- Training courses include awareness training, trust sessions, balance sheet, conflict resolution, and technical training using robots.

- Many of the employees carry radios so they can be in constant touch with other teams.

Symbols and Costumes

A visit to the Saturn plant instantly reinforces the importance of costumes in the workplace. We found out firsthand. As we approached Northfield, the administration building, several people greeted us with "How's the weather in Michigan?" Later we discovered we stood out because of our formal business suits and ties. They thought we were executives from Detroit. Saturn has its own costume—informal wear. There are no ties, jackets, or business dresses. Saturn goes out of its way to eliminate position or status symbols. Several employees noted the informal dress. One employee commented: "Here at Saturn, everyone dresses similarly. You can't tell the engineers from the line workers. The engineers work the line with the team members. They don't sit in their offices drinking coffee all day."[72]

Saturn's approach to costumes and symbols is different from most American companies. It is also different from the uniforms worn by everyone in Japan. Saturn team members have a choice in what they wear. Backstage workers have an air of pride and sense of belonging because they can dress like management.

Celebration

Saturn is currently so focused on quality and production that little time remains to celebrate what they have already accomplished. This intensity is found from the line workers on up to the top executives. Donald Hudler, vice president of Sales,

Service, and Marketing, noted, "We'll take thirty seconds to enjoy being flattered. Then we'll have to work hard to continue to get better."[73]

Though people will never forget the grand inaugural celebration when the first Saturn car was driven off the line, Saturn teams also have more traditional celebrations: team dinners, birthdays, and picnics. Fifty dollars, the amount Saturn budgets per employee for celebration and recognition purposes, is often unused. One manager stated, "We don't celebrate enough. We are often too hard on ourselves to take time for acknowledging an accomplishment."[74]

While people at Saturn acknowledge that nothing is perfect, they are clearly trying to find a balance between continuous improvement and celebration.

Saturn's Future

Saturn was named after the rocket that helped the United States leapfrog Russia's early lead in the space race.[75] GM's bet is that their new company will do the same thing in the automotive industry. Their strategy is straightforward: quality cars are built by people who care about their work and have pride in the company. While this makes so much sense, how did common sense become so uncommon in America's automobile manufacturing companies?

Saturn's uncommonness is evident in some recent challenging events: From late August to early September 1992, Saturn fell victim to a GM strike in Lordstown, Ohio. Though the Lordstown workers returned to their jobs after nine days, Saturn team members experienced a six-day furlough—the plant was forced to stop production. The striking plant supplied Saturn with more than 300 parts on a "just-in-time" system of delivery.[76] Without parts, Saturn could not function.

But team members did not stay home. They came to work and used the time for new training. When the strike ended, Saturn was six thousand cars behind production schedule. In late October 1992 (over a month and a half after the Lordstown strike), GM shook with changes in top management as old, long-term executives were replaced by new, younger people.[77] The change occurred just as GM braced for yet another projected loss in profits. As rumors began to fly about laying off workers, closing more plants, and phasing out unprofitable GM divisions, Saturn braced itself for the potential fallout.

Yet surprisingly, Saturn emerged unscathed. Through all the changes, Saturn's people hung together. Mike Bennett's comment best illustrates the unique position of Saturn, which continues the partnership with GM while also setting its sights on a brighter automotive future: "It would be a terrible mistake to absorb Saturn into the GM system, [instead] GM needs to move toward Saturnizing itself."[78] GM execs might once have scoffed at such a notion. Many, such as John D. Rock, general manager of GM's Olds division, now are taking note.

An even more recent event illustrates the depth of Saturn's commitment. In August 1993, the company announced the recall of 352,767 cars, nearly four-fifths of its total sales since Saturn began production in 1990.[79] An electrical connection in the generator system caused fires in a few vehicles. The professional way in which Saturn handled the problem was exemplary. First, the company discovered the problem itself. Second, it went public with the information immediately. Shortly thereafter, a morning program of a national network featured the Saturn recall story. The first film clip showed a dealership partner grilling hamburgers for a customer while the 25-minute repair was being completed on her car. In a nearby child-care area, her children played. In the next clip, a Saturn executive showed a close-up of the part that was to be replaced. Then a business analyst in New York was interviewed to comment on the recall. Instead of criticism, the analyst lavished praise on the company for how it was handling the situation. By sticking to its principles, Saturn received millions of dollars in free publicity and deepened consumer confidence in its cars.

With an exception of a temporary shortfall in company-wide celebrations, Saturn met or exceeded our expectations. They have turned their backstage work force into stars who share in the limelight. And they have done it without upstaging the union or the retail sales force. Whether Saturn will achieve profitability in the short-term future is open to question. The danger is America's preoccupation with immediate results. We tend to throw a lot of money at things and then pull the emerging efforts up by their roots to inspect the root system. We want to see if growth is evident immediately. Our prediction is that Saturn will succeed and join other effective companies mentioned in this book in setting a new standard for organizing human capital. Attention will be redirected from the glamorous world of financial wheeling-dealing and the corporate suite to the place where work is done, where products are created and services delivered. Norm Augustine, CEO of Martin Marietta Company, sums it up:

> "A news article once described the visit of a bright young student to the floor of the New York Stock Exchange. Thrilled by the excitement that surrounded him as billions of dollars exchanged hands every few seconds, he exclaimed, 'This is where it's at.' I would submit that 'this is not where it's at.' Not even close. Where 'it's at' is in the laboratories, the engineering facilities, on the factory floors—right where it's been for decade after decade."[80]

■ CHAPTER 18
The Challenges of 2000

The year 2000 marks the end of a millennium. As it draws near, the occasion sparks a heightened interest in the challenges the next decade will present. Predicting the future is never easy. Who would have thought that communism would end in this century? When America was supplying arms to Iraq, did anyone imagine Desert Storm? The plain fact is, even given our best efforts, there is no way to predict what the future holds. Still the crystal ball gazers keep trying, unaffected by prediction rates that are sometimes no better than those of economists or weather forecasters. We are no exception. Our principles for leading the hidden organization are anchored in the past and present. To test them against the future, we consulted three respected and credible prognosticators to see how well the principles might hold up against the future predictions of *Workforce 2000*, *Megatrends 2000*, and *The Popcorn Report*.

Workforce 2000

> By the end of the next decade [2000], the changes under
> way will produce an America that is in some ways
> unrecognizable from the one that existed only a few years
> ago.[1]

Workforce 2000, a report compiled by a respected think
tank called the Hudson Institute, analyzes and forecasts America's long-term economic and labor trends.[2] For the leaders of
America's organizations, the forward-looking document pre-
sents some disturbing news. If the eighties and nineties have
been turbulent decades for businesses, hospitals, and education, the next century will cause a whiplash. To begin with,
the majority of policies in America's organizations were created while white males dominated the work force. Women
stayed at home and raised children. Minorities held menial
jobs. Both were underrepresented in the ranks of upper management. In this inequitable dream world of the past two
decades, America's products were widely respected and
sought after by the rest of the world.

According to *Workforce 2000*, all that is going to change.
Women and minorities soon will constitute the majority of
the work force. And unless the quality of American products
improves, the world market will be dominated by our foreign
competitors. These predicted trends make it crystal clear that
existing organizational patterns, policies, and practices will
not suffice in the next century. What key challenges does the
report predict will lie ahead?

America's Labor Pool Will Contract

During the next ten to fifteen years, America's population
will grow at its slowest rate since the early thirties. The poten-

tial labor pool also will decline. The number of new job entrants will drop from 4 million today to 3.3 million in 1995.[3] The next decade's total work force will grow at a rate of 1 percent per year compared to a 2.9 percent annual increase during the seventies. This will create a seller's market.[4] Workers will move from job to job, seeking the most favorable economic and working conditions. As a result, all organizations will experience difficulty recruiting workers—particularly in behind-the-scenes job categories: secretarial-clerical, skilled crafts, technical, professional, and supervisory management. Furthermore, low-skilled job opportunities will decline more rapidly than the demand for skilled positions, creating a deficit of workers with adequate writing and verbal skills. Technical and knowledge-based workers will be the hardest to recruit. Qualified employees will enjoy the flexibility of moving from job to job, seeking the most favorable conditions.

The Work Force Will Age

Between 1986 and 2000, the number of people between ages 35 to 47 will increase by 38 percent, while the age group 48 to 53 will swell by 67 percent. The overall population will grow only 15 percent; by the year 2000, the population between 20 and 29 will become smaller.[5]

This aging of the American work force has several negative implications:[6] (a) a more rigid economy as an older, more stable work force chooses not to relocate or retrain; (b) companies powerless to expand, or new businesses unable to start up, because of the short supply of young, higher-salaried workers; (c) slow-growing or specialized companies (i.e., automobiles, metals, etc.) dealing with an older work force and therefore becoming less able to compete with other countries;

(d) older workers with limited physical and knowledge capabilities; and (e) a decreasing demand for certain goods or services consumed by young people, causing numerous companies to close or economize.

More Women and Minorities Will Enter the Work Force

Women, who now comprise half the work force, will exhibit a steadily increasing presence.[7] By the year 2000, 61 percent of women in America will be working. Three-fifths of the new entrants into the labor force will be women. Women who are married mothers will enter the work force—some by choice, others out of necessity. More women will graduate from specialized or professional schools, allowing them potentially to compete equally with their male counterparts for high-paying, high-level jobs.

Female domination of the labor force will have several influences on American organizations:[8] (a) more day care and preschools that are heavily subsidized by corporations; (b) a less mobile work force due to more two-income families choosing not to relocate their families; (c) closing of the gap between male and female wages and benefits; and (d) more creative work schedules (part-time, flexible, work-at-home, telecommuting), and restructuring of the normal work week for women and men seeking to balance work with family.

Minorities also will gain a stronger foothold in the American labor force. The report states: "Non-whites, for example, will comprise 29 percent of the net additions to the workforce and will constitute more than 15 percent of the workforce in the year 2000."[9]

The presence of black females particularly will increase, a growth so spectacular that by the year 2000, black women will outnumber black men in most organizations.[10] Despite the predicted increases, minorities will continue to suffer more economic and social disadvantages than whites.

The Pool of Immigrant Workers Will Grow

The Immigration Act of 1990 will create record levels of new immigrants. As *Workforce 2000* sees it, "At least 450,000 immigrants are likely to enter the U.S. each year for the balance of the century."[11]

Most of these will locate in cities that already hold large populations of new immigrants. California, in particular, will continue to be the largest haven for this immigrating subpopulation.

Though the immigrant population will continue to grow, their influence on the labor force will be mainly beneficial. A potential negative impact is the reduction of employment opportunities for native minorities. Although empirical evidence indicates that minority unemployment rates are not directly related to immigration patterns, the introduction of incoming workers from other countries provokes strong emotional reactions.

Megatrends 2000

John Naisbitt is among the most well-known of the American futurists. His coauthored book *Megatrends 2000* outlines several predictions for the year 2000 that have possible implications for organizations in the next century.[12]

Individual Responsibility Will Reign

A new era of individual responsibility will dawn at the millennium. Unlike the every-man-for-his-own-self philosophy of the seventies and eighties, the ethic of individual responsibility argues that *each individual is responsible for everything he or she does.* Rather than being monitored and controlled from above, new-age workers will be asked to make responsible decisions on their own.

Communities Will Replace Collectives

A community is a free association of individuals pursuing common ends with shared purpose. In a community, individual differences are expected, encouraged, and rewarded. Everyone knows who is contributing and who is not. By contrast, a collective is a place where irresponsible people can hide— assured of equal treatment—irrespective of making a less than equal contribution.

People Will Be Paid for Intelligence and Creativity

Instead of being rewarded for seniority or collective brawn, individuals will receive compensation for their ingenuity, intelligence, and creativity. Compensation will be customized, often including bonuses and stock ownership.

Consumer Interests Will Become Primary

The phrase "The customer is king" rang hollow in most organizational practices of the seventies and eighties. To successfully compete in the nineties and beyond, organizations will need to make treating the customer royally a byword rather than an afterthought.

Global Competition Will Intensify

New economic cohesion in Europe and the Pacific Rim will make it even more difficult for American organizations to compete successfully in the world marketplace. High quality and low costs will be the major factors in successful competition.

Leadership Will Replace Management

Management concentrates on short-term control and is oriented toward facts, reports, and bottom-line results. In contrast, leadership is exercised through influence or other noncoercive means. As John Naisbitt and Patricia Aburdene maintain, "Leaders think longer term, grasp the relationship or larger realities, think in term of renewal, have political skills, cause change, affirm values, achieve unity."[13] To leaders, "capital and technology are important resources but people make or break a company."[14] Leaders inspire, empower, attract, reward, and motivate people. The decade of the nineties and beyond will reward leadership rather than management.

The Work Force Will Become Highly Educated

Modern organizations were created to accommodate uneducated, unskilled workers. This is no longer the case. One-fourth of America's work force now has a college degree, and another 25 percent has had some postsecondary education.[15] This has enormous implications for how work is organized and how much say workers demand in decision making.

The Popcorn Report

Faith Popcorn is one of America's foremost trend predictors. Among other things, she predicted the AIDS crisis, the rise of cocooning (isolationism), and the failure of New Coke.[16] She offers several predictions about what organizations will face in the coming decade.

On the hope side of the hope-versus-doom argument among futurists, Popcorn sees in the distance a more decentralized, human organization with a less noticeable distinction between managers and workers.[17] American organizations that have replaced old-style management with a new participatory type will once again produce top-quality goods and services.

The corporation/customer relationship will become a closer relationship between human beings.[18] Consumers will become more vigilant and demand to know more about what is going on. Top companies will listen to what customers want and respond to their needs and desires. They will keep the consumer informed, not left in the dark.

Customers will buy goods and services from companies with a soul.[19] Customers today are fickle and prone to buy from the cheapest source or the one with the products and services perceived as offering the best value. In the 2000s, consumers will lean toward companies with the highest integrity, those with decency, ethics, and trust. Popcorn offers four steps to "find a corporate soul and win the consumer's heart."[20]

Evidence of this trend can be seen in the "Buy American" theme, which is receiving steadily increasing support.

1. *Acknowledgment*. Our industry hasn't always done everything in its power to make the world a better place.
2. *Disclosure*. This is who we were. And this is the company we are trying, with your help, to become.
3. *Accountability*. Here is how we define our areas of responsibility and who can be held accountable.
4. *Presentation*. Here is what we pledge to you the consumer: you'll find our corporate soul in all our products.

Leading Human Capital in the Twenty-first Century

As the year 2000 approaches, all these predictions about the future paint a jolting new picture. As we mentioned earlier, demographically, structurally, and spiritually, tomorrow's organizations will look very different from those of today. Such transformations do not come easily and will require courage and foresight from leaders who understand that people are an organization's most precious capital. To us, these changes will require that even more attention be given to the principles outlined in this book. Saturn's bold venture suggests that in the future, backstage may become center stage, viewed as one of the foundation pillars of organizations. If the futurists are correct, most, if not all, of our principles become even more critical guideposts for dealing seriously with the formidable challenges that lie ahead.

Managing Differently: The Year 2000

Clearly, the facts and issues arising from a changing work force and conditions of work will require that management rethink its approach to running an organization. It is fair to say that the twenty-first century will be characterized by participation, empowerment, and teamwork. John Naisbitt stated, "By the end of the decade, 40 to 50 percent of all U.S. workers will manage themselves. Empowerment will remain a watchword for the nineties."[21] *The Popcorn Report* predicts more employee participation, better customer/corporate relationships, and attention to corporate soul. *Workforce 2000* provides a demographic sketch of a different America. All these reports indicate that effectively managing hidden human resources is going to be more crucial and consequential. For this reason, we review our principles in light of these three important predictions about the future.

- **Finding a Backstage Champion.** In the future, it will be even more important for someone to represent and voice the interests of those who work behind the scenes. This person will have to deal with labor shortages, a more diverse and aging work force, and employees who want a say in their work and a stake in the organization. These factors will require more sophisticated leadership skills. If leadership is unable to understand or respond to diverse needs and concerns, serious organizational problems may occur. More and more employees will expect their leader to be trusted advocates. Changes in the work force will require leadership from all levels, especially from those who champion the interests of the unseen cast.
- **Linking Backstage to Core Mission.** Commitment and loyalty were once an integral part of America's work ethic. In the future, we're likely to see a revival of these

crucial values. Greater diversity in employee attitudes and values will make it even more important to articulate and communicate a shared sense of what the business is all about and what the organization stands for. To compete in the future labor market, companies must develop programs and policies that not only instill the mission into the everyday life of their employees, but broadcast their corporate soul to external constituencies. Successful companies of the next decade will have a well-defined core mission and widely shared values. All employees will market the corporate soul by articulating the organization's philosophical commitments to customers, peers, and neighbors. The spirit of ensemble will win out over the just-a-job mentality that now often prevails.

Ben & Jerry's provides a current example of a company with a soul. Their commitment is "to operate the company in a way that actively recognizes the central role that business plays in the structure of society by initiating innovative ways to improve the quality of life in a broad community—local, national and international."[22] It's what they call "caring capitalism." Their people go out of their way to give as much to the society as they give voluntarily to the company.

- **Hiring the Best.** Future labor shortages, especially in behind-the-scenes positions, will make successful hiring practices even more of a strategic business advantage. An aging work force, a rise in women and minority workers and a decrease in the younger labor pools will make it even harder for organizations to operate under old personnel policies.

The best companies already are developing new hiring practices to recruit a multicultural and economically diverse work force. Salaries, benefit packages, child care, elder care, and other avant-garde programs tailored to targeted recruits will become even more important issues in attracting potential workers and winning their loyalty and willingness to stay. Successful organizations of the future will cater to the individual worker's needs. Competition between companies will become fierce, especially in attracting younger talent. Recruiting the best will become a preoccupation. Finding the right fit between person and position will give companies a significant edge in attracting and retaining the best talent. They also will be prepared to take advantage of the wave of worker diversity.

Presently, our inability to unify a racially diverse population creates enormous social problems. These same issues spill into business organizations, which will be required to take the lead in changing racial diversity from a cacophony to a symphony. In many of the organizations we studied, the process has already begun. As an African-American employee at Service Merchandise observed, "I like to come to work because this is the only place where I am not discriminated against."[23]

- **Commanding and Commending Customer Service.** All of the futurists predict increased attention by the customer to seeking the best, low-cost service or product. To meet customer expectations, companies must go beyond the frontline fluff. As suggested in chapter 7, providing top-flight service must become everyone's responsibility. By engaging backstage employees in the importance of serving the customer and by expanding their definition of customer to everyone who is served—either externally or internally—organizations can take command of one of the most universal laws of business.

- **Broadening the Base of Ideas.** With a more diverse work force, the importance of soliciting ideas from workers with different cultural and racial backgrounds will become a necessity. Ideas are the lifeblood of innovation and quality. A more diverse work force potentially generates a broader array of suggestions. Employees

from different cultural backgrounds can enrich any organization's innovative capital. More experienced workers
can bring new and different alternatives for improvement.
But involving all employees in developing and suggesting
ideas will command even more time and attention. It will
require organizations to capitalize on human variety.

- **Trusting While Helping.** Trust has been lacking between most managers and workers for decades. Predictions forecast more empowerment and individual
responsibility. To achieve trust, there needs to be constant feedback and simple and meaningful incentives.
While this has often been achieved at executive levels,
few organizations have been willing to totally trust all of
their employees. Gary Wilson, maintenance coordinator
in Saturn's body shop area, sums up how various employees feel about changing the trust relationship:

> "I came to Saturn because of its vision about how
> it was going to operate, what it was intending to
> do [eliminating adversarial relationships between
> labor and management]. It's hard to see what's
> going on, not only in the auto industry but in
> U.S. business in general and not feel angry about
> the deterioration. There's got to be a better way
> [to run a business] and I want to be a part of
> that. We are on a mission to make this
> successful, so that we as a country, GM, and I
> personally can survive."[24]

Employees in the year 2000 are going to have abundant
employment options. They simply will not be a part of
any organization that has a condescending attitude toward its employees.

- **Avoiding the "That's Not My Job" Syndrome.**
With the labor pool shrinking, it will be to an employer's
advantage to seek employees who can and will perform

more than one function. Assuming employees will be better educated and will be rewarded for intelligence and creativity, companies must expect them to step over their formal responsibilities. If the customer is going to expect decency, ethics, and trust from a company, the employee also must receive the same treatment. Employees will be seeking more responsibility in the future. They will focus on making a difference rather than just making a buck.

- **Right Things, Not Tight Rules.** The better-educated and mobile workers of tomorrow will chafe under the bureaucratic rules and procedures that many of today's organizations enforce as a matter of policy. Technological advances that now play such an integral part in any organization have also made hierarchical layers and a distinct and distant chain of command obsolete. Top management is coming to realize that rigid and narrow rules and regulations no longer apply in an ever-changing, ever-demanding American society. Organizations are beginning to wake up to the fact that in order to stay competitive and profitable, employees must be empowered to make important, immediate decisions on the spot. They also need opportunities to share in decisions that affect the larger community. As employees become empowered, they will seek greater freedom to step over formal boundaries to get things done right. They will make decisions on the basis of shared values rather than merely following tight rules.

- **Appropriate Tools Guarantee Top Efforts.** Having the best technical equipment becomes more critical as the buyers' market in labor continues. Retaining the best employees will depend on providing them with the most technically advanced equipment available. Training will become more important as technological changes become even more rapid. With the influx of women, minorities, and immigrants, organizations also

will have to cultivate the people skills that make relating to people of different backgrounds second nature.
* **Celebrating Hidden Achievements.** Because future labor trends point to a more competitive market, companies that do little in the way of worker recognition may find themselves without employees. People behind the scenes must feel they are a vital part of the organization's day-to-day operations. Through celebrations, people can receive the much-deserved appreciation they desire. They will go where they feel needed, appreciated, and respected.

Changes expected in the year 2000 heighten the importance of backstage management. The best companies already have begun their transformation and are intensifying efforts to improve backstage conditions. Rick Oliver, vice president of Marketing for Northern Telecom, Inc., summarizes the implications of *Workforce 2000:*

"Companies that are not planning for their demographic changes will suffer greatly in the next decade. On the other hand, companies that are paying attention to these changes and applying the principles that you [the authors] suggest, will be the winners both in terms of their employees and their bottom line. In the nineties, how you organize, how you treat your people, and your belief systems will be more critical determinants of success than your products or even the industry you are in."[25]

Appendixes

■ APPENDIX A
Description of Organizations

Detailed Case Studies

American Airlines

With over 100,000 employees worldwide, American Airlines is one of the largest airline companies in the world. Rated number 1 in service among all domestic airlines, American has dedicated itself to continuous improvement in customer satisfaction. Though currently American is undergoing some financial restructuring, it still reports one of the largest revenues of any domestic airline company—almost $9 billion in recent listings.

American Association of Museums

Founded in 1906, the American Association of Museums, a nonprofit organization, is based in Washington, D.C. With over 11,000 members nationwide, the organization includes various topical museums, art associations, preservation societies, planetariums, zoos, and libraries. The association also oversees an accrediting system for museums and offers placement services for museum professionals.

Ben & Jerry's

For fifteen years, Ben & Jerry's has been satisfying the taste buds of individuals across the United States. With an environmentally and socially conscious mission statement and corporate agenda, Ben & Jerry's sells quality all-natural ice cream and related products. In 1978, the first ice-cream shop opened. Now, Ben & Jerry's is a $97 million corporation with three manufacturing plants in Vermont. It also boasts four company-owned shops in Vermont and eighty-nine franchised scoop shops nationwide.

Opryland USA, Inc.

Opryland USA is located in Nashville, Tennessee. Though it is known largely for its show *The Grand Ole Opry*, the company also holds interest in both radio and television stations, a theme park, and a hotel and convention center. Recently, its theme park was rated number 1 in safety over all other parks in the nation. With over 3,800 employees, Opryland operates a model quality assurance program. As a leader in the promotion of country music, Opryland has over $240 million in revenues.

Saturn Industries, Inc.

As a division of General Motors, Saturn Industries has exercised a great amount of freedom and innovation in the development of its automobile—and it has paid off. Among the numerous accolades Saturn has received, the division has reached the top three twice in the J.D. Power and Associates Customer Satisfaction Index. Saturn is the first American car to reach the top three. With close to 4,000 employees, the division hopes to expand even more with plans to possibly open another plant in the near future.

Service Merchandise

As the largest United States retail catalog store chain, Service Merchandise posts over $3.5 billion in revenues. The company maintains this dominance through the use of a sophisticated on-line computer system that permits twenty-four hour ordering by either fax or phone. With over 18,000 employees currently, Service Merchandise continues to expand as the need for catalog ordering escalates.

Vanderbilt University

As one of the premier higher education institutions in the United States, Vanderbilt University is consistently rated in the top twenty-five. With a student population of over 10,000, Vanderbilt offers students a variety of degrees and majors. The institution's law, medicine, education, and business schools are ranked among the best. With an annual revenue of over $900 million and assets exceeding $1.5 billion, Vanderbilt was rated recently as the best company to work for in the Nashville, Tennessee, area.

Hands-On Examples

Industrial Corporations

Anheuser-Busch

Anheuser-Busch is best known as the largest brewery organization in the world. It also has interest in the bakery and snack food industries with products marketed under Colonial, Rainbo, and Eagle Snacks. The company operates several entertainment attractions: Sea World parks, Busch Gardens, Cypress Gardens, and the St. Louis Cardinals professional baseball club. Anheuser-Busch posted over $10 billion in recent revenues.

Cabot Corporation

The Cabot Corporation was founded in 1882 by Godfrey Lowell Cabot. Within fifteen years after inception, Cabot had become the largest carbon black manufacturer in the world, a position it has never relinquished. Headquartered in Boston, Massachusetts, today Cabot operates a diverse group of businesses, all of which have earned leadership positions in the global markets they serve. The businesses include the chemical businesses Cab-O-Sil, Cabot Performance Materials, Cabot Plastics, and Carbon Black, and the nonchemical businesses Cabot LNG, Cabot Safety, and TUCO—all of which employ approximate 5,300 people.

First Union Georgia Servicenter

Located in Atlanta, Georgia, First Union Georgia Servicenter is a processing operation supporting First Union National Bank of Georgia in a variety of ways. Each month, the operation services more than 500,000 deposit accounts, receives approximately 50,000 telephone requests from customers, and processes over 12 million transactions. Its service affects the quality of customer service in every branch and department of First Union National Bank of Georgia.

Horace Small Apparel Company

The Horace Small Apparel Company is a subsidiary of United Uniform Services, PLC, and is headquartered in Nashville, Tennessee. Horace Small Apparel distributes uniforms and accessories, and the operation employs 1,300. Sales in 1991 totaled $95 million, with profit totaling $5.5 million.

Norco Windows, Inc.

Norco Windows, Inc., is a leading manufacturer of high-quality wood windows and patio doors based in Boise, Idaho. Norco began business in 1921 as Northern Sash and Door Company. In 1986, it was acquired by TJ International, a manufacturer and marketer of specialty building products. Norco's products are used primarily in new residential construction and in remodel and replacement projects. Its product line includes awning, custom direct set, tilt double-hung, slide-by, casement, roundtop, bow, bay, radius, and custom wood windows, as well as four styles of wood slide-and-swing patio doors. Norco's products are sold direct to home builders in selected metropolitan areas. In other markets, they are redistributed through a system of six company-owned distribution centers to 720 dealer locations.

Northern Telecom Limited

Northern Telecom, half-owned by Bell Canada, is the largest telecommunications equipment manufacturer in Canada. It is second, behind AT&T, in the North American market and among the top five telecommunications corporations in the world. With Northern Telecom Canada, Ltd. as a division, Northern Telecom specializes in digital telecommunications switching equipment. The corporation recently listed over $6 billion in revenues.

Square D

Square D recently was acquired through a somewhat hostile takeover by the French-based Groupe Schneider. Though the 1991 acquisition has allowed Groupe Schneider to become the world's largest producer of electrical products, Square D has continued its normal manufacturing of electric and industrial products and equipment for the United States marketplace. Square D manufactures components, such as transformers, connectors, surge protectors, automation products, and its trademark safety switch. Though limited in what it produces, Square D remains one of the most stable companies in the entire industry with sales topping over $1.5 billion.

Diversified Service Companies

Ameriscribe Corporation

Ameriscribe Corporation, through subsidiaries, provides on-site reprographic, mail, messenger, and other related services to their clients as well as commercial copying litigation support services and electronic publishing at their off-site locations; it also provides appellate brief and cooperative real estate prospectus printing. Located in New York City, Ameriscribe employs 2,000 workers.

Bell Atlantic Corporation

The fourth-largest provider of telephone services in the United States, Bell Atlantic became autonomous in 1983, breaking off from AT&T. It serves six mid-Atlantic states (Delaware, Maryland, New Jersey, Pennsylvania, Virginia, and West Virginia) and the District of Columbia. Several innovative features, such as Caller ID, were developed by Bell Atlantic. The company provides cellular and beeper/pager services through their Mobile Systems. Recently the company set its sights on international markets, a shift that has added to the over $12 billion in revenues most recently posted.

Dahlin Smith White

Located in Salt Lake City, Dahlin Smith White is an advertising agency specializing in business-to-business and high-tech advertising. John D. Dahlin is president and founded the agency approximately six years ago. The creative shop employs ninety people and reported revenue of $60 million in 1991.

Walt Disney Company

Disney is the largest producer of family entertainment through its numerous theme parks and resorts and its film industry business. Disney promotes several consumer products emphasizing the Disney name and publishes *Discover* magazine. The company's theme parks range from operations in the United States, Japan, and Europe to the cruise ship *Queen Mary* and the *Spruce Goose* airliner. Films are its most influential division, enjoying successive hits and profit making in a diversified line. Disney has posted close to $6 billion in recent revenues.

Extended Systems

Extended Systems is dedicated to providing products to enhance the life, capability, and functionality of customers' existing computer resources. Founded in 1984, Extended Systems distributes its products worldwide, with regional sales offices located in several major metropolitan areas in the continental United States.

Jewish Hospital HealthCare Services, Inc.

Jewish Hospital HealthCare Services owns and/or manages seven separate health care facilities. These facilities include a nursing home, rehabilitation center, and five hospitals totaling 1,300 beds. During the latter part of the eighties, the company nearly doubled its gross revenues. Total profits have recently increased from approximately $400,000 to $15 million in 1991.

MedTrac, Inc.

MedTrac is a medical and disability cost management firm whose primary function is to help employers control medical costs for their health care and workers' compensation programs. Headquartered in Nashville, MedTrac has regional offices in Atlanta, Detroit, and Minneapolis, with more offices opening around the United States.

Morrison Knudsen

Morrison Knudsen, based in Boise, Idaho, operates one of the leading general contracting services worldwide. Through design operations and engineering consultation and development, the company focuses on large contracts. Projects include railroad machinery and systems, generalized mining, and ecological accidents. The company's clientele range from private owners to foreign governments. It includes among its clients governmental agencies in the United States at both local and federal levels. Morrison Knudsen showed recent revenues of over $1.5 billion.

Octel Communications Corporation

Octel Communications, headquartered in Milpitas, California, manufactures voice-processing systems. Founded in 1984, Octel specializes in telephone and telegraph apparatus. They employ 1,048 persons and reported sales of $127.8 million in 1991.

Stevens Aviation

Stevens Aviation was founded over four decades ago and has been a major, high-quality force in corporate and commercial aviation from its inception. Stevens offers aircraft maintenance and overhauls; structural modifications; avionics upgrades; interiors completions and refurbishment; new and used aircraft sales and brokerage; charter operations; strip and paint services; engine, propeller, and component overhauls; Beech Aircraft distribution and service center operations; Aerospatiale sales and service; fleet management; full-service

FBO operations, including fueling, VIP concierge, ground handling, and hangar storage; and wholesale parts sales. Stevens Aviation is owned by NTC Group, a privately held conglomerate with interests in aviation services, textile manufacturing, and industrial power transmission systems.

TJ International, Inc.

Headquartered in Idaho, TJ International makes and markets specialty building products for the light construction industry. Products include wooden structural components, such as roof and floor joists and beam headers, as well as lumber products, columns and posts, and wood windows and patio doors. Products are sold to architects, contractors, developers, distributors, dealers, and industrial users for constructing warehouses, schools, shopping centers, office buildings, apartments, condominiums, townhouses, and single-family and manufactured housing. TJ International employs approximately 3,000 individuals.

Financial and Consulting Companies

Alexander and Alexander

As an international insurance brokerage and risk management firm, Alexander and Alexander conducts business in over seventy countries around the world. It is the second-largest international brokerage firm and the world's leading retail insurance broker and also operates several management consulting and human resources services. Revenues top $1 billion.

Dodge Group, Inc.

Founder Frank Dodge first served as president and CEO of McCormack and Dodge. In 1983 McCormack and Dodge was acquired by Dunn and Bradstreet, and Frank Dodge departed to start Frank Dodge Associates in Massachusetts. The newly formed Dodge Group combines the experience of several top software developers into a very integrated software company. The Dodge Group offers software applications in finance and accounting, customer service, and management areas. Sales are expected to climb as this upstart company continues expanding into American and European markets.

Kidder, Peabody and Company, Inc.

With General Electric as its parent company, Kidder, Peabody is one of the world's leading investment banking and brokerage firms. It concentrates on a very distinctive clientele of corporations and high-net-worth individuals, while specializing in high-yield sales and trading, investment banking, and asset management and investment services. Kidder, Peabody has shown strong economic performance, which recently accounted for 24 percent of the over $55 billion in total GE revenues.

McKinsey and Company

As the world's largest independent management firm, McKinsey and Company stands out in the field of management consulting. Founded in 1926 by a University of Chicago accounting professor, the firm has worked with over 150 of the largest corporations in America and abroad. McKinsey's mission is to help clients make improvements in their personal and professional performance, while building a company that itself can attract and retain employees. Currently, the company has over fifty offices in twenty-five countries. Of the more than 4,500 employees, over half are consultants. McKinsey continues expanding its client representation and recently posted over $900 million in fees.

Nonprofit Organizations

Harvard University

As the oldest and one of the most prestigious higher education institutions in the United States, Harvard's endowment of more than $4 billion is one of the largest in the world. Because of its unique history and international acclaim, only 18 percent of the potential undergraduate students that apply are accepted. Harvard boasts thirty-three Nobel laureates and thirty Pulitzer Prize winners.

Yale University

Considered Harvard's archrival, Yale also enjoys a proud and honored history in America's higher education community. Founded in 1701 and one of the oldest universities, Yale ranks consistently within the top five collegiate institutions in the United States. With roughly 10,000 students enrolled, Yale has schools in medicine, divinity, law, art and architecture, music, and engineering.

Secondary Research

American Telephone and Telegraph (AT&T)

The parent company of the Bell System prior to Bell's breakup in 1983, AT&T operates in one of the most high-tech markets in the world. Its primary purpose is the movement of information and the provision of products and services necessary for global communication. Over $40 billion in revenues was reported recently.

American Transtech

A division of AT&T, American Transtech specializes in telemarketing and financial services. It provides administrative information for corporate shareowner accounts, stock transfers, and employee benefit plans. American Transtech also is involved in market research and data base management. It is the largest transferor of stock and second-largest telemarketing service in the United States. American Transtech shares in AT&T revenues.

Amoco Corporation

Amoco is a major petroleum and gasoline company with large interests in chemical production. It is the largest holder of natural gas reserves in North America. Formally Standard Oil (a Rockefeller legacy), Amoco is an integrated company with major investments in the United States. It also operates in more than forty countries. Despite paying more than $128 million in restoration damages on the *Cadiz* disaster, Amoco posted over $28 billion in recent revenues.

Averitt Express

Located in Cookeville, Tennessee, Averitt Express conducts most of its business in the southeastern region of the United States. In a highly competitive carrier industry, the company continues gaining market share with increased contracts and route expansions. Recent sales have exceeded $140 million with operating revenues over $56 million. Currently Averitt Express employs more than 2,000 in fifty centers in nine southeastern states.

Avis, Inc.

Next to Hertz, Avis is a leader in the car rental industry, pushing Hertz for the top spot. In 1990, Avis was named best in the car rental category by *Financial World*. In the European market, Avis holds first place with over 30 percent market share. Its Wizard System is used in the hotel industry and in the automobile rental business. With over $1.2 billion in recent sales, Avis continues to show profitability.

Avon Products, Inc.

Avon is the world's leading door-to-door marketer of cosmetics, toiletries, and fragrances. Operating in a fluctuating, trendy industry, Avon continued its global expansion by entering into several former Eastern European countries and China. The company produces jewelry, clothing, children's toys, and fitness videos. After fighting off a takeover attempt by Chartwell Associates, Avon shows prospects for a profitable future, with recent revenues over $3 billion.

Baldor Electric Company

Known for its industrial motors, Baldor Electric also produces industrial grinders, dental equipment, and various other electronic products. During the early eighties when the motor industry market took a downturn, Baldor successfully maintained profits and investments. It received unprecedented earnings through quality control and just-in-time manufacturing, which allowed the company to cut costs while maintaining production. In the late eighties, Baldor began exporting products to the Far East, including Japan. The company recently produced $290 million in revenues.

Becton Dickinson and Company

One of the leading suppliers of medical and diagnostic supplies and equipment, Becton Dickinson offers a broad range of health care products. The company is the world's leading producer of single-use medical devices, producing more hypodermic needles and syringes than any other company. Internationally, Becton Dickinson operates plants in Canada, Ireland, France, and Brazil. Following an attempted hostile takeover by Sun Company in the late seventies, Becton

Dickinson divested itself from nonmedical businesses. Becton Dickinson remains strong fiscally with recent revenues of over $2 billion.

Carlisle Plastics, Inc.

Carlisle Plastics, Inc., is a manufacturer of trash bags and other plastic products. Located in Victoria, Texas, the manufacturer has experienced phenomenal growth since 1985, with revenues tripling and cash flow climbing to $49 million in 1991. Carlisle Plastics, Inc., employs approximately 1,300 workers and expects $265 million in sales in 1992.

Chaparral Steel

Chaparral Steel evolved from a joint venture by Texas Industries and Co-Steel in 1973 to create a technologically advanced steel mill for manufacturing structural beams and reinforcement bars from scrap steel. The company also casts billets, which are used in the different bar mills. Due to the development of the bar mill market, the company recently began export operations. Over 7 percent of its shipments are now to overseas destinations. From an employee base of nearly 1,000, Chaparral Steel has posted over $400 million in revenues.

Ciba-Geigy Canada, Ltd.

Ciba-Geigy Canada, Ltd., is an innovative and responsible chemical company that provides products for health, agriculture, industry, and vision. Headquartered in Mississauga, Ontario, Ciba-Geigy Canada is a leading member of the worldwide Ciba-Geigy organization, with affiliates in some eighty-six countries on five continents, employing more than 90,000 people.

Corning

Corning is managed by its founding Houghton family (1851), which controls roughly 15 percent of the company's stock. Known largely for its glass and ceramic cookware, the company's laboratories develop fiber optics, and glass for televisions, computers, and eyeglasses. The company currently produces over 60,000 products worldwide. It has approximately nineteen joint ventures. Some of these are with foreign companies, such as Samtel in Italy and Vitro SA in Mexico. Of the four main divisions, Corning's communications segment has shown the highest profits in recent reports, propelling Corning to almost $3 billion in revenues.

Cypress Semiconductor Corporation

Cypress Semiconductor Corporation designs, makes, and sells a broad line of high-performance digital integrated circuits, which are fabricated using proprietary 0.65, 0.8, and 1.2 micron CMOS (complementary metal-oxide-silicon) technologies. Cypress' products generally are used as critical components to enhance the performance of advanced electronic systems made in four market sectors: computers, military and aerospace, telecommunications, and instrumentation.

Delta Airlines

Delta Airlines is one of the top airline companies in the world and among the most fiscally sound. In an attempt to expand its service, Delta bought several routes from Eastern and Pan Am. With these routes, the company has surpassed other major airlines in cities served. With over 61,000 employees and revenues of over $9 billion, Delta has earned the distinction of having the industry's lowest customer complaint record.

Diamond International Corporation Fiber Products Division

Diamond International Corporation Fiber Products Division, located in Red Bluff, California; Plattsburgh, New York; Palmer, Massachusetts; and Natchez, Mississippi, is a manufacturer of cardboard egg cartons.

Eastman Kodak

Eastman Kodak is the world's largest producer of photographic products. But the bulk of its revenues originate from information systems relating primarily to business products, chemicals production developed primarily for manufacturers using EK products, and health and household products (through the acquisition of Sterling Drug). Despite maintaining debt from Sterling Drug and a recent court order to pay Polaroid $925 million for patent infringement, Eastman Kodak's financial future continues looking healthy. Revenues were recently projected at $19 billion.

Ericsson GE Mobile Communications

Ericsson is 80 percent L. M. Ericsson of Sweden and 20 percent General Electric. Ericsson GE Mobile Communications is a division located in Lynchburg, Virginia, and specializing in car phones, bay stations, radios, and wireless telephones. The Lynchburg division employs approximately 1,700 people.

Federal Express

Federal Express provides overnight delivery of documents and packages throughout three continents, an international scope enhanced through the 1989 acquisition of Tiger International. In 1990, Federal Express was recognized by the United States Department of Commerce with the Malcolm Baldridge Award for quality. Despite continued losses in international profits, Federal Express boasted roughly $7.6 billion in recent revenues.

Florida Power and Light Company

Florida Power and Light provides electricity service to over 3 million customers in the lower south coastline area of Florida. The only U.S. company to win the coveted Deming Award, it is the fourth-largest electric utility company in the United States. Until recently, FPL Group had investments in the insurance business, real estate, cable television, and the Florida citrus industry, but it has decided to focus on more utility-related business, such as alternative energy sources. Florida Power and Light has posted sales around $5 billion.

Ford Motor Company

Ford produces cars, trucks, and tractors, as well as plastic, glass, and electronic components for vehicles listed under the names of Ford, Mercury, Lincoln, and Jaguar (a recent acquisition). Ford also participates in the financial services industry, and until recently, it was a player in the aerospace technology industry. Located in Dearborn, Michigan, the Ford Motor Company has endured financial hardship, but prospects for future profits look hopeful. The company recently showed revenues of over $97 billion.

Four Seasons Hotels, Inc.

Four Seasons Hotels, Inc., specializes in luxury hotels and resorts in Canada, the United States, and London. This Toronto-based hotelier also owns resorts that offer oversize guestrooms and access to championship golf and tennis facilities in the Caribbean, and has plans for developments in Mexico City, Paris, Singapore, and Tokyo. Four Seasons Hotels boast the poshest rooms in the hotel industry and, in 1992, reported revenues of $163.70 million.

General Electric

One of the largest conglomerates in the world, General Electric traces its roots to Thomas Edison, inventor of the light bulb. Under the GE corporate umbrella, major divisions operate and produce several products and services in aerospace technology, aircraft engines, medical equipment, broadcasting, appliances, lighting, and financial services. Recently GE's lighting and electric divisions entered into the European and former Eastern Block countries. General Electric boasted close to $58 billion in revenues.

General Mills

General Mills, with interests including the Olive Garden and Red Lobster restaurant chains, is a leading producer of consumer foods. Other interests include the Big G cereals such as Cheerios and Lucky Charms, Betty Crocker mixes, Yoplait yogurt, Bisquick, and Gold Medal flour. To compete more aggressively in the European cereal market, General Mills partnered with Nestlé and has secured part of the market share held by Kelloggs. General Mills claims recent revenues at nearly $7 billion.

General Motors

General Motors (GM) produces automobiles, trucks, diesel locomotives, aircraft engines, and satellites. It also operates in the financial services industry and mortgage banking. As the largest automotive maker in the world, GM has taken a hard economic beating. Recently the company began streamlining its automotive operations by closing plants that have not shown profitability in past years. Under the GM name, car models such as Chevrolet, Buick, Cadillac, Oldsmobile, and Pontiac account for GM's sales. Also under GM is the new Saturn car division, which has been highlighted previously. The company posted recent revenues hovering around $123 billion.

Hospital Management Professionals

In 1981, Hospital Management Professionals, Inc. (HMP), was formed as an employee-owned, full-service manager of hospitals for their prospective board of trustees. HMP recognized the need for many hospitals to become a part of a larger network and secure experienced, stable management leadership uncompromised by other, sometimes conflicting agendas, including ultimate outside ownership or diversion of patients to other hospitals. That concept has proven to be most successful. Today HMP has joined with another company from Quorum Health Group. It is the largest management company of nonprofit hospitals in the United States.

Hewlitt-Packard

Hewlitt-Packard (HP) is the world's largest and most diversified manufacturer of electronic measurement and testing equipment and the world's second-largest workstation manufacturer with over 26 percent of the market. HP is also a leader in factory automation and data base management of software. The chairman of HP is David Packard, and the president and CEO is John A. Young.

Hudson Institute

As a nonprofit research institute, Hudson specializes in public policy analysis. Members are elected from various business, academic, and government sectors. The public policy issues that Hudson examines range from areas of national security and economics to education and technology. All studies conducted by the institute are funded through grants obtained from various sources, with emphasis on long-term or long-range outlook and impact. The *Workforce 2000* report may be the most widely recognized study that Hudson Institute has completed recently.

Johnsonville Foods

Once known as Johnsonville Sausage, the company specializes in meat packaging and sausage. CEO Ralph Stayer greatly increased the family-owned company's sales and revenues, posting recent sales of over $25 million. Though known for its products, Johnsonville Foods has made a name for itself in employee empowerment and product quality. The company sets new standards for employee involvement through innovations such as employee teams and committees, dissolution of its quality-control department, and employee performance-based profit sharing. Though the current market remains tight, Johnsonville Foods continues sharing strong profits, and its future holds similar expectancy.

Kiwi International Airlines

Kiwi International Airlines is an employee-owned airline that employs approximately 208 workers, all of which average twenty years experience with airline and owner operations. Most of the capitalization for Kiwi was invested by employees who will be responsible for operating the airline. Executive offices are located in Newark, New Jersey, and Robert Iverson is the chief executive officer.

Lechmere, Inc.

Headquartered in Woburn, Massachusetts, Lechmere, Inc., is a retail home-appliance and electronics chain. Founded in 1913, the chain has 4,000 employees and reached sales of $470 million in 1991. The chief executive officer is C. George Scala, and J. Kent Flummerfelt is president.

Manugistics, Inc.

A computer software and services company in Rockville, Maryland, Manugistics has 275 employees. The CEO is William M. Gibson. Manugistics set records for both revenues and profits during fiscal year 1991, in part by remaining loyal to its values, employees, and clients.

Maritz Corporation

A management consulting firm established in 1894, Maritz operates from Fenton, Missouri, a suburb of St. Louis. The company offers motivational and incentive services to major corporations within the United States and Europe. Based on its motivational and training programs and marketing research operations, Maritz has enjoyed recent sales of over $1 billion. Maritz has over 135 offices in the United States and approximately 5,500 employees. Though founded almost 100 years ago, the company is still run by the Maritz family, with William Maritz as its current president.

Marriott Corporation

One of the world's largest hoteliers, Marriott operates about 700 hotels, and it ranks first as a provider of food and services management for the business, health care, and education industries. Recently Marriott divested itself of its airline catering, fast-food, and family restaurant businesses and its holdings in the cruise line industry. Marriott has turned attention toward retirement communities and employee-sponsored day-care facilities.

Martin Marietta

As the country's eighth-leading defense company, Martin Marietta's operations include aerospace, information technologies, construction materials, and specialty chemical products. Its contracts range from the Titan launch vehicle series and the Peacekeeper missile to mail-sorting machines. Martin Marietta is also responsible for the *Magellan* spacecraft, which began mapping the surface of Venus in 1990. *Fortune* magazine ranks Martin Marietta as eighty-third on their Fortune 500 industrial corporation's list.

MBNA America Bank, National Association

MBNA America is the fourth-leading issuer, marketer, and servicer of premium and standard bank credit cards in the United States. It markets credit cards through professional, fraternal, educational, and special interest associations, including 223 medical and 70 bar associations. These markets allows them to reach approximately 77 million potential cardholders. MBNA also offers credit card bank agent services to financial institutions representing approximately an additional 12 million potential customers.

McDonald's Corporation

This company operates, licenses, and services the largest chain of fast-food restaurants in the world. Aside from restaurants in the United States, McDonald's also has operations in the rest of North America, South America, Europe, Asia, and Australia. The company owns at least 60 percent of the more than 11,000 restaurants cited in December 1990 and holds leases on the rest. McDonald's recently posted over $6.5 billion in revenues. In addition to the food chain division, the corporation is involved heavily in the development, building, and day-to-day maintenance of Ronald McDonald Houses. These facilities provide places of residence, counseling, and support for families with hospitalized children.

Microsoft Corporation

Microsoft Corporation is the leading developer of personal computer (PC) systems and applications software in the world. The company was founded in 1975 and produced the basic, critical PC operating system MS-DOS. Located in Redmond, Washington, Microsoft employs 4,037 people.

Motorola

The United States' current leader in the production of semiconductors, Motorola is also the world's leading supplier of mobile phones, cellular phone systems, and pagers. The electronics company also specializes in the development of two-way radios. Due to Motorola's aggressive business stance, the company is the only non-Japanese supplier of cellular phones and pagers to Nippon Telegraph and Telephone. Though its semiconductor division recently lost some market share due to late shipments, Motorola continues to outpace its competitors. The company employs over 100,000 people in U.S. facilities and abroad and has earned over $10 billion in recent revenues.

New York *Daily News*

One of the oldest newspaper companies in the United States, once boasting a circulation over 1 million, the *News* has seen better days. A bitter strike in the winter of 1990 by delivery and printing workers left the New York *Daily News* standing financially on shaky ground. During 1991 the company looked hopeful, following its takeover by Robert Maxwell, but due to his recent death, the publishing empire that bears his name has suffered financial hardship. The *News*'s financial future remains cloudy.

Nissan Motor Corporation, U.S.A.

As the parent Japanese subsidiary of Nissan Motor Company of Tokyo, Nissan of America operates several plants and firms in various regions of the United States. With a strong market share of light automobiles and trucks, the company also produces the Infiniti luxury car. Nissan cars are recognized worldwide for their easy handling, low maintenance, high gas mileage, and affordable prices. Along with Honda and Toyota, Nissan is one of the largest importers of cars into the United States, and its success helped encourage American auto makers to upgrade their manufacturing standards of automobiles.

Oxford Chemicals, Inc.

A subsidiary of Diversey U.S. Holdings, which is itself a subsidiary of Canada's Molson Companies, Limited, Oxford Chemicals specializes in production of several home-use chemical compounds from insecticides to environmental sanitation systems. A diverse corporation, Molson owns holdings not only in chemicals, but in breweries and lumber products. Oxford Chemicals, Inc., boasts sales of over $35 million.

Pepsico, Inc.

Pepsico is a major force in three different markets: soft drinks, fast-food restaurants, and snack food. Pepsico's soft drink division, which claims 33 percent of the total U.S. market and 15 percent of the international market, boasts such names as Pepsi, Diet Pepsi, Mountain Dew, and Slice. Pepsico's restaurant segment has more units than any other restaurant system in the world. The segment consists of Pizza Hut, Kentucky Fried Chicken, and Taco Bell. Pepsico's snack food segment (Frito-Lay) accounts for approximately 13 percent of the total U.S. snack market. Pepsico, Inc., is headquartered in Purchase, New York, and employs approximately 308,000 workers.

Planned Parenthood Federation of America

A social welfare organization, Planned Parenthood provides counseling and information on a variety of effective means for fertility control, producing and promoting various educational and training programs directed at increasing the public's knowledge about human reproduction. The federation also initiates research on biomedical, socioeconomic, and demographic variables most commonly associated with fertility. Planned Parenthood operates roughly 800 centers that offer medically supervised services and maintains a budget of over $330 million.

Quality Food Centers

Quality Food Centers is the largest independent supermarket chain in Seattle/King County, Washington, with thirty-two supermarkets in operation as of December 31, 1991. The chain emphasizes superior customer service, high-quality produce and meat, and convenient store locations in stable and growing areas. All stores are open seven days a week, twenty-four hours a day. Quality Food Centers offer a full line of food items as well as a limited number of nonfood items. All stores have photo processing and automated teller machines. Quality Food Centers employs approximately 2,400 workers.

Randall Food Markets, Inc.

Randall Food Markets, Inc., is the leader in the Houston grocery business. Robert Onstead is chairman of this organization, which was founded in 1955. Today, Randall Food Markets, Inc., has forty-four locations throughout the Houston area.

Reflexite Corporation

Reflexite Corporation is a technology-based business competing in world markets. The CEO is Cecil Ursprung. The company is 59 percent employee owned. Located in New Britain, Connecticut, Reflexite's sales topped $31 million in 1991.

Remington Products

Established in 1979 and currently owned by Victor Kiam II, Remington manufactures electric shavers, shaving aids, knives and shavers, blades, and various grooming products for both men and women. With an employee base of over 1,700 and sales topping $400 million, Remington continues to write a successful ending to a company story that almost ended in bankruptcy. Kiam, who obtained Remington in the eighties, is largely credited for having turned the company around and making it a profitable and competitive shareholder in the grooming industry. The company recently broadened its market interests to include Eastern Europe and Asia.

Romac and Associates, Inc.

Romac and Associates, founded in 1966 in Boston, Massachusetts, is a recruiting firm, providing permanent, temporary, and contract staffing services. The company specializes in entry-level to top-level positions within accounting/finance, banking, and data processing. Romac and Associates has offices throughout the United States.

Sara Lee Corporation

Though known largely for its frozen dessert and bakery items, Sara Lee stands as an extremely diversified company. In addition to Sara Lee foods, the company produces packaged meats under such familiar brands as Rudy's Farm, Jimmy Dean, and Hillshire Farms; coffee and grocery items, under the Merrild Kaffe, Maison Du Cafe, and Pickwick brands; Hanes, Leggs, Coach, Champion, and Fuller Brush consumer personal products; and Kiwi, Radox, and Royale Ambree household products. Due to its diversity, Sara Lee remains stable fiscally and boasts over $12 billion in recent revenues.

Scandinavian Airlines of North America (SANA)

With Scandinavian Airlines System (SAS) as its parent company, SANA holds a strong interest in the foreign airlines industry operating in North America. A major force in the European air industry, SAS maintains flight services for passengers, freight, and mail spanning over eighty cities in fifty countries. The company holds the honor of being the designated airline carrier for Denmark, Norway, and Sweden. Aside from the airline division, SAS operates a chain of hotels and is involved in the catering and restaurant business. It also holds investments in travel-related and financial services.

Scandinavian Service School (SSS)

The Scandinavian Service School operates a management consulting service to top companies, primarily in Europe. A company that specializes in service, SSS helps corporations examine their service policies and techniques and provides expert consultation on areas of improvement. SSS has worked with several large corporations, such as British Airways, Volkswagen, Abbey Life Britain's Thistle Hotel chain, and Scandinavian Airlines System. The school boasts a high success rate with those companies that have enlisted its help and hopes to broaden its scope of clientele by expanding into North America.

Spartan Express, Inc.

Founded in 1966 and located in Greer, South Carolina, Spartan is a short-haul carrier. It has an operating revenue of approximately $70 million.

Springfield Remanufacturing Company

Springfield Remanufacturing Company, located in Springfield, Missouri, remanufactures old diesel and gasoline engines for manufacturing, industrial, and farm machinery and equipment. The company sales were approximately $60 million for 1991.

Stanley Works

Based in New Britain, Connecticut, Stanley Works is the world's leading manufacturer of hand tools and assorted hardware. Stanley is divided into two divisions. The Home Improvement and Consumer Products Division specializes in producing various hardware for the home and the builder. The Industrial and Professional Products Division manufactures industrial and hydraulic tools and assorted doors and storage facilities. In the eighties, Stanley purchased over twenty businesses to consolidate the hardware market. The company has enjoyed a sound fiscal operation, with sales dipping only slightly during the recent economic recession. With over 17,000 employees, Stanley sales topped almost $2 billion in 1990.

Stride Rite

A maker of athletic and casual footwear, Stride Rite recently became the leading marketer of children's footwear in the United States with top-selling brand names such as Keds and Top-Sider. Two years ago the company sold its J. M. Herman division in order to consolidate. Stride Rite manufactures most of its own products at plants in the United States and Puerto Rico, but also imports footwear from overseas. In April 1992, Arnold Hiatt retired as CEO after having the post for over twenty years. Stride Rite recently posted over $570 million in revenues.

Sulzer Brothers, Ltd.

The 150-year-old Sulzer Brothers, Ltd., is the world's leading manufacturer of weaving machines. The company also produces heating and air-conditioning equipment and paper-making machinery. Although its base is Zurich, Sulzer Brothers will begin manufacturing its air-jet weaving machines in Japan in 1993.

Summitt Health, Ltd.

Summitt is an integrated health-care company, operating several acute-care hospitals and nursing facilities largely within the western region of the United States. Five of their acute-care hospitals are located in Saudi Arabia, under contract with the royal government. Summitt also operates retirement hotels, hemodialysis centers, home health care agencies, substance abuse centers, and urgent care centers. With over 5,000 employees, the company has nearly $400 million in recent sales. Through this integrated health care approach, Summitt maintains it can offer communities sound medical care covering a wide range of areas.

Textron, Inc.

One of the oldest conglomerates in the United States, Textron is diversified in products and services for government and public consumption. Textron's interests range from manufacturing helicopters and aircraft parts to strategic weapons and aerospace technology. The company produces golf carts and automotive parts along with providing financial services and insurance. Textron recently posted nearly $8 billion in revenues.

United Electric Controls Company

A family-owned business for over sixty years, United Electric Controls manufactures various electromechanical and pressure controls, temperature and pressure probes, and electromechanical recorders. With over 400 employees and over $32 million in recent sales, the private company continues to hold a strong and stable presence in the marketplace. Due to recent sagging sales, the company implemented a new employee program incorporating several Japanese work techniques. Along with those adaptations, the company instituted a bold new ideas program to stimulate worker creativity and cost-savings production.

United States Steel (USS)

A subsidiary of USX Corporation, USS is the largest steelmaker in the nation. USX was founded originally as United States Steel by J. P. Morgan in 1901, but when investments took the company into oil production through the acquisition of Marathon Oil and Texas Oil and Gas, the corporation reorganized as USX, with United States Steel a subsidiary. USS operates several plants, which produce sheet, strip, tin mill products, plates, and pipe and tubing. The majority of USS plants are located in the northern region of the United States. Despite having low sales in a depressed steel market, USS posted over $6 billion in recent revenues.

University of Florida

Located in Gainesville, Florida, the University of Florida was established in 1853. Today there are approximately 34,198 students at this state university.

Westinghouse Electric Corporation

Despite a shaky financial history and repeated losses in sales, Westinghouse remains a strong presence in the market. A diversified company with products and services falling into six major categories (electronic systems, business units, environmental systems, financial services, power systems, and Group W Broadcasting), Westinghouse recently acquired office furniture maker Knoll International and broadened its base in the furniture business. It has also begun several joint ventures with foreign companies to secure interests in other markets. With over 115,000 employees, Westinghouse posted nearly $13 billion in recent revenues.

White Storage and Retrieval Systems

Located in Kenilworth, New Jersey, White Storage and Retrieval Systems manufactures automated retrieval systems for factories and offices. The company employs 400 people and reported $50 million in annual revenues for 1991. Chief executive officer is Donald Weiss.

Xerox Corporation

The leading producer of copying and duplicating machines, Xerox also produces other business equipment and supplies, which complement its copiers. In 1989, Xerox received the prestigious Malcolm Baldridge Award for quality. Through its renowned Palo Alto Research Center, the company has developed and begun marketing its new DocuTech Production Publisher, which combines copying, printing, and scanning technology within computer systems. Along with these technological divisions, Xerox also holds interest in the financial services sector. With a strong fiscal history, Xerox has shown close to $17 billion in recent revenues.

■ APPENDIX B
Chapter Notes

Introduction—Tapping Hidden Resources

1. Interview with Faye Bartlett, operator, Vanderbilt University, December 1990.

2. U.S. Department of Labor, Bureau of Labor Statistics, *Handbook of Labor Statistics*, 1983 and 1985.
Note: The backstage ratio was derived from U.S. labor statistics, consulting, and research. The onstage/backstage ratio can vary in some organizations.

3. Paul B. Carroll, "Culture Shock—Story of an IBM Unit That Split Off Shows Difficulties of Change," *Wall Street Journal*, July 23, 1992.

4. Interview with Timothy Epps, vice president of Human Resource Services, Saturn Corporation, April 1992.

Chapter 1 Somebody Nobody Knows

1. Studs Terkel, *Working People Talk about What They Do All Day and How They Feel About What They Do* (New York: Pantheon Books, 1974).

2.–4. Charles Kuralt, *On the Road with Charles Kuralt* (New York: Putnam Publishing Group, 1986).

5.–7. Studs Terkel, *Working People Talk.*

8. Interview with Saturn Corporation employees, July 1992.

9. Per Ola and Emily d'Aulaire, "Now What Are They Doing at That Crazy St. John the Divine," *The Smithsonian*, December 1992.

10. Studs Terkel, *Working People Talk.*

11. U.S. Department of Labor, Bureau of Labor Statistics, *Handbook of Labor Statistics*, 1983 and 1985.
Note: The backstage ratio was derived from U.S. labor statistics, consulting, and research. The onstage/backstage ratio can vary in some organizations.

12. Jolie Solomon, "Managers Focus on Low-Wage Workers," *Wall Street Journal*, May 9, 1989.

13. Barbara Garson, *All the Livelong Day: The Meaning and Demeaning of Routine Work* (Garden City, NY: Doubleday, 1975).

14. Studs Terkel, *Working People Talk.*

15. Barbara Garson, *All the Livelong Day.*

16. Interview with former AM line worker, June 1992.

17. Staff, *Personnel Management: Policies and Practices*, Englewood Cliffs, NJ: Prentice Hall, 1981.

18. Consulting performed by the authors.

19. Studs Terkel, *Working People Talk.*

20. Alan Farnham, "The Trust Gap," *FORTUNE*, December 4, 1989.

21. Studs Terkel, *Working People Talk*.

22. Alan Farnham, "The Trust Gap."

23. John R. Emshwiller, "Business Loses Billions of Dollars to Employee Theft," *Wall Street Journal*, October 5, 1992.

24. Molly Ladd-Taylor, "Women Workers and the Yale Strike," *Feminist Studies*, Fall 1985.

25. K. Crowe, et al., "The Night the Lid Blew Off," *Newsday*, October 30, 1990.

26. Staff, "Employee Turnover—Measurement and Control," *Small Business Report*, February 1987.

27. Jolie Solomon, "Managers Focus on Low-Wage Workers."

28. Barbara Garson, *All the Livelong Day*.

29. Interview with a former employee of Oxford Chemical, June 1992.

30. Dick Schaff and Margaret Kaeter, "Quantifying Quality," *Training* (Supplement) March 1991.

31. Charles Kuralt, *On the Road*.

32. According to the *1992 World Almanac*, average annual pay was $23,602 in 1990. Assuming a 4% increase in 1991, and a 4% increase in 1992, the 1992 average salary is $25,528. 100 backstage employees × $25,528 annual salary × a 10% productivity increase = $255,280. 75 million workers × $25,528 annual salary × a 10% productivity increase = $191.46 billion in added economic value.

Chapter 2   Identifying the Hidden Organization

1. Dennis Brisselt and Charles Edgley, *Life as Theater: A Dramaturgical Source Book*, 2nd edition (New York: Aldine de Gruyter, 1990).

2.–3. Interview with Mac Pirkle, artistic director, Tennessee Repertory Theatre, April 1991.

4. Jim Cavanaugh, *Organization and Management of the Non-professional Theater Including the Backstage and Front-of-House* (New York: Richards Rosen Press, Inc., 1973).

5. Interview with Mac Pirkle.

6.–7. Jim Cavanaugh, *Organization and Management.*

8.–9. Interview with Mac Pirkle.

10. Interview with Chicago Bulls Organization spokesperson, July 1992.

11. Interviews with American Airlines employees, May 1990.

12.–22. Desert Storm information compiled from Brian Duffy and Kenneth T. Walsh, "The Gulf War's Final Curtain," *U.S. News and World Report*, March 4, 1991; Stephen Budiansky et al., "No Time to Back Down," *U.S. News and World Report*, March 4, 1991; Warren Cohen and Douglas Pasternak, "Fighting Numbers," *U.S. News and World Report*, March 11, 1991; Mike Tharp et al., "Countless Unsung Heroes," *U.S. News and World Report*, March 18, 1991.

23.–26. Consulting performed by the authors.

27. Interview with Service Merchandise employee, January 1990.

Chapter 4   Finding a Backstage Champion

1. John F. Love, *McDonald's: Behind the Arches* (New York: Bantam Books, Inc., 1986).

2. Interview with Ben & Jerry's employees, November 1992.

3. Interview with Pat Shappert, supervisor of Housekeeping, Opryland Hotel, April 1991.

4. Comments submitted by William J. Agee, chairman and CEO, Morrison Knudsen Corporation, June 1992.

5.–14. Larry Kreider story compiled from interviews with Larry Kreider, vice president of Purchasing, May 1989, and Service Merchandise employees, October 1992.

15.–20. Donna Kane story compiled from interviews with Donna Kane, vice president of Corporate Planning, and Jewish Hospital HealthCare Services employees, December 1991.

Chapter 5   Linking Backstage to the Core Mission

1. Interviews with American Airlines employees, May 1990.

2. Ronald Henkoff, "Cost Cutting: How to Do It Right," *Fortune*, April 9, 1990.

3. Alan Farnham, "The Trust Gap," *Fortune*, December 4, 1989.

4. Rosabeth Moss Kanter, "Championing Change: An Interview with Bell Atlantic's CEO Raymond Smith," *Harvard Business Review*, January/February 1991.

5. Interviews with Opryland employees, July 1990.

6. Opryland mission statement.

7. Lee G. Bolman and Terrence E. Deal, *Searching for Leadership: Another Search Party's Report*. In print.

8. Interview with Frank Dodge, president and CEO, Dodge Group, Inc., November 1992.

9.–10. Interview with Walt Minnick, president and CEO, TJ International, August 1992.

11.–15. Ronald C. Yates, "Workers Hold Cards in This Game," *Chicago Tribune*, August 16, 1992.

16.–17. Larry Jabbonsky, "Things Are Looking Up at Pepsi," *Beverage World*, October 1992.

18. Ronald Henkoff, "Cost Cutting."

19. Carol Clurman, "More Than Just a Paycheck," *USA Weekend*, January 19–21, 1990.

20. Staff, "With an ESOP, They Try Even Harder," *Personnel*, January 1990.

21. Barbara Fitzgerald-Turner, "Manugistics Tests for Its Values," *Personnel Journal*, October 1992.

Chapter 6   Hiring the Best

1. Donald D. DeCamp, "Are You Hiring the Right Kind of People," *Management Review*, May 1992.

2.–3. Interview with Al Becker, director of Public Relations, American Airlines, May 1990.

4.–5. T. J. Rogers, "No Excuses Management," *Harvard Business Review*, July/August 1990.

6. Interview with Extended Systems employees, October 1992.

7. Interview with Jon Gullette, associate vice chancellor of Operations, Vanderbilt University, February 1990.

8. Interview with Opryland employee, April 1991.

9. Comments submitted by William J. Agee, chairman and CEO, Morrison Knudsen Corporation, June 1992.

10. Ron Zemke, "Contact! Training Employees to Meet the Public," *Training*, August 1986.

11. Alfred Borcover, "Grumps Needn't Apply: For Disney 'Cast,' It's Always Showtime," *Chicago Tribune*, August 2, 1991.

12.–13. Interview with Jim Robertson, director of Staffing, Octel Communications, December 1992.

14. Interview with Frank Dodge, president and CEO, Dodge Group, Inc., November 1992.

15. Barbara Duncan, "At Disneyland, Customer Service Is Not a 'Fantasy,' " *Bank Marketing*, March 1988.

16. Thomas J. Murray, "Getting Mickey Organized," *Business Month*, December 1987.

17.–18. Interview with Steve Townes, executive vice president, Stevens Aviation, November 1992.

19.–20. John Hinrichs, "Commitment Ties to the Bottom Line," *HR Magazine*, April 1991.

21.–26. J. Case, "Collective Effort," *Inc.*, January 1992.

27. "Stock Options: The Employee Benefit of the '90s," *John Naisbitt's Trend Letter*, September 17, 1992.

Chapter 7 Commanding and Commending Customer Service

1. David Wessel, "Sure Ways to Annoy Consumers" from *The American Way of Buying*, A Wall Street Journal *Centennial Survey*, *Wall Street Journal*, November 6, 1989.

2. Information taken from *Legendary Service Training*, Blanchard Training and Development, Escondido, CA, 1989.

3. U.S. Department of Labor, Bureau of Labor Statistics, *Handbook of Labor Statistics*, 1983 and 1985.
Note: The backstage ratio was derived from U.S. labor statistics, consulting, and research. The onstage/backstage ratio may vary in some organizations.

4. Ron Zemke, "Contact! Training Employees to Meet the Public," *Training*, August 1986.

5. Otis Port and John Casey, "Questing for the Best," *Business Week: The Quality Imperative*, *Special Issue*, 1991.

6. Interview with Ben & Jerry's employees, November 1992.

7. Paul L. Blocklyn, "Making Magic: The Disney Approach to People Management," *Personnel*, December 1988.

8.–9. J. Laabs, "Ben & Jerry's Caring Capitalism," *Personnel Journal*, November 1992.

10. George Gendron, "What It Takes," *Inc.*, November 1992.

11.–12. Interview with John Dahlin, president of Operations and Administration, Dahlin Smith White, November 1992.

13. Chris Lee, "The Customer Within," *Training*, July 1991.

14. Interviews with Service Merchandise employees, March 1990.

15. Interview with Larry Shoaf, senior vice president, Alexander and Alexander, November 1992.

16. Eric R. Blume, "Customer Service," *Training and Development Journal*, September 1988.

17. Terrence E. Deal and Allen A. Kennedy, *Corporate Cultures* (Reading, MA: Addison-Wesley Publishing Company, Inc., 1982).

18. Interview with Bill Boesch, vice president of Cargo, American Airlines, May 1990.

19.–20. Interview with Lt. Col. Jack Stevenson, U.S. Army, August 1992.

21.–22. Interview with Laurie Shappert, manager of Marketing Support, Opryland, July 1990.

23. Paul L. Blocklyn, "Making Magic."

24. Michelle Neely Martinez, "Disney Training Works Magic," *HR Magazine*, May 1992.

25. Interview with Ann McNamara, vice president of Personnel and Legal Counsel, American Airlines, May 1990.

26. Larry Armstrong and William C. Symonds, "Beyond 'May I Help You?'" *Business Week: The Quality Imperative Special Issue*, 1991.

27. Interview with Norco Windows employees, November 1992.

28. Eric R. Blume, "Customer Service," *Training and Development Journal*, September 1988.

29. Consulting performed by the authors.

30. Robert A. Ferchat, "Productivity in a Customer Vein," *Executive Speeches*, June 1988.

31. Toni Mack, "Caviar Yes, Chardonnay No," *Forbes*, October 28, 1991.

32. Interview with Tom Adkinson, director of Public Relations, Opryland, June 1990.

Chapter 8 Broadening the Base of Ideas

1.–2. Consulting performed by the authors.

3. Jack Welch, "What I Want Business to Do in '92: Create a Company of Ideas," *Fortune*, December 30, 1991.

4. P. Rogers, "Breaking All the Rules," *Dairy Foods*, September 1992.

5.–8. Michael Gates, "American Airlines, Do People Make the Difference?" *Incentive*, May 1989.

9. Interviews with American Airlines employees, May 1990.

10. Aaron Sugerman, "Keeping the Skies Friendly," *Incentive Marketing*, December 1986.

11. Michael A. Verespej, "Who Can Argue?"

12.–14. Interview with Walt Minnick, president and CEO, TJ International, September 1992.

15.–16. Interviews with TJ International employees, September 1992.

17. Rosabeth Moss Kanter, "Championing Change: An Interview with Bell Atlantic's CEO Raymond Smith," *Harvard Business Review*, January/February 1991.

18.–20. George Gendron, "What It Takes," *Inc.*, November 1992.

21. Peter F. Drucker, "The New Productivity Challenge," *Harvard Business Review*, November/December 1991.

22. Information retrieved from Kathryn McDonald, manager of Meter Reading, South, Florida Power and Light, December 1992.

23. Interview with John Dahlin, president of Operations and Administration, Dahlin Smith White, November 1992.

24.–25. "More Companies Look to Creativity, Innovation as Valuable Business Tool," *John Naisbitt's Trend Letter*, August 15, 1991.

26. David Woodruff and Jonathan B. Levine, "Miles Traveled, Miles to Go," *BusinessWeek: The Quality Imperative Special Issue*, 1991.

Chapter 9 Trusting While Helping

1. Story told to William A. Jenkins by Professor Everett Nicholson at Purdue University, West Lafayette, Indiana.

2. Warren Bennis, "What I Want Business to Do in 1992: Concentrate on Trust," *Fortune*, December 30, 1991.

3. Interview with American Association of Museums employee January 1988.

4. Thomas A. Stewart, "GE Keep Those Ideas Coming," *Fortune*, August 12, 1991.

5. Ronald Henkoff, "Cost Cutting: How to Do It Right," *Fortune*, April 9, 1990.

6. Brian Dumaine, "Unleash Workers and Cut Costs," *Fortune*, May 18, 1992.

7. Steve Rogers, "For Averitt Express the Driving Force Is People," *Advantage Magazine*, May 1989.

8. John Byrne, "Profiting from the Nonprofits," *Business Week*, March 26, 1990.

9. Interview with Gary Jones, director of Power Monitoring and Control Systems, Square D Company, November 1992.

10. Interview with Terry Jackson, Manager, First Union Georgia Servicecenter, August 1992.

11.–12. Interviews with Ben & Jerry's employees, November 1992.

13. Interview with Jennifer Martin, parks operation supervisor, Opryland, July 1990.

14. Interview with Kathy Roadarmel, employee relations manager, Opryland, July 1990.

15.–16. Michael Gates, "American Airlines, Do People Make the Difference?" *Incentive*, May 1989.

17. Golden Wrench Award proposal, taken from Robert Crandall's speech at American Airlines Annual Meeting, May 1989.

18. Staff, "Growth Strategies at Remington," *The Journal of Business Strategy*, January/February 1989.

19. Larry Armstrong and William S. Wymonds, "Beyond 'May I Help You?'" *Business Weekly: The Quality Imperative Special Issue*, 1991.

20. Staff, "Avis ESOP's Fable," *The Economist*, July 1989.

21.–22. Joann DeMott, *Making Daily Management Work: A Leadership and Managerial Perspective*, Consulting Notebook, 1991.

23. Booker T. Washington, *Up from Slavery* (Corner House Publishers: Williamstown, MA, 1978).

Chapter 10   Avoiding the "That's Not My Job" Syndrome

1.–3. Consulting performed by the authors.

4. Dana Welchsler Linden, "Can This Kiwi Fly?" *Forbes*, September 14, 1992.

5. Consulting performed by the authors.

6. Speech by Gail Neumann, vice president of Human Resources and General Counsel, Nissan Corporation, March 1990.

7.–8. Dave Kielinski, "The Hidden Human Costs of Total Quality," *Business Ethics*, May/June 1992.

9. Consulting performed by the authors.

10. Interview with Chuck Raper, director of Administration, McKinsey and Company, June 1992.

11. Interviews with Opryland employees, July 1990 and April 1991.

12.–14. Brian Dumaine, "Who Needs a Boss?" *Fortune*, May 7, 1990.

15. Brian Smith, "Management's New Gurus," *Business-Week*, August 31, 1992.

16. James R. Healey, "U.S. Steel Learns from Experience," *USA Today*, April 10, 1992.

17. John Southerst, "First, We Dump the Bosses," *Canadian Business*, April 1992.

18.–19. D. Keith Denton, "Multi-Skilled Teams Replace Old Work Systems," *HR Magazine*, September 1992.

Chapter 11   Right Things, Not Tight Rules

1. John J. Keller, "Defying Boss's Orders Pays Off for Physicist and His Firm, AT&T," *Wall Street Journal*, June 25, 1991.

2. John M. Cowan, "Metaphor of the Month Award," *Speechwriter's Newsletter*, September 1992.

3. Interview with Hyman George Rickover, on *60 Minutes*, CBS, December 9, 1984.

4. Consulting performed by the authors.

5. Ronald Henkoff, "Cost Cutting: How to Do It Right," *Fortune*, April 9, 1990.

6. E. J. Muller, "Spartan Express," *Distribution*, August 1992.

7. Robert A. Ferchat, "Shooting for the Moon," *Vital Speeches*, September 15, 1989.

8. Interview with McKinsey and Company employees, June 1992.

9. Dawn Gunsch, "Employees Team Up with HR," *Personnel Journal*, October 1991.

10.–13. Timothy W. Firnstahl, "My Employees Are My Service Guarantee," *Harvard Business Review*, July/August 1989.

14. Consulting performed by the authors.

15.–17. Bob Filipczak, "Beyond the Gates of Microsoft," *Training*, September 1992.

18. John Carey, "Getting Business to Think about the Unthinkable," *BusinessWeek*, June 24, 1991.

19.–20. R. Hof, "From Dinosaur to Gazelle," *BusinessWeek Special Issue, Reinventing America*, 1992.

21. Patricia Sellers, "Getting Customers to Love You," *Fortune*, March 13, 1989.

Chapter 12 Don't Steal the Show

1.–2. Information taken from *Legendary Service Training*, Blanchard Training and Development, Escondido, CA, 1989.

3. Consulting performed by the authors.

4.–5. *Tonight* show with Johnny Carson, NBC, May 29, 1992.

6. John Taylor, "Actions Speak Louder," *Forbes*, October 12, 1992.

7. Interview with Terry Warren, president and CEO of MedTrac, November 1992.

Chapter 13 Appropriate Tools Guarantee Top Efforts

1.–2. Thomas A. Stewart, ed., "The New Century American: Where We Stand," *Fortune Special Issue*, Spring/Summer 1991.

3. Rosabeth Moss Kanter, ed., "Service Quality: You Get What You Pay For," *Harvard Business Review*, September/October 1991.

4. Otis Port and John Carey, "Questing for the Best," *BusinessWeek: The Quality Imperative Special Issue*, 1991.

5. *Webster's Ninth New Collegiate Dictionary* (Springfield, MA: Merriam-Webster, Inc., Publishers, 1985).

6. Interview with Courtney Reynolds, former corporate planner, Morrison Knudsen, February 1992.

7. Interview with Chuck Raper, director of Administration, McKinsey and Company, June 1992.

8. Allen Halcrow, "Federal Express: A Commitment to Training Has Helped Federal Express Keep Profits and Customer Satisfaction High," *Personnel Journal*, January 1992.

9. Chris Sullivan, "The White-Collar Productivity Push," *Datamation*, January 15, 1990.

10.–11. Jason Zweig, "Bag Man," *Forbes*, August 13, 1992.

12. Gail E. Schaves, "A Swiss Athlete Gets in Fighting Trim," *BusinessWeek: The Quality Imperative Special Issue*, 1991.

13. D. Heatherman and B. Kleinen, "Training Plus Technology: the Future is Now," *Training and Development*, September 1991.

14. Erick Calonius, "Smart Moves by Quality Champs," *Fortune*, Spring/Summer, 1991.

15. Louis Kraar, "Twenty-five Who Help the U.S. Win," *Fortune Special Issue*, Spring/Summer 1991.

16. Stephen Covey, *The Seven Habits of Highly Effective People: Restoring the Character Ethic* (New York: Simon and Schuster, 1989).

17. Interview with Kim Igoe, director of Museum Assessment Programs, American Association of Museums, January 1990.

18. Jaclyn Fierman, "Shaking the Blue-Collar Blues," *Fortune*, April 22, 1991.

19. Ronald Henkoff, "Where Will the Jobs Come From," *Fortune*, October 19, 1992.

Chapter 14   Dressing the Hidden Cast

1. Ruth Simon, "Behind the Scenes at the Magic Kingdom," *Forbes*, July 13, 1987.

2. Jennet Conant, "Style's Hidden Persuaders," *People Weekly*, Spring 1990 Extra.

3. Interview with Jon Gullette, associate vice chancellor of Operations, Vanderbilt University, April 1990.

4.–5. Interview with Doug Small, CEO, Horace Small Apparel Company, November 1992.

6. Tina Beaudoin, "G & K Services: Spiffing Up Corporate Images," *Management Review*, December 1988.

7.–8. Matthew Schifrin, "The Big Money in Mailrooms," *Forbes*, August 3, 1992.

9.–10. Subrata N. Chakravarty, "White Slacks and Carbon Black," *Forbes*, October 26, 1992.

11.–12. Interview with Opryland employees, June 1990.

13. Dace Embrekte, "More Companies Allowing Workers to Dress Casually," *The Tennessean*, June 14, 1992.

14. Interview with Donna Kane, vice president of Corporate Planning, Jewish Hospital HealthCare Services, December 1991.

15. Consulting performed by the authors.

16.–17. Daniel Boyle, "Employee Motivation That Works," *HR Magazine*, October 1992.

18. Interview with Bill Boesch, vice president of Cargo, American Airlines, May 1990.

19. Interview with Pat Shappert, supervisor of Housekeeping, Opryland, June 1990.

20. Ralph Kilmann and Ines Kilman, *Making Organizations Competitive* (San Francisco: Jossey-Bass, 1991).

Chapter 15   Celebrating Hidden Achievements

1.–4. Interview with Mac Pirkle, artistic director, Tennessee Repertory Theatre, April 1991.

5. Interview with Bill Boesch, vice president of Cargo, American Airlines, May 1990.

6. Interview with Annie Hayes, damage and defective clerk, Service Merchandise, March 1990.

7. Interview with Vanderbilt University employee, May 1990.

8. Consulting performed by the authors.

9. Interview with Rob Beltramo, business consultant, May 1992.

10. Interview with Terry Jackson, manager, First Union Georgia Servicenter, August 1990.

11. David Campbell, *If I'm in Charge Why Is Everyone Laughing?* (Greensboro, NC: Center for Creative Leadership, 1974).

12. Interview with Ann McNamara, vice president of Personnel and Legal Counsel, American Airlines, May 1990.

13. Interview with Al Becker, managing director of External Communications, American Airlines, May 1990.

14. Golden Wrench Award proposal, excerpts taken from Robert Crandall's speech at American Airlines Annual Meeting, May 1989.

15. Interview with Bill Boesch.

16. Michael Gates, "American Airlines, Do People Make the Difference?" *Incentive*, May 1989.

17. Comments submitted by William J. Agee, chairman and CEO, Morrison Knudsen Corporation, June 1992.

18.–22. J. Laabs, "Ben & Jerry's Caring Capitalism," *Personnel Journal*, November 1992.

23.–25. Interviews with Ben & Jerry's employees, November 1992.

26. Ben & Jerry's One World, One Heart Festival Program, San Francisco, 1992.

27. J. Laabs, "Ben & Jerry's Caring Capitalism."

28.–31. John Dahlin, "What It Takes," *Inc.*, November 1992.

32.–33. Interview with John Dahlin, president of Operations and Administration, Dahlin Smith White, November 1992.

34.–35. Interview with Jerry Lukach, plant manager, Norco Windows, November 1992.

36. Bridget O'Brian, "Advertisers' Fights Don't Usually Involve Such Strong-Arm Tactics," *Wall Street Journal*, March 11, 1992.

37. Interview with Steve Townes, executive vice president, Stevens' Aviation, November 1992.

38. Consulting performed by the authors.

39. Alan Farnham, "The Trust Gap," *Fortune*, December 4, 1989.

40. Consulting performed by the authors.

41. Harvey Cox, *The Feast of Fools* (Cambridge, MA: Harvard University Press, 1969).

42. Interview with Bill Boesch, vice president of Cargo, American Airlines, May 1990.

Chapter 16   The Hidden Cast Speaks

All quotes in chapter 16, unless otherwise noted, came from focus group meetings organized by William A. Jenkins and Terrence E. Deal. The ten focus groups consisted of three to five employees each, from three different companies.

1. Paul Sweeney, "Now They've Got to Treat Folks Right," *Southern Exposure*, March/June 1985.

2. *The Bulletin of Vanderbilt University: Owen Graduate School of Management*, 1991/1992.

3. Stephen R. Covey, *The Seven Habits of Highly Effective People: Restoring the Character Ethic*. (New York: Simon and Schuster, 1989).

Chapter 17   Saturn: A Look to America's Future

1. S. C. Gwynne, "The Right Stuff," *Time*, October 29, 1990.

2. James B. Treece, "Here Comes GM's Saturn," *BusinessWeek*, April 9, 1990.

3. David Woodruff, "At Saturn, What Workers Want . . . Fewer Defects," *BusinessWeek*, December 2, 1991.

4. S. C. Gwynne, "The Right Stuff."

5. James B. Treece, "Here Comes GM's Saturn."

6. William J. Cook, "Ringing in Saturn," *U.S. News & World Report*, October 22, 1990.

7. Lindsay Chappell, "GM Combs Saturn Suppliers for New Players," *Automotive News*, August 24, 1992.

8. Interview with Saturn Corporation employees, August 1992.

9. S. C. Gwynne, "The Right Stuff."

10. Beverly Geber, "Saturn's Grand Experiment," *Training*, June 1992.

11. Interview with Timothy Epps, vice president of Human Resource Services, Saturn Corporation, April 1992.

12.–13. Interview with Saturn Corporation employees, June 1992.

14. S. C. Gwynne, "The Right Stuff."

15. Tim Martin, "Saturn Corporation Continues to Win Buyers," *The Tennessean*, July 8, 1993.

16.–17. Lindsay Chappell, "Saturn Gaining Fans and Kudos: Dealers Added; Output Climbs," *Automotive News*, March 23, 1992.

18. Tim Martin, "Saturn Corporation Continues to Win Buyers."

19. Interview with Saturn Corporation employees, June 1992, and Editorial, "Saturn's Successes," *The Nashville Banner*, June 24, 1992.

20. Lindsay Chappell, "Saturns Headed to Taiwan," *Automotive News*, February 10, 1992.

21. Micheline Maynard, "Following the Leader," *USA Today*, July 21, 1992.

22. Beverly Geber, "Saturn's Grand Experiment."

23. Micheline Maynard, "Following the Leader," and Jim Henry, "Saturn's Cupboard Is Stripped Bare," *Automotive News*, August 17, 1992.

24. Micheline Maynard, "Fulfilling Buyers' Wishes, Saturn's Well Runs Dry," *USA Today*, August 18, 1992.

25. Micheline Maynard, "Following the Leader."

26. Liz Pinto, "Simplicity Is Key to Labor Tranquility of Saturn," *Automotive News*, September 7, 1992.

27.–28. Staff, "Reinvent U.S. Schools as Saturn Did Cars," *The Tennessean*, September 20, 1992.

29. James B. Treece, "Here Comes GM's Saturn."

30. Staff, "General Motors' Long-Shot Bid to Beat Japan on Costs," *BusinessWeek*, March 12, 1984.

31. S. C. Gwynne, "The Right Stuff."

32. Saturn Corporation Mission Statement submitted by Saturn Corporation, June 1992.

33.–34. Liz Pinto, "Simplicity Is Key to Labor Tranquility at Saturn."

35. Staff, "United Auto Workers Control Highlights," *The Nashville Banner*, July 30, 1985.

36.–37. Beverly Geber, "Saturn's Grand Experiment."

38.–41. Interview with Saturn Corporation employees, June 1992.

42. James B. Treece, "Here Comes GM's Saturn."

43. Don Hinkle, "Employees Cheer Saturn Leaving Line," *The Tennessean*, July 31, 1990.

44.–47. David Woodruff, "At Saturn, What Workers Want . . . Fewer Defects."

48. S. C. Gwynne, "The Right Stuff."

49. James B. Treece, "Here Comes GM's Saturn."

50. Interview with Saturn Corporation employees, June 1992.

51. Information submitted by Saturn Corporation and interview with Saturn Corporation employees, June 1992.

52. Beverly Keel, "Saturn Mission Like a Religion for Employees," *The Nashville Banner*, October 9, 1990.

53.–54. Interview with Saturn Corporation employees, June 1992.

55. David Woodruff, "At Saturn, What Workers Want . . . Fewer Defects."

56. Interview with Timothy Epps, vice president of Human Resource Services, Saturn Corporation, April 1992, and Saturn Corporation employees, June 1992.

57.–58. Interview with Saturn Corporation employees, June 1992.

59. Bob Battle, "Union and Non-Union Labor to Build Saturn," *The Nashville Banner*, December 6, 1985.

60.–67. Interview with Saturn Corporation employees, June 1992.

68.–70. James B. Treece, "Here Comes GM's Saturn."

71. William J. Cook, "Ringing in Saturn" and James B. Treece, "Here Comes GM's Saturn."

72. Interview with Saturn Corporation employees, June 1992.

73. Micheline Maynard, "Following the Leader."

74. Interview with Saturn Corporation employees, June 1992.

75. William J. Cook, "Ringing in Saturn."

76. Tonya Kennedy, "Saturn Production Resumes Tuesday," *The Nashville Banner*, September 7, 1992.

77.–78. Tim Martin, "GM Shouldn't Touch Saturn, Analysts Advise," *The Tennessean*, October 27, 1992.

79. Staff, "A Glitch in Saturn's Smooth Orbit," *U.S. News & World Report*, August 23, 1993.

80. Consulting performed by the authors.

Chapter 18   The Challenges of 2000

1.–2. Hudson Institute, *Workforce 2000: Work and Workers for the Twenty-first Century* (Indianapolis: Hudson Institute, 1987).

3.–4. Jill Kanin-Lovers, "Meeting the Challenge of Workforce 2000," *Journal of Compensation Benefits*, January/February 1990.

5.–11. Hudson Institute, *Workforce 2000*.

12.–15. John Naisbitt and Patricia Aburdene, *Megatrends 2000: Ten New Directions for the 1990's* (New York: Avon Books, 1990).

16.–20. Faith Popcorn, *The Popcorn Report* (New York: Doubleday, 1991).

21. "The Global Network: Washington, D.C.," *John Naisbitt's Trend Letter*, April 16, 1992.

22. J. Laabs, "Ben & Jerry's Caring Capitalism," *Personnel Journal*, November 1992.

23. Interview with Service Merchandise employee, January 1990.

24. Beverly Geber, "Saturn's Grand Experiment," *Training*, June 1991.

25. Interview with Richard Oliver, vice president of Marketing, Northern Telecom, March 1992.